MOST OF 14TH STREET
IS GONE

Most of 14th Street Is Gone

The Washington, DC Riots of 1968

J. Samuel Walker

OXFORD
UNIVERSITY PRESS

OXFORD

UNIVERSITY PRESS

Oxford University Press is a department of the University of Oxford. It furthers
the University's objective of excellence in research, scholarship, and education
by publishing worldwide. Oxford is a registered trade mark of Oxford University
Press in the UK and certain other countries.

Published in the United States of America by Oxford University Press
198 Madison Avenue, New York, NY 10016, United States of America.

Library of Congress Cataloging-in-Publication Data
Names: Walker, J. Samuel, author.
Title: Most of 14th Street is gone : the Washington, DC riots of 1968 / J. Samuel Walker.
Description: New York, NY : Oxford University Press, 2018. |
Includes bibliographical references and index.
Identifiers: LCCN 2017034091 | ISBN 9780190844790 (hardback : alk. paper) | ISBN 9780190844813 (ebook)
Subjects: LCSH: Riots—Washington (D.C.)—History—20th century. | Washington (D.C.)—History—20th
century. | African Americans—Washington (D.C.)—History—20th century. |
Poor People's Campaign.
Classification: LCC F200 .W235 2018 | DDC 975.3/041—dc23
LC record available at https://lccn.loc.gov/2017034091

3 5 7 9 8 6 4 2

Printed by Sheridan Books, Inc., United States of America

This book is dedicated with love to my grandchildren, Charlotte and Jack

CONTENTS

Preface   ix

Introduction   1

1. The Other Washington   5

2. The Specter of Urban Violence   25

3. A City in Flames, April 4–5, 1968   49

4. "Smoldering Ruins Block after Block,"
    April 6–12, 1968   82

5. "A City of Remorse"   97

6. The Long Recovery   118

Notes   137

Essay on Sources   173

Index   179

PREFACE

I HAVE BEEN A RESIDENT of the Washington, DC suburbs for nearly five decades, but I knew little about the city's long and fascinating history until I started working on this book. I arrived in the area to attend graduate school at the University of Maryland in 1969, a year and a half after the riots that followed the death of Martin Luther King Jr. My only acquaintance with the 1968 disorders in Washington was the description my wife-to-be, Pat, provided of a bus trip that took her to the Greyhound bus station through the middle of the troubled areas on the worst day of the rioting. She was traveling from New Jersey to visit a college friend who lived in the Maryland suburbs, and as the bus drove through the city, she observed burning buildings and looters carrying goods from stores. Without any advance warning that the riots were raging, she was more than a little startled by what she saw. Her friend Ann waited at the bus station while Ann's father, doubtless with considerable anxiety, sat in his car some distance away because the streets were blocked. Pat, dragging her suitcase through the streets, did not feel frightened, though she did become increasingly uneasy. Eventually, she and Ann made their way safely to the car and to the suburbs.

Although the signs of the destruction the disorders left behind were still clearly evident in 1969, I paid little attention. In later years, I was aware of the problems that existed in the burned-out areas, but I often drove downtown on 7th Street NW without knowing much about what had happened there after King's assassination. I began to think seriously about it only after I decided that the riots would be a good topic for a book. As I conducted my research, I found a story filled with controversy, tension, drama, and human interest.

I am greatly indebted to those who provided assistance along the way. Don Ritchie drew on his vast knowledge of American political history to steer me in fruitful directions. Pete Daniel and Blair Ruble offered much-valued encouragement. Archivists in every institution I visited were enormously helpful. Joellen ElBashir, curator of manuscripts at the Moorland-Spingarn Research Center at Howard University, responded to my requests in a prompt and informative manner. Anne McDonough, Laura Barry, and Jessica Smith of the Historical Society of Washington, DC, made the collections at the Kiplinger Library easily accessible. The staff at the National Archives is always a source of valuable information, and, with rare exceptions, offers friendly assistance. I am especially grateful to David Langbart for his sleuthing abilities and to Carly Docca for her rescue mission. Allen Fisher of the Lyndon B. Johnson Library shared his large supply of expertise to guide my research in the collections of the library. Ray Smock and Jody Brumage of the Robert C. Byrd Center for Congressional History and Education made a trip to Shepherdstown pleasant and productive. Moira Fitzgerald of the Beinecke Rare Book and Manuscript Library at Yale University and Aryn Glazier of the Dolph Briscoe Center for American History at the University of Texas at Austin provided much appreciated assistance in my search for good photographs. I am greatly indebted to Emery Pajer for his skills in drawing the maps that appear in this book.

I am deeply grateful to Nancy Toff, my editor at Oxford University Press. She showed an interest in this topic in an informal conversation when it was little more than a vague notion in my mind. Since then, she has shared my growing enthusiasm even as she gently pushed me to fully explore its various dimensions. The prompt information she provided about the status of my book proposal, despite a breakdown in email communication between New York and Italy, furnished the basis for an exceedingly pleasant celebratory dinner on the shores of Lake Como with friends and family.

The members of my family were, as always, wonderfully supportive. My grandchildren, Charlotte and Jack, will read this book eagerly, I'm sure, at least as far as the dedication page. They might be a little surprised to find the Washington riots of 1968 included in their bedtime reading.

Introduction

IN APRIL 2015, the city of Baltimore, Maryland, suffered an eruption of rioting and looting that was the worst urban violence it had experienced in forty-seven years. It came as a rude shock to city and state officials and to tourists who had enjoyed the downtown attractions of "Charm City" during the previous three decades. The opening of glittering Harborplace, the world-class National Aquarium, the impressive Maryland Science Center, and the much-admired Orioles Park at Camden Yards between 1976 and 1992 had transformed Baltimore. From an object of scorn that its own mayor described as burdened with a "poor image," the city emerged as a must-see destination that drew millions of visitors every year.

The 2015 riots occurred a short distance but a world away from Harborplace. The immediate cause was the death of Freddie Gray, a twenty-five-year-old resident of a neighborhood scarred with empty row houses, closed factories, high crime rates, and other signs of urban distress. Gray was arrested and thrown into a police van without being strapped into a seat. He suffered a severe spinal cord injury while in custody and lapsed into a coma shortly after arriving at the police station. He died a few days later. Gray's death led to a week of peaceful protests that focused on complaints about police brutality, which had been a disturbingly common problem in Baltimore for years. On the day of Gray's funeral, the protests turned violent. The scores of people who participated threw rocks and bottles at police officers, burned squad cars, and looted and burned stores. Order was restored only after Mayor Stephanie Rawlings-Blake declared a curfew and Governor Larry Hogan sent in National Guard troops.

Amid a series of charges and countercharges about the causes of and response to the riots, it seemed clear that the underlying source of the violence was the conditions that prevailed in the affected areas of the city. "I think we, as a country, have to do some soul-searching," President Barack Obama declared. He pointed out that the Baltimore riots were a part of larger and wider currents. "This is not new. It's been going on the decades," he said. "And without making any excuses for criminal activities that take place, . . . you have impoverished communities that have been stripped away of opportunity." If urban decay was not new, however, serious rioting in major cities, with few exceptions, had been rare occurrences in the late twentieth and early twenty-first centuries. The last time Baltimore had endured a severe outbreak of urban violence was in 1968.[1]

The Baltimore riot of 1968 was but one of many serious urban disturbances in the United States during the mid- and late 1960s. The worst of them occurred in New York City in 1964, in Los Angeles in 1965, and in Newark, New Jersey, and Detroit in 1967. In 1967 alone, disorders occurred in 164 cities, large and small, across the country. Although the visible effects in many cases were not extensive, the aggregate costs of the riots were disturbingly high: eighty-three deaths, 1,897 injuries, and property damage that ran into the tens of millions of dollars. The disorders also produced the unquantifiable hardships of dislocation of residents, disruption of communities, and fear of further and perhaps greater turmoil. The outbreaks of urban violence and destruction between 1964 and 1967 were distressing to President Lyndon B. Johnson and many other Americans, not only because of the deaths, injuries, and property damage they caused but also because of what they highlighted about the troubled state of race relations in America. "The summer of 1967 again brought racial disorders to American cities, and with them shock, fear and bewilderment to the nation," the Report of the National Advisory Commission on Civil Disorders concluded in a study published in early 1968. "Discrimination and segregation have long permeated much of American life; they now threaten the future of every American."[2]

Shortly after the National Advisory Commission's report appeared, riots broke out in more than one hundred American cities following the assassination of Martin Luther King Jr. in Memphis, Tennessee, on April 4, 1968. The most serious and most alarming of the 1968 disorders occurred in Washington, DC. The violence in Washington was particularly noteworthy for two reasons. On a local level, it stood out because of the deaths, injuries, and enormous destruction it caused. On the day after King's death, rioting raged out of control in and around three of the city's major commercial strips. Before calm returned, thirteen people were dead, thousands were injured, and nearly eight thousand were arrested. The consequences of the immense property damage from the riots extended not only to store owners but also to residents of ghetto areas who lost their homes, belongings, and jobs.

Leonard Downie Jr., a managing editor with the *Washington Post*, underlined the impact of the disorders in the capital ten years after they occurred. "Left behind were hundreds of burned-out buildings, whole blocks that looked as though they had been bombed into oblivion, vital centers of commerce for black Washington that had been reduced to rubble, small businesses and lifetimes of investment by their owners that had been obliterated," he wrote. "Years were to pass before the rebuilding would substantially begin, before fears growing out of the riots would subside, before new living patterns would emerge for both black and white citizens of Washington."[3]

The second consideration that distinguished the Washington riots in 1968 and gave them national importance was that they took place in the capital city. Restoring order in the streets required the intervention of more than fifteen thousand National Guard and US Army troops. People across the country could open their local newspaper to see photos of armed soldiers guarding the Capitol Building against potential threats from American citizens. Richard Starnes, the Washington correspondent for the Scripps-Howard chain, suggested that local citizens were disheartened and deeply saddened by the unusual and disconcerting sight. "They are not watching armed men patrol the streets of some seedy banana republic," he remarked. "They are watching them patrol the capital of the United States."[4]

Despite the breadth and depth of much outstanding scholarship on the history of the capital city, the riots of April 1968 that traumatized Washington have not received the attention they merit.[5] What happened in the capital and in other cities in the United States at the same time deserves careful treatment. It had a major impact on the cities that sustained the costs as well as on government planning for the disquieting prospect of more outbreaks of a similar nature. It seems axiomatic that evaluating the roots of and the response to the 1968 riots is one essential step toward effectively addressing the urban woes that can lead to violence. The alternative is to face the prospect that, as author and television host Tavis Smiley put it in 2015, "protests and riots—uprisings—could become the new normal."[6]

In my approach to this topic, I attempt to answer the questions that I regard as most critical to understanding the causes and consequences of the 1968 riots in Washington. Some questions consider the events and circumstances that led up to the violence on the streets. What economic, social, and political conditions prevailed in Washington in the 1960s? How did the alarmingly explosive disorders that took place in the United States in 1967 influence national and local policies and preparations for dealing with further urban violence? Other questions relate to the outbreak and proceedings of the 1968 riots in Washington. What triggered them? Was the response well-considered and appropriate, and why did it stir bitter controversy? What were the costs of the riots and who were the primary victims? Who were the rioters and what were their motivations? How did the riots end? What lessons were learned? Finally, some questions bear on what happened in the wake of the Washington disorders. What efforts were made to rebuild the devastated areas and how successful were those efforts? Why did severe riots in the capital and in major cities around the nation become rare occurrences after April 1968?

In the title and throughout this book, I use the term "riot," often in plural form because there were multiple "riots" in Washington in April 1968. I think the word most accurately describes the events I cover, and my usage is consistent with the definition found in dictionaries. The *Oxford Dictionary of English*, for example, defines a riot as a "violent disturbance of the peace by a crowd."[7] Some scholars have suggested that the term should be avoided because it plays down the legitimate grievances of rioters and offers support for claims that urban disorders were aimless and unjustified. They prefer the terms "rebellion" or "uprising" to emphasize that rioters logically sought redress from the intolerable conditions they faced. I use the term "riot" in a descriptive, not a pejorative, way, and I do not use it as a code word to denigrate the severity of the problems that were day-to-day realities in the poor neighborhoods of the capital. What happened in Washington in 1968 fits very well with the dictionary definition and with common usage of the term "riot." Further, words such as "rebellion" and "uprising" strongly imply that riot participants took to the streets with at least some vague political objective in mind. This attribute did not apply to any significant extent to the Washington riots. I use the words "disorders" and "disturbances" as synonyms for "riots," and again, without any intention of understating the root causes of the violence and destruction of 1968.[8]

I

The Other Washington

FROM THE TIME OF ITS FOUNDING, the city of Washington, DC, served as the focal point for America's great experiment in democracy. Over a period of 150 years, it grew from a shabby, muddy, and altogether unimpressive outpost to the beautiful monumental city that was familiar to most Americans from school trips, family vacations, books, photographs, films, and television programs. Tourists who visited the capital personally and citizens who enjoyed its sights vicariously could take pride in, or at least acknowledge, the Capitol dome and the rituals of representative government it symbolized, the majesty of the White House and the power it conveyed, and the towering columns of the Supreme Court building that perhaps suggested the imposing mysteries of judicial review. They could honor Presidents George Washington, Thomas Jefferson, and Abraham Lincoln at their respective monuments; marvel at the wonders of the Smithsonian Institution, the Library of Congress, the National Archives, and other Washington cultural landmarks; and pay homage to the soldiers, sailors, and Marines who fought valiantly in America's wars.

This was the Washington, DC, that attracted millions of visitors from around the country and around the world. It was, wrote Russell Baker in the *New York Times* in 1963, "a showcase of the American experience" and the "heart of democracy."[1]

Washington was also a residential city that was much less familiar, even invisible, to short-term visitors. Residential Washington had a long, shadowy, and frequently contentious history. Baker found that "behind the noble postcard façade that Washington shows the American tourist is a city racked by change, trouble, and danger." The most enduring and perplexing problem that confronted the capital, which became more prominent in the 1950s and early 1960s, was racial inequality. In a city whose monuments celebrated freedom, democracy, and fairness of opportunity, the status of its black citizens and the battle for civil rights were particularly urgent and momentous. Haynes Johnson, an editor with Washington's *Evening Star* who later received a Pulitzer Prize for his reporting on the struggle for racial justice, commented in 1963 that "what happens in the capital affects Negroes everywhere" and could not "be dismissed as of only local interest." The reason, he argued, was that "Washington is the crucible of our democratic system," and that "if democracy fails in Washington, it will fail in all of our cities."[2]

In 1800, when the federal government moved from Philadelphia to its new home in Washington, the nation's two most important public buildings were still under construction. The Capitol and the President's House at the other end of Pennsylvania Avenue represented the prevailing high hopes that Washington would grow into a glittering centerpiece of America's bold venture in popular government. But the capital city made painfully slow progress toward fulfilling the grand plans and elegant conceptions of its designer, Pierre L'Enfant.

Washington remained an insult to L'Enfant's vision until after the Civil War. Instead of wide thoroughfares, it had muddy, unpaved, and unsafe streets. Instead of a National Mall graced with fine buildings, it had pigpens, rubbish heaps, and cattle grazing on the grounds of the unfinished Washington Monument. Instead of a scenic canal that served as a commercial link between the eastern and western parts of the city, it had a malodorous, open sewer that ran parallel to Pennsylvania Avenue. Instead of gardens, parks, and promenades, it had swamps, tree stumps, and untended vegetation. A reporter from Sacramento described the capital in 1864 as "ill-kept, noisome, and stinking" and suggested that "the man in the moon would hold his nose going over it."[3]

Washington transformed itself into a city of distinctive splendor only gradually. The halting process of developing the capital received a major setback when British troops burned the Capitol, the President's House, and other government buildings in 1814. The executive mansion, by then commonly referred to as the "White House," had been rebuilt with a modified design by 1818. The damaged sections of the Capitol were repaired and improved, and the building was finally finished with a wooden dome covered with copper in 1826. Congress agreed in 1850 to enlarge the Capitol to provide for the growing number of members from states recently admitted to the Union. Rising above the expanded House and Senate wings was a new cast-iron dome, completed in 1866, that became the most readily recognizable architectural structure in America.[4]

Meanwhile, other harbingers of monumental Washington appeared around the city. Support for a suitable memorial to George Washington gained momentum after 1833, when the Washington Monument Society decided to solicit donations from the American people. But the level of contributions was disappointing, and the monument stood as a partially completed eyesore until Congress stepped in to provide funding in 1876. A handsome addition to the mostly undeveloped National Mall was the Smithsonian Institution's turreted "Castle," which was completed in 1855. Other buildings that opened in the late nineteenth century earned places among Washington's monumental icons. They included the Pension Building (later the National Building Museum), the State, War, and Navy Building (later the Eisenhower Executive Office Building), and the Library of Congress.[5]

The most important enhancements to the city after the Civil War were often invisible or at least not obvious to casual visitors. Between 1871 and 1873, Alexander Shepherd, the vice president of the Board of Public Works for what was then the territorial government of the District of Columbia, took charge of providing desperately needed civic improvements. Shepherd, whose influence far exceeded his rather modest position and invited comparisons with machine bosses in other cities, was confident, determined, and brazenly inattentive to budgetary constraints. Under his leadership, streets in central Washington were graded, paved, and lighted. Sewers were built. The putrid city canal was filled in and paved over; it later became Constitution Avenue. Water mains were installed in parts of the city where they had never existed. Thousands of trees were planted. Those and other projects were completed in about three years, and the quality of design or construction on some streets and sewers was bad enough to soon require rebuilding. But Shepherd's achievements offered modern services that were new and welcome amenities in the city of Washington.[6]

The creation of monumental Washington was far from finished. It received new impetus in the early twentieth century. Senator James McMillan of Michigan, chairman of the Senate Committee on the District of Columbia and a longtime advocate of improving the city's infrastructure and public spaces, was instrumental in bringing about momentous changes.

They included enhancing the landscape of the Mall, extending it from the Capitol to the Potomac River, adding a reflecting pool, and constructing a memorial to President Lincoln at the far western end.[7]

Another critical step in the development of monumental Washington occurred in 1926, when Congress approved the expenditure of $50 million for new federal buildings. Much of the money was used to clean up the area known as "Murder Bay," located between Pennsylvania Avenue and the Mall east of 15th Street. Murder Bay had long been infamous for its gambling dens, brothels, saloons, and high crime rate; it also included mostly run-down residential sections. By the late 1930s, the area's rude streets had been replaced by a line of far less interesting but far more reputable government buildings known collectively as the Federal Triangle. Other notable additions to the city's monumental profile during the New Deal era included the Supreme Court building, the National Gallery of Art, and the Jefferson Memorial. By that time, the central core of the city was clearly defined by its museums, monuments, and other tourist attractions. Their common theme was to emphasize the accomplishments of American freedom and democratic government.[8]

The residential city of Washington did not aspire to such lofty goals, and its history was in many ways a rebuke to the ideals that the monumental city celebrated. It was home to a growing population that sought employment, decent shelter, safety, and perhaps even comfort. But large portions of the "other Washington" did not deliver those minimal objectives; they offered instead substandard housing, limited employment prospects, and, in the case of black citizens, rank discrimination. The gradual construction of the monumental core of the city displaced and isolated some residential areas, further accentuating the dividing lines between the two Washingtons. The attractions on the Mall became the leading and often exclusive destination for tourists, and for them much of the rest of the city remained obscure and vaguely sinister.

The permanent population of the capital expanded from 3,210 residents, including 623 slaves, in 1800 to 61,122, including 1,774 slaves, in 1860. The Civil War generated the first large-scale migration to the capital; by 1870, the population had nearly doubled to 109,199. The wartime surge occurred partly because of the arrival of troops, businessmen, contractors, laborers, and others to protect, feed, and minister to the needs of the city and to support the war effort. Although many did not remain after the war ended, some did.

The segment of the population that poured into Washington in the greatest numbers and that was the least welcome was made up of former slaves. During the war, as many as forty thousand African Americans fled their owners and flocked to the capital city, especially after Congress abolished slavery in the District of Columbia in April 1862. Individuals, families, and sometimes large groups of slaves of all ages left Maryland and Virginia and headed for the capital. The migrants made their way to Washington in hopes of finding jobs and opportunities, and many of them stayed.[9]

The fugitives from slavery generally were desperately poor and uneducated, and the city lacked the resources and, for the most part, the will to offer much assistance. The mayor of Washington, Richard Wallach, announced in 1862 that the city would offer aid to local black citizens. But he complained that many of the recently arrived refugees were "idle, dissolute, and reckless," and that imposing the "burden of supporting the multitude" on the city "would be an intolerable grievance." Black leaders took sharp issue with the view that Wallach expressed and applauded migrants for their willingness to work, often in low-paying government jobs in hospitals, stables, fields, and streets. Nevertheless, despite relief efforts carried out by local citizens, especially churches, and the federal government, most former slaves who settled in Washington suffered wretched living conditions in camps, alleys, and shanties.[10]

The massive influx of people and the jumble of wartime activities left the city of Washington in shambles. Housing was scarce and expensive, and some areas, by any measure, were shameful slums. The superintendent of the police department graphically described the miseries of conditions in "Murder Bay" in 1865. "Here," he observed, "crime, filth, and poverty seem to vie with each other in a career of degradation and death. Whole families . . . are crowded into mere apologies for shanties" where "their roofs afford but slight protection [and] from beneath a few rough boards used for floors, the miasmatic effluvia from the most disgustingly filthy and stagnant water . . . renders the atmosphere within these hovels stifling and sickening." The capital had never had adequate water supplies, sewage treatment, garbage disposal, animal control, street lighting, police protection, or other public services that were commonly found in other cities. After the war, epidemics of violent crime and disease made already deplorable living conditions even worse.[11]

The primary reason that Washington was in such lamentable straits was the failure of Congress to provide sufficient funding for fundamental requirements. The US Constitution gave Congress exclusive jurisdiction over governing the District of Columbia, and through the years, the legislative branch had been at best parsimonious and at worst neglectful in exercising its responsibilities. When Alexander Shepherd engineered the projects that took important strides toward making Washington into a modern city during the 1870s, he paid little heed to the costs. He believed that Congress would be so pleased with the improvements that it would agree to cover the bills. Congress, however, balked at paying all the steadily mounting expenses, and within a short time the District of Columbia's territorial government went bankrupt. One result was that in 1874, Congress created a new government, codified by the Organic Act of 1878, headed by three commissioners appointed by the president. But final control over District affairs remained in the hands of congressional committees in the House and Senate. Under this system, residents of Washington were denied the right to select their own leaders. Congress agreed to pay for one-half of the city's budget; the other one-half would come from tax assessments on local citizens. This arrangement remained in effect until 1973, when Congress granted partial home rule to the District of Columbia.[12]

Despite the financial woes that faced the new government, Shepherd's improvements made Washington a much more agreeable place to live. One local newspaper editorialized in 1873 that the "city of Washington, which was a disgrace to the country, has blossomed into a beauty and a loveliness so that it is to-day the most attractive city in the Union." As a residential community, the city prospered as never before. The basis of the local economy was, as always, federal employment, and the number of civilian jobs in government agencies more than doubled between 1871 and 1881. The 13,124 jobs in the federal government in 1881 represented nearly 20 percent of total employment in the city. But Washington's growth did not come from government expansion alone. Other recently arrived residents who represented a wide variety of professions, vocations, and crafts settled in the city. The total population of the city increased to 147,091 by 1880 and to 230,402 by 1890, more than twice the level of 1870.[13]

As the population of Washington expanded after the Civil War, some new and several distinctive neighborhoods developed within the city. Areas around Rock Creek, which meandered in a southwesterly direction between 16th Street and 27th Street in the northwestern quadrant of Washington, had long been a swampy wasteland in which poor black citizens lived in squalid conditions. The land was bought up by developers, who drained the swamps and built stately homes for affluent whites. The area's appeal was extended by the creation of Rock Creek Park in 1890. The port of Georgetown, often called a city despite its small size, was located at the western end of the capital. It predated the founding of Washington and guarded a measure of its independence until it became fully a part of the city in 1895. For the most part, it offered far fewer desirable homes than the newer neighborhoods to its north and east. The nucleus of ostentatious wealth in Gilded Age Washington was the area around Dupont Circle, located about a mile north of the White House. Many "nouveau riche" families migrated to Washington from around the country, attracted in large part by the absence of a well-established and snobbish high society that denied them entry in other cities. They built huge mansions in what had been a working-class neighborhood, effectively forcing the previous residents to move elsewhere. By 1900, the *Evening Star* commented, the Dupont Circle area was the "storm center of high society."[14]

Other sections of the District of Columbia also underwent dramatic changes in the late nineteenth century. The city of Washington expanded past its northern border (Boundary Street, later Florida Avenue) into mostly rural, agricultural areas of Washington County, which was a part of the District. The extension of streetcar service attracted middle-class workers to new subdivisions by enabling them to commute to their downtown jobs. As Washington County steadily urbanized, the dividing lines between city and county disappeared, and the District of Columbia became a single entity.[15]

Another neighborhood that was thinly populated before the Civil War and that thrived in the postwar era was the U Street corridor, which ran roughly between North Capitol Street and 15th Street in the northwestern quadrant of the city. This general area was later called "Uptown" and, still later, "Shaw," with boundaries that were never well defined. The construction of streetcar lines running north and south on 7th Street and 14th Street encouraged residential development in a city with an acute shortage of housing. Citizens from working-class and professional backgrounds, both black and white, moved into the area, and it grew rapidly. Those with sufficient income could purchase or build handsome homes on newly paved streets. Poorer residents, in contrast, often lived in alleys that sat behind the houses that faced streets and were invisible to most passersby. One especially prominent addition to the Shaw area was an enclave of Victorian mansions called LeDroit Park. The developers initially sold their stylish homes only to whites, and they built a high fence to keep blacks out of the neighborhood.

The population of the Shaw area at first was rather evenly divided by race, but it gradually became predominantly black as many whites relocated to newer sections of the city farther north or across the District line to the Maryland suburbs. By the mid-1890s, this trend had foiled the developers' plan to keep LeDroit Park exclusively white. At the same time, black entrepreneurs established businesses to serve the local community and to spare black customers the inconvenience and often the discomfort of shopping at downtown, white-owned stores. Between 1895 and 1920, the number of a wide assortment of businesses owned by blacks in Shaw increased from fifteen to three hundred.[16]

Along with prosperous commercial strips on U, 7th, and 14th Streets, the Shaw neighborhood was the site of local cultural institutions and cherished leisure activities. Its borders included several majestic theaters that featured films, floor shows, musicals, and vaudeville, and that hosted many of the greatest stars in popular music. The prominence and excellence of the entertainment that the Shaw area provided earned it the title of "Black Broadway." In addition to theaters, the U Street corridor was the location of Washington's major-league baseball park, opened in 1911 and eventually named for team owner Clark Griffith. It stood conspicuously at U Street and Georgia Avenue, where the Senators, with rare exceptions, struggled to compete in the American League.

A more important asset to the community was Howard University, the first college "south of the Mason-Dixon Line dedicated to a biracial education." It was chartered by Congress in 1867 and located just north of U Street at 5th Street NW. The cultural and intellectual contributions of Howard's faculty were critical elements that supported Shaw's status as the "undisputed center" of black Washington and the city's claim to be the heart of "American Negro civilization."[17]

Other sections of the District of Columbia that were heavily black did not fare nearly as well as the Shaw area. Shepherd's public works projects had not included the Southwest, Southeast, or Northeast quadrants of the city, and they failed to benefit from the improvements he sponsored. The Southwest section was a relatively small triangle of land between the Potomac River and its juncture with the "Eastern Branch" (later named the Anacostia River). It had been largely an impoverished area since the founding of the city, and conditions had greatly worsened during and after the Civil War because of the large numbers of freed slaves who settled there. The situation in much of the Southeast and Northeast quadrants that branched out from the Capitol on the west side of the Anacostia River was similar. An article in the *Evening Star* in 1890 graphically described the hardships facing some residents of the city: "In a filthy back yard, a disease breeding hole, some one had at some time put up some boards in such a manner as to give a poor imitation of a very poor cow shed. In that three people lived after a fashion."

In the late nineteenth century, a growing number of Washingtonians expressed concern about serious poverty in their midst. They were motivated both by humanitarian impulses and by public health considerations. The focus was the alleys in which many destitute citizens lived. Jacob Riis, who had won fame as author of *How the Other Half Lives* (1890), a book about poverty in New York, told a congressional committee after touring slums in Washington in 1903: "I confess I had no idea there were such things as I saw in this city yesterday when I went in several alleys and witnessed the way the colored people are living. The inside of these houses is too dreadful to even conceive." Photographers took ironic shots of the Capitol dome rising over appalling, nearby slums. Expressions of concern, congressional hearings, newspaper articles, dramatic photographs, and expert studies did not, however, produce effective action to deal with the problem.[18]

One other distinctive section of the District of Columbia was its least populated and most obscure. This was the area that lay across the Eastern Branch, which was separated from the city by the river and settled fitfully and sparsely. One developer, John W. VanHook, tried during the 1850s to lure employees of the Navy Yard, located on the other side of the river in Southeast, but had little success. The property he and other investors purchased was divided into smaller parcels that were designated for sale to whites only. He also built a fine home overlooking the Eastern Branch that, appropriately enough, was sold by his creditors to Frederick Douglass, the famed black abolitionist, writer, orator, and advocate of civil rights. The Southeast neighborhoods east of the river subsisted as a lightly populated, mixed-race area. Well into the twentieth century, they remained isolated and largely forgotten.[19]

In the immediate wake of the Civil War, race relations in the capital were in a state of transition. Congress extended the right to vote and to serve on juries to African American males in the District of Columbia. In 1869 and 1870, local ordinances approved by the city council (which, along with the mayor, then governed the capital) outlawed racial discrimination in a variety of public establishments, including theaters, restaurants, pubs, and hotels. Within three years, those measures were extended to other types of businesses. Washington officially took important steps toward providing equality for and prohibiting discrimination against black residents and visitors. The reality of its treatment of black citizens, however, was quite at odds with legal requirements. After the early 1870s, the status of blacks in the nation's capital, as elsewhere, steadily declined and Jim Crow restrictions became increasingly common. Restaurants and hotels refused black patrons, theaters banned them altogether or seated them in separate sections, and many churches practiced strict segregation. Trade unions denied membership to African Americans, and the local social register removed them from its lists of city elites.

Conditions reached a low point after Woodrow Wilson was inaugurated as president in 1913. Under his administration and with his tacit approval, some federal agencies officially segregated working areas, lunch rooms, toilets, and other facilities. "The effect is startling," reported the National Association for the Advancement of Colored People (NAACP). "Those segregated are regarded as a people apart, almost as lepers." Even in agencies in which segregation was not imposed, black employees suffered from loss of jobs, demotions, diminished status, and other setbacks. A Georgia congressman championed the idea of totally excluding blacks from government employment. The indignities that black citizens suffered in the late nineteenth and early twentieth centuries, whether as petty as society puffery or as serious as job discrimination, drove an ever-widening wedge between the city's black and white populations. Increasing unfamiliarity was a fertile breeding ground for mutual suspicion, misunderstanding, and ill will.[20]

The denial of civil rights to black citizens and the increasingly rigid segregation that characterized race relations in Washington did not go unchallenged. Some of the city's sizable contingent of African American citizens, along with their white allies, fought against measures and social conventions that relegated blacks to a starkly inferior position in the nation's capital. They formed organizations and speakers' bureaus, wrote articles in prominent publications, established newspapers, and sought to build greater racial unity within a black population long characterized by sharp class distinctions. Their efforts met with little success until the New Deal era, when strong support from First Lady Eleanor Roosevelt and other prominent government officials led to limited, but symbolically meaningful, improvements. Secretary of the Interior Harold Ickes, for example, prohibited racial segregation in the cafeteria in his agency's office building, and more important, required his department's contractors to hire workers on a nondiscriminatory basis.

During the 1930s, civil rights advocates applied a direct-action approach to promote their cause in Washington and elsewhere. One tactic that proved effective was boycotting merchants who practiced discrimination. The owner of a hot-dog stand on U Street, for example, refused to hire black workers until a boycott that drastically diminished his sales enabled him to see the error of his ways. Similar protests against other businesses in predominantly black neighborhoods, including chain grocery stores and pharmacies, did not always have the desired impact on the targeted merchants, but they made an impression on smaller local retailers who could ill afford a prolonged reduction in income. Meanwhile, the local chapter of the National Negro Congress, an organization founded in 1936, assumed a leading role in protesting job discrimination, dismal living conditions in black neighborhoods, and police brutality in the capital.[21]

Despite some encouraging developments, progress in combating discrimination remained slow and uncertain. During World War II, the crusade against the racist doctrines of Nazi Germany called attention to racial attitudes and discriminatory practices in the United States and in its capital. But the war against Nazism did not produce major advances for blacks in the city. This was evident in June 1945, when the District's board of recreation decided to formally prohibit blacks and whites from using the same recreational facilities, including parks, playgrounds, and tennis courts. The official policy of segregation incited strong protests, including an eloquent dissent from a white army officer whose children had always played with black neighbors. "How can we explain to these children that they must not enter the playground with Negroes, even if the colored children invite them?" he asked. "If the Nation's capital permits segregation in recreation, I say we have fought this war in vain." Reason and common sense did not prevail; the board stuck with its decision.[22]

After World War II, civil rights advocates staged protests and won legal battles that loosened the stranglehold of institutional racism in Washington. In one particularly important case, they challenged the standard practice among most restaurants of denying service to African Americans. Although the Reconstruction-era laws that prohibited racial discrimination in restaurants and other public places were still on the books, businesses had long ignored them with impunity. In January 1950, a group of four local citizens, three black and one white, walked into Thompson's Restaurant, a cafeteria located at 14th Street and New York Avenue in the city's downtown area, a short distance from the White House. They entered for the purpose of testing the enforceability of the nineteenth-century laws. The most prominent of the activists was eighty-six-year-old Mary Church Terrell, a charter member of the NAACP, a writer and speaker of international renown, and a resident of Washington for six decades. When Terrell and her companions went to pay for the items they selected in the cafeteria line, the restaurant manager informed them that "we don't serve colored people here." He said that allowing African Americans to eat in the cafeteria was forbidden by his company's policy and, he claimed incorrectly, by the laws of the District of Columbia.[23]

As planned, the cafeteria's refusal to serve Terrell and her colleagues led to a lawsuit against the Thompson restaurant chain. The case first went to Municipal Court, where Judge Frank H. Meyers ruled that although the nineteenth-century laws had never been repealed, they were no longer valid because they had not been enforced for so long. Several months later, the Municipal Court of Appeals overruled Meyers by affirming the legitimacy of one of the Reconstruction-era ordinances. The case then went to the US Court of Appeals for the DC Circuit, which ruled in a 5–4 vote that Meyers's decision was correct and that the responsibility for anti-discrimination legislation in Washington should be left to Congress. "I consider today's majority decision in the Thompson Restaurant case a tragedy for the United States," commented Terrell. "Clearly the matter is up to the Supreme Court to resolve."

On June 8, 1953, the Supreme Court resoundingly reversed the DC Circuit's decision. By a vote of 8–0, the justices found that the 1870s laws were still valid and "presently enforceable." Four days later, Terrell and her companions who had been turned away in 1950 marched into Thompson's and selected what they wanted to eat. In a gesture of respect and good-will, the cafeteria manager, who had replaced the man who had refused them service, picked up Terrell's tray and delivered it to her table. While the Thompson case proceeded through the courts, civil rights advocates, including Terrell, had used boycotts and picketing to force Hecht's, one of the city's leading department stores, and other reluctant downtown retailers to serve African Americans at their lunch counters.[24]

The desegregation of Washington restaurants was an important step forward in the campaign against racial restrictions in the capital and offered hope for breaching other discriminatory barriers. But despite gradual progress in combating Jim Crow, one critical area of *de facto* racial division in the city—housing—remained intractable. The population of the District grew substantially in the first five decades of the twentieth century, reaching a record total of 802,178 in the 1950 census. The black population increased at an even faster rate than the white population, and by 1957, Washington had become the first city in the country with an African American majority.

The trend was a result both of black influx into the capital and white flight to the suburbs of Maryland and Virginia. By early 1961, 54 percent of the city's residents were African American.[25]

The black migrants who settled in Washington came largely from the rural South. They joined millions of African Americans who left the South and made their way to northern cities that they hoped would be a "promised land." During their journeys, they faced immense unknowns, difficulties, and dangers. The Great Migration began in earnest during World War I, quickened during World War II, and continued through the 1960s. The vast movement occurred in part because mechanical cotton-picking machines greatly reduced the need for agricultural labor and in part because of the oppressive racial conventions that prevailed in the South. The prospects of good jobs and less onerous living conditions were powerful incentives. The problem was that the promised lands of the North often turned out to be mirages.[26]

African Americans who moved to Washington during the Great Migration, like their predecessors during the Civil War, were usually poor. They were generally better educated than those who stayed behind, though in many cases, they faced a difficult adjustment in moving from rural areas in the South to a large city. The reasons they settled in Washington varied, but the presence of extended family members was often decisive. Although the capital did not have the heavy industry that provided job opportunities in northern cities, government agencies were a significant source of employment, or at least hope. Washington's large black population and its geographical proximity to the South might have been additional attractions.

The city was grievously ill-equipped to fulfill the hopes and aspirations of African American migrants. Employment opportunities were limited, though they expanded after World War II, especially in the federal government. Housing was glaringly inadequate in both quantity and quality. The new arrivals all too often had no choice but to live in grim slums that were congested, and ironically, overpriced. Conditions in areas of the city that had long been plagued with dreadful housing further deteriorated as more people poured in. A house that appeared perfectly respectable to passersby might be home to several families instead of the one family for which it was designed. Alley dwellings around the city were particularly noticeable and shocking to those who paid attention. Although the residents of alleys often took pride in a sense of community, the lives they led were precarious and short of sanitary, plumbing, and electrical services that more-prosperous citizens took for granted. Plans to replace alleys with low-cost public housing, despite good intentions, were largely unproductive.[27]

The population pressures and severe housing shortages in Washington affected black citizens of all classes and income levels. The poor neighborhoods in which many blacks lived inevitably spilled over into adjacent areas that were more affluent. African American residents of greater means might have moved in turn to more desirable locations, but they were usually prevented from purchasing homes in white areas by custom, hostility, and contractual arrangements that sought to keep blacks out. One widely employed approach to blocking racial integration was the restrictive covenant, which forbade a white owner from selling a house to a black buyer. In 1948, the Supreme Court ruled that covenants were legally unenforceable, but they continued to be informally effective for many more years.

There were other high barriers that African Americans had to overcome if they wanted to buy a home in a white neighborhood. The Federal Housing Administration, which enabled families of modest means to secure loans to purchase houses, had a policy of providing assistance only for property in "racially homogeneous neighborhoods." But it also was loath to guarantee loans or support construction in black neighborhoods because it regarded them as bad credit risks.[28]

If African American families managed to clear those hurdles and move into a white area, they often were greeted with malice from their new neighbors. Residents of areas of Maryland and Virginia adjacent to Washington did not greet new black neighbors with mob violence, as occurred in other suburban communities in the North. But in Montgomery County, Maryland, just across the District line, blacks who bought homes received threatening phone calls that hardly made them feel welcome. In 1964, the eminent historian John Hope Franklin encountered racial hostility when he taught summer school at the University of Maryland in College Park, about eight miles from downtown Washington. He rented a house in nearby Hyattsville, Maryland, that was owned by another professor who was out of town. When Franklin arrived for the summer term, he was told of rumors that some of his temporary neighbors were so angry about the presence of a black family in their midst that they planned a protest demonstration. Members of the university's history department were concerned enough that they organized teams to guard the property and make certain the Franklins "were not molested." Although the Franklin family was not harassed, twelve-year-old "Whit" found that the neighborhood children were far from hospitable. Franklin assumed that the children acted on the instructions of their parents, whom he later characterized as "local yokels." The undisguised hostility toward and limited mobility for African Americans in Washington mirrored the same attitudes, restrictions, and residential patterns in other cities throughout the North. With no other options, even relatively well-off African Americans were forced to share housing with relatives or to pay excessive charges to live in substandard dwellings.[29]

Many of Washington's formerly mixed-race neighborhoods became increasingly poor and more heavily black. This was evident, for example, in sections of the city east of the Anacostia River, where many apartment complexes were built on the cheap after World War II to meet the housing shortage. As a result, the area changed rapidly, as a report of the District of Columbia government pointed out, from "a low density neighborhood of single-family homes [to] one of predominantly rental accommodations housing a young and transient population." The report showed that this development created serious problems: "The population influx accompanying housing construction strained the capacity of schools, streets, and other publicly provided facilities and services, and contributed to the decline of adjacent enclaves of single-family homes." Neighborhoods around the city that lay east of Rock Creek Park faced similar difficulties. Living conditions in the once-thriving U Street corridor deteriorated. Large single-family, middle-class homes were divided into apartments or made into boardinghouses. Many businesses closed or moved out of the area.[30]

The Southwest quadrant, which was largely but not exclusively black, remained the most depressed area in the city. A study commissioned by the District of Columbia government called it "a rundown, dilapidated, substandard neighborhood" that "provided dramatic pictures of tragic poverty in a land of affluence." In 1950, a survey of about 5,600 "dwelling units" in the area showed that "more than 43 percent had outside toilets, more than 70 percent had no central heating, more than 44 percent had no baths, and more than 21 percent had no electricity." During the 1950s, the District's Redevelopment Land Agency (RLA), which Congress had created in 1949 to undertake urban renewal projects, made plans to replace Southwest with a new community of modern homes and apartments for middle- and high-income residents, shopping centers, restaurants, and a limited number of public housing units for low-income families. The bulldozers quickly cleared the area of its previous housing and its previous residents. Some critics denounced Southwest redevelopment as "Negro removal" because the RLA made no effective provisions to relocate the approximately 23,500 people who had lived there.

The displaced residents scattered around the city. The largest number wound up in public housing in neighborhoods close to those they had involuntarily vacated. Others moved across the Anacostia River or to Shaw. An investigation of the former Southwest residents found that the overwhelming majority occupied dwellings that, physically, were substantial improvements over those they had left. But the dislodged families also reported dissatisfaction, alienation, and a profound nostalgia for the communities they had departed. Despite more comfortable living conditions, most regretted that they had been forced out of their homes in Southwest. Whether or not the former residents were happy in their new neighborhoods, Southwest redevelopment had unfavorable consequences by increasing already intense population pressures in other areas of the city.[31]

The situation in Washington in the mid-twentieth century was not entirely bleak for its black citizens, however. Some neighborhoods maintained a strong sense of community, and African American churches were especially vital in meeting both spiritual and mundane needs of the areas they served. The continuing expansion of the federal government after World War II created an ample supply of new jobs. By 1950, the government was the city's largest source of employment for black men and an important provider of jobs for black women. Although most of the jobs held by black federal employees were clustered at the lower end of the pay scale, they offered a reliable paycheck and career opportunities that expanded the city's middle class.

The desegregation of public facilities proceeded at a sluggish but steady pace. Restaurants that served black patrons in the wake of the Thompson's cafeteria decision were joined by theaters, bowling alleys, skating rinks, barbershops, and other previously segregated businesses that opened their doors to customers of all races. The District of Columbia's board of recreation gradually and reluctantly integrated the use of its parks, playgrounds, tennis courts, and swimming pools. One of the last holdouts was the privately owned Glen Echo Amusement Park, a popular destination for young people that was located a short distance from the District line in Maryland. Park management refused to change its whites-only policy even in the face of protests by Howard University students and local residents that went on for several weeks in the summer of 1960. Finally, under pressure from US attorney general Robert F. Kennedy, the park agreed in early 1961 to admit black patrons.[32]

Although ending Jim Crow and the affronts it imposed on black citizens of all classes was a necessary and salutary step forward for the Washington community, it was not an unambiguous blessing. As the use of restrictive covenants and other obstacles to selling homes to blacks diminished, middle- and upper-class African Americans bought homes in neighborhoods in the city and its suburbs that previously had been closed to them. This was a favorable development for blacks who could afford to move, but it caused a greater concentration of poverty in the areas they left. Meanwhile, the pace of white flight from the city to the suburbs also accelerated, which produced similar effects. The white population of the District decreased by 33.3 percent between 1950 and 1960, and the trend continued in later years.[33]

Much of the white abandonment of the city was the result of the appeal of the suburbs, but it also was a response to growing problems in the city. One critical issue was the declining quality of education in Washington, especially after the Supreme Court's landmark 1954 decision on school segregation in *Brown v. Board of Education of Topeka, Kansas*. During most of the first half of the twentieth century, the doctrine of "separate but equal" had applied in Washington's public schools. But, as elsewhere around the country, the "equal" part of the formula was a sham; the inequalities that the capital's black schools suffered included clearly inferior physical plants, student-teacher ratios, and expenditures per student. They were so meagerly funded that a report on the system published in 1949 recommended that three-quarters of the entire education budget for the District be allocated to upgrading the buildings and facilities of black schools.

The *Brown* decision made integration of the District's schools imperative. The city's board of education announced immediately that it would open the new academic year in the fall of 1954 with integrated schools. But the practical requirements of integrating the system after decades of slighting the needs of African American students proved to be overwhelming. There were difficult social adjustments for students who had never shared a classroom with children or teachers of a different race. Some white parents were dismayed to find that their children were assigned to schools largely attended by black students. More important, it was soon obvious that the education that most black students had received did not measure up to that of whites in the same grades, and this caused enormous difficulties for teachers. White parents were greatly troubled by this discrepancy. "Both of our children were in grade school, capably staffed and progressive," one father recalled. "Our first trial came . . . when the deterioration of the school curriculum became apparent in spite of the heroic efforts of principal and teachers alike." The basic problem, he explained, was that "the influx of colored children slowed down the pace of the whole school curriculum" and this meant that his "children did not work to their full capacity." As a result of their concerns about the value of the education their children received, an unintended effect of school integration, many families left the city to settle in suburban areas. In 1950, the enrollment of the District of Columbia's school system was 49.3 percent white and 50.7 percent black. In 1961, it was 18.5 percent white and 81.5 black.[34]

Another major concern that spurred white flight to the suburbs was rapidly increasing crime rates in the District of Columbia. This was a part of an alarming national trend; between 1958 and 1964, the incidence of crime in the United States expanded by 30 percent, a rate that was "five times as fast as the population." Experts agreed that the most important reason was the growth in the country's population, especially the young urban population, after World War II. As the postwar baby boom generation reached its teens, the incidence of major crimes, though not necessarily violent crimes, surged. A critically important contributor to unlawful behavior was "environmental conditions" in urban ghettos. Low income, high unemployment, poor schools, decrepit housing, and other afflictions that were all too prevalent in struggling urban areas generated alienation and hopelessness that often led to crime. Informed observers pointed out that although crime rates were also increasing in rural areas and affluent suburbs, they remained well below those in cities. The trends of the early 1960s clearly indicated a close relationship between youth, poverty, and crime.[35]

The crime rate in Washington rose faster than that of cities of a similar size between 1959 and 1965, according to the Federal Bureau of Investigation (FBI) crime index, which included murder, rape, robbery, aggravated assault, breaking and entering, larceny of at least $50, and automobile theft. The increase was 116 percent in the District of Columbia, compared with an average of 63.3 percent in other cities with similar populations. In 1965, the capital achieved the unwanted distinction of the fastest-growing crime rate in the nation. The crime index showed an increase of 6.3 percent across the country and 4 percent in cities of more than 250,000, but it shot up by 11 percent in Washington.

The dismaying increase in crime rates triggered a palpable increase in fear of crime in the city. Much of it was rooted in white fear of black crime. In Washington, police records showed that in 1962, about 85 percent of those arrested for serious offenses were African Americans. "It is a matter of record that Negroes *do* commit the greatest number of serious crimes, and they commit them far out of proportion to their percentage of the population," Haynes Johnson, a strong supporter of racial equality, wrote in 1963. "These figures are one of the reasons why many white men think of crime and the Negro as synonymous."[36]

Crime statistics were not exact, definitive, or free of racial bias, and they obscured the fact that as many as 80 percent of the crimes in Washington were committed "by Negroes against Negroes." But they were indicative of a troubling problem that worried a growing segment of the local population, both white and black. "I keep reading that Washington is a jungle. *We* don't consider it a jungle," commented an African American schoolteacher in 1963. "It's our home, so the problem is closer to us than to anybody, and we want to solve it more than anybody." In December 1966, the President's Commission on Crime in the District of Columbia, which President Lyndon B. Johnson had established the previous year, concluded that the "high incidence of crime in Washington fully justifies grave concern by the community." A few months later, the *Los Angeles Times* ran a story under the headline "Crime Fears Hold Tight Grip on Residents of Washington." One example it gave was that the FBI decided not to allow shopping arcades on the street level of its soon-to-be-constructed headquarters building on Pennsylvania Avenue "because they could provide a lurking ground for muggers." The growth of crime in Washington speeded white, and increasingly, as housing options gradually opened, middle-class black departure from the city's neighborhoods. The effect was to further concentrate poverty and its ill effects in ghetto areas.[37]

When Russell Baker published a series of articles on the nation's capital in the *New York Times* in 1963, he concluded that it was "a city racked by change, trouble, and danger." One chronic problem that was distinctive to the capital was the lack of a municipal government with power to perform its own administrative functions. Walter N. Tobriner, president of the city's three-member board of commissioners, complained: "The basic problems are complicated by the fact that here we have a government charged with responsibility but practically powerless to carry out that responsibility." The congressional committees that controlled the city's purse strings were often indifferent to the needs of the population and unreasonably tightfisted in funding the local government. The severe limitations on the capital's authority to manage its own affairs made it unique among American cities. But there were also important similarities between the "other Washington" and sizable urban centers around the country, especially in their struggles to deal with the chronic

problems of high unemployment, serious poverty, inferior schools, inadequate housing, loss of population, declining tax bases, and growing
crime. After the mid-1960s, those problems were joined by acute concern
about rioting in the streets as serious outbreaks of urban violence spread
across the United States.[38]

2

The Specter of Urban Violence

AS URBAN GHETTOS AROUND the country erupted in rage in the mid-1960s, the prospects of similar violence in the nation's capital became an increasingly acute concern for federal and local government officials. As early as the winter of 1962, Attorney General Robert F. Kennedy warned that unless steps were taken to improve conditions in Washington's poor neighborhoods, there would be "a major explosion in the District of Columbia." Chuck Stone, a highly regarded African American journalist, made the same point about the capital in different terms in 1963: "Just give us an equal chance to attain middle-class standards," he commented, "and we'll give you all the middle-class morality you want."[1]

The first major riot of the 1960s that commanded national attention occurred in New York City's Harlem neighborhood in July 1964. It came just two weeks after President Johnson signed the Civil Rights Act of 1964, which banned discrimination on the basis of race, religion, sex, or national origin in public accommodations and employment. It was one of Johnson's proudest achievements. The riot in Harlem erupted after an off-duty white policeman shot and killed a fifteen-year-old black student in murky circumstances. This tragedy set off six days of furious rioting in which several thousand African American protesters looted stores, damaged cars, threw bottles and rocks, and engaged in a running battle with police. Although only one person was killed in the melee, hundreds were injured. Within a short time, fierce racial violence also broke out in Philadelphia and Rochester, New York.[2]

The rioting was in no way related to the passage of the civil rights law. But a growing number of white Americans saw a vaguely articulated connection between the battle against racial discrimination, street violence, and urban disorders in black neighborhoods. This led to what was soon termed "white backlash." Pollster Louis Harris reported in September 1964 that "anxiety among white Americans over the race issue is rising in intensity." He found that the increasing concern was fueled by "worry about safety in the streets, which many people now relate to Negro outbreaks in Northern cities this past summer."[3]

The riots that occurred in Harlem and other cities in the summer of 1964 were preludes to the more severe urban violence, in terms of loss of life and property, that erupted during the following three summers. An outburst of violence that stunned the entire country and that contributed mightily to white backlash took place in the Watts section of south-central Los Angeles in August 1965. It began just a few days after Johnson signed the Voting Rights Act, which prohibited racial restrictions that had long denied the right to vote to African Americans in the South. The law represented the president's second great civil rights triumph.

The Watts riot came as a harsh awakening to Johnson and his supporters. "The Los Angeles riot, the worst in the United States since the Detroit riot of 1943, shocked all who had been confident that race relations were improving in the North," wrote the National Advisory Commission on Civil Disorders, which Johnson created in 1967, in a retrospective analysis. The upheaval in Watts raged out of control for five days, and when it ended, the costs were immense—thirty-four people killed, hundreds injured, $35 million in property damage, and about four thousand arrests. Johnson initially reacted with incredulous self-pity. "How is it possible after all we've accomplished?" he wondered. But he soon supplied his own answer. He told John A. McCone, who was set to chair a state of California investigation of the Watts outbreak, that ghetto residents "have absolutely nothing to live for, 40 percent of them are unemployed, these youngsters live with rats and have no place to sleep. . . . You just have no idea of the depth of the feeling of these people." Johnson added that the solution was "to find some way to wipe out these ghettos and find some housing and put them to work." But he also publicly drew parallels between the Watts rioters and members of the Ku Klux Klan. "They are both," he said, "lawbreakers, destroyers of constitutional rights and liberties, and ultimately destroyers of a free America."[4]

The crisis of urban violence worsened in 1966. "The events of 1966 made it appear that domestic turmoil had become part of the American scene," the National Advisory Commission on Civil Disorders commented. Riots of varying intensity occurred in thirty-eight American cities during the summer, including Minneapolis, Atlanta, Philadelphia, Chicago, and Cleveland. Nearly all of them were set off by a "minor incident fueled by antagonism between the Negro population and the police." They typically included looting, burning, rock-throwing, sniper fire, injuries suffered by both civilians and police, and occasional loss of life among residents of the riot areas. Most Americans were deeply troubled by the violence that had become so commonplace in cities around the country, and white backlash took on new virulence. One poll taken in late summer 1966 showed that 70 percent of white Americans thought that blacks were "trying to move too fast" in fighting for civil rights, and another indicated that 90 percent opposed new civil rights legislation.[5]

Urban ghettos exploded with unprecedented scope and fury in 1967. In May, the FBI provided an ominous report to the White House on the prospects for the coming season. "All signs point toward recurrent racial convulsions throughout the country this summer," it advised, "more than likely on an even wider scale than in previous years—marked by plundering, arson, destruction, and attacks on law enforcement officers." It acknowledged that "most of the riots of the past three years have been spontaneous eruptions," but it blamed subversives, especially communists, for fanning "the fires of racial discord and animosity." The FBI's claim that communists contributed to unrest among black citizens and promoted violence was consistent with its long-standing position that subversive elements were key players in the civil rights movement. Among the "demagogues" it listed in its May 1967 report as contributors to racial violence were comedian Dick Gregory, boxing champion Cassius Clay (who had long before changed his name to Muhammad Ali), and Martin Luther King Jr. Although the FBI was far off base in condemning those figures as extremists, its predictions about the high probability of "another riotous summer" proved to be painfully accurate. In June, July, and August of 1967, there were, in categories later introduced by the National Advisory Commission on Civil Disorders, eight major riots. This group was defined by disorders in which there were "(1) many fires, intensive looting, and reports of sniping; (2) violence lasting more than two days; (3) sizeable crowds; and (4) use of National Guard or federal forces." There were also twenty-seven "serious" and one hundred "minor" disturbances; the total number for the summer was 136.[6]

By any definition, the worst of the riots occurred in Newark, New Jersey, and Detroit. On July 12, a minor incident involving a taxi driver arrested in Newark set off an angry reaction from city residents who protested what they regarded as police brutality. The riots that ensued lasted for five days as outnumbered police and poorly trained National Guard troops tried to restore order. When the violence finally ended, 26 people (24 African Americans and 2 whites) were dead, 1,100 were injured, and 1,400 were arrested. Property damage totaled more than $10 million, most of which was stolen or ruined inventory from stores. Six days later, an even more costly outbreak of rioting flared up in Detroit. Again, it began with routine arrests and soon escalated into massive turbulence that required the intervention of federal troops. By the time the disorders wound down on July 27, 43 people had died, 33 of whom were African Americans and 10 of whom were whites. Of those who lost their lives, 17 were identified as looters, 2 of whom were white; 7,200 individuals were arrested. The property damage was estimated at about $40 million, including 2,509 stores that were destroyed or looted of food, liquor, furniture, appliances, clothing, and other merchandise.[7]

Despite the warnings that the riots of the summer of 1967 were likely, they were a demoralizing blow for the Johnson administration. As Joseph A. Califano Jr., special assistant to the president for domestic affairs, later wrote, they demonstrated that the White House's support for civil rights and its war on poverty "could not calm the mean streets of urban ghettos." The Newark and Detroit outbursts were especially discouraging. "The senseless deaths and tragic destruction in those two cities," Califano commented, "slapped Lyndon Johnson with a violent reminder that his ambition to do something for poor blacks, whether one side or another thought it was too much or too little, might in any case be too late." The crisis in the cities left Johnson with few options. As he had suggested after Watts, he believed the only way to solve the problem of urban rioting was to "wipe out these ghettos." This was the same position that civil rights leaders and their supporters had advocated for years. But support for domestic spending programs, especially as the costs of the Vietnam War skyrocketed, was slipping badly. A telling example was strong congressional resistance to, and indeed ridicule of, a bill to exterminate rats in urban slums. White backlash intensified as a result of the riots while support for civil rights declined. "Shockingly, large numbers of Americans, including many liberals," Vice President Hubert Humphrey told Johnson in July 1967, "are displaying extremely hostile racial attitudes."[8]

Johnson tried to steer a middle path between white anger and fear on the one hand and black resentment and frustration on the other. In a televised address to the nation on July 27, 1967, as the Detroit riot was ending, he made clear his support for stern action against urban violence. "Let there be no mistake about it—the looting, arson, plunder and pillage which have occurred are not a part of a civil rights protest," he declared. "There is no American right to loot stores, or to burn buildings, or to fire rifles from rooftops. That is a crime—and crime must be dealt with forcefully, and swiftly, and certainly." Having affirmed his position on law and order, the president reiterated his belief that the "only genuine, long-range solution for what has happened lies in an attack . . . upon the conditions that breed despair and violence." He denounced Congress for cutting funds for his programs to address urban woes and fight the war on poverty. "This is not a time for angry reaction," Johnson argued. "It is a time for action, starting with legislative action to improve the life of our cities."[9]

Johnson announced that he had appointed a Special Advisory Commission on Civil Disorders (soon to be the *National* Advisory Commission on Civil Disorders). Its charge was to "investigate the origins of the recent disorders in our cities" and to make recommendations "for measures to prevent or contain such disasters in the future." He named as chairman Otto Kerner, the governor of Illinois. Kerner, a longtime friend of Johnson, a general during World War II, and a Democratic machine politician, was highly desirous of obtaining a federal judgeship. The president, who would later appoint him to the US Court of Appeals in Chicago, reasoned that Kerner was not likely to stray far from his administration's positions. The vice-chairman of the commission was John V. Lindsay, the liberal Republican mayor of New York and a veteran of the front lines of racial unrest in his city. Other members of the commission included Democratic senator Fred Harris of Oklahoma, Republican senator Edward W. Brooke of Massachusetts (the first African American elected to the Senate since Reconstruction), and Roy Wilkins, executive director of the NAACP. The eleven members of the Kerner Commission were proven leaders who, not incidentally, were also mostly political moderates. By establishing the commission, Johnson hoped to preempt the possibility of a congressional investigation that could seek to embarrass the administration. He also hoped that the investigation would suggest ways to deal with the urban crisis, or at least "buy time." There were no obvious or immediate solutions, which made the fear of crime and racial violence that had been growing across the country for the past several years even more prevalent and intractable.[10]

An editorial aired on both radio and television by station WTOP in Washington on July 26 and 27, 1967, called the riots in Detroit, Newark, and other cities "the biggest shock to America in a quarter-century." Local officials and citizens were gravely concerned that the same kind of shocking events could occur in the capital. Residents of ghetto areas recognized that the conditions they faced mirrored those of other cities, and they saw the disorders around the country as a possible "forecast for Washington." The fear of crimes against individuals remained very much alive in Washington, and the intensified worries about riots in the streets were a highly unwelcome addition. The similarities in the fundamental causes of both kinds of violence increased the level of unease.

An article in the *Washington Post* in early June 1967 suggested that the city's leaders were "awaiting summer with apprehension, but not without hope." The apprehension arose from the fact that "Washington has all the tinder-box ingredients to flare into street violence and riots—jobless youth, poverty, rundown housing, an alienated underclass, racial prejudice, fourth-rate slum schools, white-cop hatred." The hope of avoiding violence rested on some unique Washington assets, including "a large Negro middle class," the presence of the federal government and its concern about conditions in the slums, the lack of "an abrasive white minority," and the geographical separation of ghetto areas. For Washington's citizens, the question of whether the city's advantages would outweigh the "tinder-box ingredients" was the great imponderable in the summer of 1967. One disturbing portent was a study conducted in six unnamed northern cities that showed that growing numbers of African Americans believed that riots were the best way to obtain relief from their problems.[11]

With the city on edge, rumors abounded. This was particularly apparent on a late July day shortly after the Detroit riot. Stories circulated in the city that the National Guard was deploying in the streets, that the Key Bridge linking Georgetown and Virginia was burning down, and that riots were breaking out in several sections of the city. Other rumors claimed that 80 percent of the black officers in the Metropolitan Police Department had refused to report for duty, that federal employees had been sent home, and that the Marines had set up camp on the National Mall. All those reports were false, and John B. Layton, who had been chief of police since 1964, pleaded for calm. "The community is disturbed about the riots in other cities," he said. "The greatest service any citizen can give is not to repeat rumors he hears."[12]

While hoping to be spared violence in the streets, the District of Columbia government and the White House made rudimentary preparations to deal with disorder if it occurred. Stephen J. Pollak, the adviser to the president on national capital affairs, told Johnson that he had consulted with the commanding general of the Military District of Washington, which was responsible for defending the city, to make certain that troops would be available if needed. Walter N. Tobriner, president of the District's board of commissioners, advised Layton that in the event of a riot to minimize the use of firearms and avoid mass arrests. Tobriner and Layton agreed that if a riot occurred, federal troops should be called out "at the earliest possible stage." They also recommended that regular troops rather than National Guard units should be mobilized if the police force needed assistance. The National Guard was inadequately trained in riot control and had performed with widely recognized and dangerous ineptitude in Newark and Detroit.[13]

The Washington police faced a test of their readiness to handle neighborhood turmoil when a potentially serious disturbance began on the night of July 31, 1967. A fire broke out from unknown causes in a used-furniture store on 7th Street NW in the Shaw neighborhood, an area that the *Washington Afro-American* described as "a prime example of urban blight in its most visible and shocking form." By the time the fire department arrived, a crowd of two to three hundred, mostly young people, had gathered, and some threw stones and bottles at firefighters and police. The police managed to disperse the crowd, but within a short time, they received reports of serious vandalism in the same general area. For the rest of the night, bands of youths smashed store windows, set cars on fire, stoned police cruisers, and looted two liquor stores. Police restored order by about 5:00 a.m. and arrested twenty-eight suspects, eleven of whom were juveniles. The night's activities produced only limited damage and few injuries, and the disturbance fell into the "minor disorder" category that the Kerner Commission later devised. Nevertheless, the "rampage," as the *Evening Star* labeled it, was troubling as a potential harbinger of more damaging disorders.[14]

The Shaw disturbance also underscored the tensions between black citizens and the Metropolitan Police Department. The President's Commission on Crime in the District of Columbia, which Johnson had established in July 1965, reported in December 1966 that "a substantial segment of the community believes that Negroes in the custody of the police are physically mistreated." It also condemned frequent "verbal abuse" by police officers, especially the use of "trigger words such as 'boy' or 'nigger.'" When Layton took over as police chief, he pledged that under his leadership, "this department is totally committed to improvement efforts in all the dimensions and phases of police-community relations." Layton was a career Washington policeman who had risen through the ranks from patrolman to chief, and he was well liked and respected by the members of the police force who worked for him. But he was hindered by a blind spot on the question of making certain that officers were duly considerate toward all residents of the city. In July 1966, he denied that there was any need to ban offensive trigger words by District policemen, a step that departments in other cities had taken. At the same time, he failed to recognize that use of the word "boy" in addressing black males was highly insulting. He later directed the District police to avoid certain disrespectful trigger words, but he left "boy" off the list.[15]

After the July 1967 disturbance, militants complained that the police had overreacted and flaunted their weapons by "waving shotguns and poking them in kids' stomachs." A short time later, Harry C. McPherson, the White House staff counsel and chief speechwriter, heard about the same problem in an informal conversation with three black youths whom he had known for nearly a decade. McPherson had been among the last members of Johnson's staff to become worried about growing crime in the District, but in 1966 he had decided that the situation was serious enough to move his family home from the Capitol Hill area to the Maryland suburbs. He remained deeply concerned about civil rights and police abuses, and he sent Johnson a memo about the comments of the young men with whom he had talked. They were ages seventeen, eighteen, and nineteen, and they lived in a poor area of the city with families on welfare. McPherson asked them "what really griped Negro people most about their lives." They unanimously agreed that the primary grievance was not bad housing, job shortages, or poor schools. Rather, it was the police who "really make people mad." The youths said that the police in some precincts "get you in a station house and really bounce you around." One of them had been picked up for allegedly stealing a bicycle. "I didn't know nothing about it," he said. "They took me to the precinct and rapped me around. Took their knuckles and banged me on the head til it was ringing." McPherson's report highlighted an issue that the Johnson administration had to navigate between goals that conflicted when the police abused their authority. It had to provide, within the limits of federal jurisdiction, adequate protection for public safety while guarding against both the substance and perception of police brutality.[16]

In an atmosphere of tense uncertainty over crime and the potential for serious riots, the city of Washington acquired a measure of home rule. Since the 1870s, the city's top executives were the three commissioners appointed by the president. But much effective power in governing the city remained firmly entrenched in Congress, especially the House Committee on the District of Columbia. The committee, dominated by Chairman John L. McMillan of South Carolina and other congressmen from southern states, adamantly opposed home rule for the District of Columbia. The committee was notorious for using its hearings as a platform for blaming the capital's problems, especially crime, on its black majority. An unnamed newspaper editor commented in 1963 that "many members of the committee are segregationists and want to do everything they can to make Washington less attractive to Negroes and a prize example of the failure of integration." Sterling Tucker, a prominent black leader and head of the Washington Urban League, pointed out the "anomalous situation where America's only predominantly Negro city is ruled by enemies of the Negro."[17]

Every president since Harry S. Truman had proposed home rule for the District of Columbia, and the Senate had voted in favor of it five times. But appeals for self-government never managed to overcome the opposition of the House committee. President Johnson was determined to succeed where his predecessors had failed, partly because of his affection for the city and partly because he thought home rule would be a deterrent to civil unrest. He and his wife, Lady Bird, had lived most of their adult lives in Washington, spending weekends in their native Texas. "I love this capital city," Johnson declared in July 1965. "I love its beauty and simple dignity, and all the meaning that is present in its past and that is present in its promise." He made similar remarks to a group of visitors two years later. "This has been my home for longer than any other place. This is my home," he said. "I have a strong feeling for the District of Columbia." Johnson was also a steadfast advocate of home rule because he believed it might reduce the chances of riots. "The clock is ticking," he warned, "when people feel mistreated and they feel injustice" but have "no vote and no voice in their government."[18]

The president's efforts to win approval for a self-government bill in 1965 fell short, even though, Califano recalled, "Johnson contacted more members than I believe he ever talked to on a piece of legislation." In early

1967, he decided to use legislative legerdemain to at least partially achieve his goal. He bypassed the House Committee on the District of Columbia by wielding his executive authority to reorganize the District government, which meant that his proposal would be considered by the more sympathetic House and Senate Government Operations Committees. The plan would take effect unless one house of Congress voted to disapprove it. The White House compromised McMillan's influence by leaking information about shady deals he had arranged for his personal benefit. After another round of hard lobbying, the House voted not to reject Johnson's plan on August 9, 1967, and that settled the issue. As a result of the reorganization, the president would appoint a single commissioner, an assistant commissioner, and a nine-member city council, subject to Senate approval. Their independence to govern the capital would be seriously curbed, however, by the continuing role of Congress, which retained authority over the city's laws, taxes, and budget.[19]

Johnson quickly decided that he wanted to appoint an African American as commissioner (the job title soon evolved into "commissioner-mayor" and, informally at least, to "mayor"). The candidate whom he selected within a short time was fifty-two-year-old Walter E. Washington, a veteran official in the District of Columbia government who was then serving as chairman of the New York Housing Authority under Mayor Lindsay. His appointment and confirmation made him the first black mayor of a large American city. Washington had come a long way from his boyhood home of Jamestown, New York, an industrial city in the western part of the state. His parents had moved there from Georgia when they were newly married teenagers, and years later, Washington was uncertain about why they had chosen to settle in Jamestown. His mother died suddenly of appendicitis when he was seven; his father, who was known for his friendly manner, worked at odd jobs, such as cook, metal worker, and waiter.

There were few blacks in Jamestown when Washington grew up and little overt discrimination. Black and white students attended the same schools, went to the same dances, and played on the same teams. Washington was an indifferent student who was well liked by his classmates. He was an outstanding long-distance runner on the track team; he also achieved distinction for his dancing and orchestra-directing skills. When he graduated from high school, he was restless and unsure about what he wanted to do. Eventually, he and a friend came up with the idea of attending Howard University, in part because jobs were scarce in Jamestown and mostly because they thought it would be a good place to meet girls. "I guess there were maybe three or four Negro girls our age in all of Jamestown, and most of them were my sisters," his friend later remarked. "We really wanted to meet some classy Negro girls." Washington hitchhiked to the District of Columbia, but he soon ran out of money and returned to Jamestown. He found a job and, with his father's encouragement and assistance, saved money to go back to college. This time he thrived. He waited on dining hall tables to help pay his bills, but that did not prevent him from participating in campus activities. He joined a fraternity and was elected to the student council. After he earned his undergraduate degree, he graduated from Howard Law School. While attending Howard, he also met his wife, Bennetta, the daughter of a prominent Washington minister.[20]

In 1941, Washington took a job as a junior housing assistant with the National Capital Housing Authority, which administered public housing in the District. Over a period of twenty-five years, he worked his way up to become executive director of the agency. During his career, he won praise for his openness, willingness to listen and respond to complaints from citizens, and impatience with mindless bureaucratic "gymnastics." He pioneered services that later became widely used features of public housing, such as day-care centers, career counseling, credit unions, and tenant councils. He earned an enviable reputation in his field, and for that reason, Lindsay recruited him to head the New York Housing Authority. Washington was known to be outgoing, even-tempered, and levelheaded. He was comfortable in crowds "among jeans or dinner jackets." Some critics faulted him for limited executive experience, for a lack of personal dynamism, and for spending most of his career with an agency that was not held in high regard. But Washington's appointment was greeted with enthusiasm. The *Washington Post* commented that he had "the kind of experience, the general credentials and the sort of personality that any community might look for in a chief municipal executive." The *Evening Star* hailed him as a "super choice." Marion Barry Jr., a fiery civil rights activist, offered a similar view. "Of all the names of black people for the position, Walter Washington is the best," he declared. "I hope he continues to be innovative and creative and can get the city really moving."[21]

Johnson's selection as assistant commissioner (the title gradually lost favor to "deputy mayor") was Thomas W. Fletcher. He was the former city manager of San Diego, where he had led efforts to revitalize the city's downtown area. During his tenure, San Diego was named an "All-American City" by *Look* magazine. Fletcher was known as an outstanding administrator as well as an expert on urban problems. He had just joined the US Department of Housing and Urban Development as a deputy assistant secretary when Johnson appointed him to the new post. "He is well trained for his task," the *Post* editorialized, "and his professional life has been devoted to problems of exactly the sort that he will deal with in the District."[22]

Johnson carefully considered candidates to fill the nine positions on the city council. He soon decided that the council, in keeping with the population of the city, should have a black majority. Among the five black members he selected was Walter E. Fauntroy, a prominent local minister and civil rights leader, who was named vice-chairman. Johnson's choice for council chairman, John W. Hechinger, was a reluctant nominee. He was the president of a prosperous building supply and home improvement chain in the Washington area. He was also a civic leader of renown and accomplishment. Hechinger played a key role in desegregating the local chapter of the Boys' Club, of which he was a trustee, and served as an officer in several other community organizations. He was a board member of the District of Columbia's Redevelopment Land Agency, where he became closely acquainted with the issues surrounding urban renewal.

Hechinger tried valiantly to decline the chairmanship of the city council, citing his commitment to the family business, his other obligations, and his political inexperience. But Johnson refused to take a "no" answer, and he marshaled all of his legendary persuasive powers. He told Hechinger that after "the terrible trouble we've had in our urban communities," he needed "someone who cares about his city and who is an administrator, a businessman, to chair this council." He informed Hechinger that he had "extracted pledges" from the other council members "that they will work closely with you so that this first pilot government gets off the ground properly." As Hechinger began to weaken, Johnson expressed sympathy with the difficulty of his decision. Then the president went on at length about the tough decision he was facing about whether to authorize the bombing of Haiphong in North Vietnam. "I wish I could spend more time on the problems of Washington, but I can't," he said. "I need you right here to help me make this city the way it ought to be." Califano, who witnessed the exchange, later wrote, "Poor John Hechinger didn't know what his mind was with this presidential rush." Hechinger recalled that "within the next five minutes of all that jazz, I accepted." The press was notified immediately that, pending Senate approval, the city council had a chairman.[23]

There was one other important post in the new District government that was not a presidential appointment but that had potentially enormous consequences for fighting crime and preparing for urban disorder. A short time after taking office, Mayor Washington, in consultation with the White House staff, created the new position of director of public safety, to whom the chief of police was subordinate. This was a controversial move and an inherently awkward arrangement, and it came about because of widespread citizen objections to the racial attitudes of members of the police department. Hechinger raised alarms when he learned of a white police officer assigned to the Southeast section of the city whose behavior was abusive. The patrolman routinely cursed city residents and often used racial slurs. Several residents of the neighborhood and anti-poverty workers aired their grievances about the officer for more than two hours at a city council meeting. Faced with an obviously volatile situation that concerned the council, Chief Layton responded by doing nothing effective about it.

This episode and other cases of continuing police disrespect for black citizens convinced Hechinger that Layton should be replaced. He told Washington and Fletcher that making the change would help demonstrate that the mayor was clearly in charge of the new government, which seemed especially important because the "black community didn't feel comfortable with Layton." To Hechinger's frustration, Washington elected to leave Layton in place and establish the new post of director of public safety. "The decision was a textbook example of poor management—solving a personnel problem by creating an office that is superior to the one you can't control in order to avoid a hard, unpopular decision," Hechinger later wrote.[24]

Despite the jurisdictional ambiguities that were built into the new position, the mayor found a well-regarded law enforcement professional to fill it. On December 1, 1967, Mayor Washington announced that he had appointed Patrick V. Murphy as director of public safety, in charge of the police department, the fire department, and the District's Office of Civil Defense. Murphy had begun his career as a patrolman in the New York City police department in 1945 and, like Layton, he had moved up to a high-ranking position. He had served as deputy chief inspector and as commander of the New York Police Academy. When he was passed over for promotions, he took a job as the assistant director of the Justice Department's Office of Law Enforcement Assistance, an agency that Johnson had created to help fight crime. Murphy was told by Attorney General Ramsey Clark that his nomination as director of public safety was supported by the "highest level of the White House." He was "flattered but not overjoyed" about the prospects of the job.

Director of Public Safety Patrick Murphy and Mayor Walter Washington, April 11, 1968. *U.S. News & World Report Collection, U9-18976-23A, Library of Congress*

Murphy was well aware that his relationship with Layton was likely to be complicated. He decided that the chief "was not an evil or even an unpleasant man," but he was not convinced that Layton had prepared his force for the prospect of rioting in the coming summer. He was equally concerned about the chief's apparent insensitivity toward black residents. Murphy had made his own views clear in a speech he gave before coming to Washington. He said that "racial injustice is the major cause of crime in the United States" and that "the method of policing many Negro communities has always been a major aspect of racial injustice."[25]

Murphy was known as an inspirational and cool-headed leader. But he reacted angrily when he learned that Layton had failed to report an incident to him in which several members of the police force who had been drinking heavily fired off random gunshots as they passed the home of the president of Howard University in their car. At a press conference, he blistered Layton for his "typical police department coverup," which he regarded as a "big inexcusable error." When he met with Layton, he delivered the message emphatically: "Chief, don't you understand? I'm your *boss*." Nevertheless, lines of authority remained ill defined, and Murphy's attack on Layton generated resentment among police officers. The District of Columbia Police Wives' Association, which reflected the opinions of members of the police force, complained bitterly to Mayor Washington that Murphy had "lowered the image and morale of the Police Department" and demonstrated "poor judgement and unbelievable lack of descretion [*sic*]." It was not an auspicious start in the new city government's campaign against crime and civil disorder in Washington.[26]

The new regime confronted a formidable array of problems when it took office in the fall of 1967. Walter Tobriner, who was completing a six-year tenure as president of the now-abolished board of commissioners, confided to friends that he worried that the "modern urban crisis may be insoluble." Schools in Washington performed with distressingly poor results. A study of the school system by Columbia University's Teachers College found that "education in the District is in deep, and probably worsening, trouble." The housing crisis was as recalcitrant as ever. Robert G. Kaiser of the *Washington Post* reported in September 1967 that "more than a quarter of a million people live in substandard housing: thousands in houses without much plaster or heat, without a bed or soap in a sink." In Clifton Terrace Apartments, located five blocks north of U Street in Northwest Washington, tenants had to put up with filth, crumbling ceilings, peeling paint, missing light fixtures, obscene graffiti, leaking roofs, empty faucets, and often no heat in the winter. They paid about $105 a month, which was not expensive but not cheap either, and their rent did not include their elevated gas bills for using their stoves to heat their apartments. The owner of the once-elegant apartment complex was eventually sentenced to sixty days in jail for his failure to provide heat to his tenants. Mayor Washington commented privately that he "was truly shaken to see the misery and suffering," and he added that "one of the things that troubles me is that Clifton Terrace is not an isolated case."[27]

In addition to the city's education and housing woes, the new District government was greeted with other serious problems that required attention. The capital had the highest per capita infant mortality in the country. Kaiser described the local air quality as "far dirtier than experts say is safe or comfortable." The Potomac River after a rain storm was "in effect, a large, open sewer." Crime rates continued to soar. They increased by 41.1 percent in May 1967, compared to one year earlier, and by 39.8 percent in June 1967, over the same period. Although aggravated assaults were down, robbery, burglary, larceny, and car theft were up substantially. Lurking behind those discouraging indicators about conditions in the city was the ever-present and perhaps growing threat of severe urban violence on the streets of the nation's capital.[28]

Even as the District of Columbia government was getting organized, the Johnson administration was aggressively, at times frantically, making plans for dealing with the prospects of a major outbreak of rioting the following summer. After the shocking events of 1967, the president demanded that federal agencies take action "to be certain that civil disturbance problems were under control and receiving proper attention." The point man for carrying out the president's order was Attorney General Clark, who served as the "director of federal government activities relating to civil disturbances." Clark was a dedicated proponent of advancing civil rights and protecting civil liberties, and he was convinced that, in the long run, the only effective way of preventing unrest was to eliminate poverty and terrible living conditions in urban ghettos. But he was also responsible for promoting law and order, and he took several steps to achieve that goal. One was to search for ways to improve communications among federal officials in the event of disturbances. Another was to hold a series of meetings in early 1968 with mayors and chiefs of police of more than a hundred cities. Patrick Murphy, who had suggested the conferences when he was still at the Justice Department, explained that their purpose was to exchange information, to settle the "frazzled nerves" of local leaders, and to emphasize the pressing need for improving police performance.

Clark's most striking innovation was to establish a secret intelligence-gathering section within the Department of Justice, called the Interdivisional Information Unit (IDIU). Its function was to collect information about what was happening in the black community. It focused its surveillance activities on "black nationalist and similar groups" in hopes that advance warnings would enable the government to be better prepared for disturbances and to coordinate responses with state and local officials. In creating this unit, Clark bypassed the FBI, which came under his jurisdiction as attorney general, in large part because he distrusted what he regarded as J. Edgar Hoover's excessive use of wiretapping. Further, Clark recognized that the FBI would have trouble "penetrating the largely Negro operations covered" because it had only 40 black agents out of a total of about 6,300. He planned to use lawyers who worked in ghetto areas for Great Society welfare agencies, US attorneys based in urban centers, and local officials to provide information through a far-reaching surveillance network. The IDIU established a "situation room" to gather and process the intelligence it received and to improve communications among federal, state, and local law enforcement agencies.[29]

At the same time the Justice Department formed its domestic intelligence unit, the US Army stepped up preparations for urban disorders, including surveillance activities. Although it began collecting intelligence on civilians in the United States earlier, it greatly expanded its programs after the Newark and Detroit riots in 1967. It acted with the full knowledge and encouragement of the White House and the Justice Department. In a report of February 1968, an army "Task Group" argued that extensive domestic intelligence activities were made necessary by the dangers of "demonstrations and violent attacks upon the social order" that could lead to "a situation of true insurgency" if they came under the control of "external subversive forces." In contrast to the Justice Department but like the FBI, the army was much inclined toward the conclusion that civil unrest was likely to be incited by communists or other groups it regarded as subversive. Its very broad definition of subversives included such organizations as Martin Luther King's Southern Christian Leadership Conference and the NAACP and individuals who criticized the Vietnam War. The army collected massive banks of information from police and FBI records; Justice Department, Secret Service, and Civil Service Commission files;

subscriptions to hundreds of newspapers and magazines, including underground publications; and the use of undercover agents.[30]

Among the most prominent black leaders targeted for surveillance was Stokely Carmichael, chairman of the Student Nonviolent Coordinating Committee (SNCC) in 1966–1967. He was a charismatic and militant advocate of "black power," a term he coined and made famous. The meaning of the phrase was ambiguous. In some cases, Carmichael explained it as a call for black unity, but at other times he used it as a summons to "smash everything Western civilization has created." In either event, the concept of black power heightened already intense fears of racial violence among white Americans. Carmichael's position on racial issues and his condemnation of the Vietnam War led to careful surveillance of his activities by the army, the Justice Department, the FBI, and other agencies. His inflammatory rhetoric also stirred much anger within the Johnson administration. Some officials were convinced that Carmichael had played a role in inciting riots and demanded that Clark take legal action against him. The attorney general replied that "he had put lawyers in every division of the Justice Department to work on the evidence against him, but they had come up empty-handed." He refused to pursue a weak case that would probably acquit Carmichael and enhance his status. Clark's argument went down poorly with some of his cabinet colleagues and with the president. Like the army and the FBI, Johnson was inclined to vastly overestimate the role of communists and other outside agitators in provoking or fueling urban unrest.[31]

Domestic intelligence that extended beyond militants like Carmichael to include American citizens who represented no credible threat of organized violence was only a part of the army's preparations for urban disorder. The army also responded to the 1967 upheavals by making, for the first time, detailed plans for deployment of troops in cities where riots occurred. It was keenly aware that state and municipal police were the first line of defense against urban violence and that the National Guard was the primary backup if police forces were unable to restore order. But it also knew that the introduction of federal troops had been necessary in Detroit and could be again in the disturbances that were expected in 1968. The army conducted extensive training programs in riot control for both regular army and National Guard troops and officers. It provided military supplies to National Guard units that were essential for riot control, such as gas masks and communications equipment.

Most important, the army decided on rules of engagement for operating in the environment of a major civil disturbance. The basic principle was to "avoid appearing as an invading, alien force rather than a force whose purpose is to restore order with a minimum loss of life and property and due respect for the great number of citizens whose involvement is purely accidental." Troops would be instructed that they would "not load or fire their weapons except when authorized by an officer in person or when necessary to save lives." Army policymakers anticipated that, subject to the judgment of commanding officers at the scene, "riot control agents," such as tear gas, would be used before live ammunition. If firing shots became imperative, soldiers should aim "to wound rather than to kill." Finally, unless full martial law was declared, police rather than soldiers would apprehend lawbreakers, and police officers would accompany troops to make arrests.[32]

The Johnson administration's preparations for the summer of 1968 focused on responding to urban riots rather than preventing them. This was consistent with the assumption that serious disturbances were likely to recur. Ramsey Clark, however, took a more optimistic view. He told the cabinet on March 13, 1968, that the attitude of police chiefs was "good," that the army was "ready," and that if Congress provided money for a summer jobs program, "we have an excellent chance to prevent major riots this summer." His boss was less sanguine. In an informal meeting with college students a few weeks earlier, the president had offered his judgment that "we will have several bad summers before the deficiencies of centuries are erased." He commented that "we are making the biggest attempt ever made in the history of this land . . . to attack illiteracy, ignorance, and discrimination," but he added that there would "still be millions in poverty after we do all we can." Asked by one student what could be done to prevent the outbreak of riots during the coming summer, Johnson hesitated and then answered, "We can't avert it." He could not see "that anything could prevent more trouble in the cities this year and in the future."[33]

The president's assessment was remarkably frank, especially in an election year in which he was expected to run for another term in the White House. The Republican Party was obviously hoping to capitalize on public fears of crime and urban unrest by making law and order a prominent campaign issue. In the wake of the Newark and Detroit riots, the newsletter of the Republican Congressional Committee, which worked to elect party candidates to Congress, accused Johnson of acting with "unpardonable vacillation, indecision and even indifference" in the face of urban calamity.[34]

Presidential aspirant Richard Nixon took up the same theme in a highly visible article in *Reader's Digest* in October 1967. He raised the question "How did it happen that last summer saw the United States blazing in an inferno of urban anarchy?" Nixon's answer was the "decline in respect for public authority and the rule of law in America." He echoed Johnson in acknowledging that urban problems were decades in the making and would take a long time to fix. Nixon offered three solutions for dealing with the urgent issue of urban violence: improved training and better pay for police; increasing the number of police on the streets; and winning the trust and "active help of the law-abiding majority of the Negro community." The potency of law and order as a political issue was apparent in a Gallup poll published in late February 1968. It found that the public ranked "crime and lawlessness," including rioting and looting, as the most important domestic problem in the country "for the first time since the beginning of scientific polling in the mid-thirties."[35]

In an atmosphere of public anxiety and political posturing, the Kerner Commission released its report on civil disorders on March 1, 1968. After Johnson established the commission in July 1967, it held a series of closed hearings to collect information that generally lasted entire days and sometimes continued well into evening hours. Some commissioners and staff members also made visits to cities to observe conditions and conduct interviews. After gathering a massive amount of material, the commission rushed to complete and publish its findings. It hastened to finish its work in part because its limited funds were running low and mostly because, anticipating the outbreak of riots in the summer, it wanted to pressure the Johnson administration into increasing its expenditures on urban issues. Governor Kerner had proven to be, as Califano recalled, "a loyal but weak chairman." Mayor Lindsay, who served as vice-chairman and whom the president disliked, had assumed a leading role in the commission's deliberations. He insisted that the final report be written in a way that commanded attention and produced front-page headlines.

The Kerner Commission report carried out Lindsay's wishes. It began with a statement that set the tone for a gloomy and disquieting presentation: "Our nation is moving toward two societies, one black, one white—separate and unequal." It followed with a harsh indictment of white society for creating the conditions that spawned rioting in the ghettos. "What white Americans have never fully understood—and what the Negro can never forget—is that white society is deeply implicated in the ghetto," the report declared. "White institutions created it, white institutions maintain it, and white society condones it." The Kerner Commission held out hope that the trends it described could be reversed and that "deepening racial division is not inevitable." But it warned that proceeding on the "present course will involve the continuing polarization of the American community and, ultimately, the destruction of basic democratic values."[36]

After analyzing the 164 disturbances that occurred in the first nine months of 1967, including 136 during the summer, the commission concluded that there was no "typical" riot. "The disorders of 1967 were unusual, irregular, complex and unpredictable social processes," it wrote. Nevertheless, it detected some patterns. It found that riot participants acted "against local symbols of white American society, authority and property in Negro neighborhoods—rather than against white persons." The most obvious symbols of white authority were police officers. The commission listed twelve "deeply held grievances" in ghetto areas, and reported that police actions rated first in the relative intensity of complaints. It acknowledged that the role of police in ghettos was "one of the most difficult in our society." The commission also suggested that hostility to police officers was often a symbolic substitute for other problems and that the legitimacy of objections to police behavior was difficult to evaluate. Nevertheless, it made its position clear: "Police misconduct—whether described as brutality, harassment, verbal abuse, or discourtesy—cannot be tolerated even if infrequent. It contributes directly to the risk of civil disorder."

The Kerner report emphasized that, other than resentment toward police, bleak living conditions and limited opportunities were the leading causes of disorders. The second- and third-ranking grievances of ghetto residents in terms of intensity were the shortage of good jobs and inferior housing. The commission offered a wide range of recommendations to ease the urban crisis that echoed the proposals that many black leaders had advanced for years. Some of the commission's suggestions, such as hiring more black police officers, applied to local governments. But many of them came under a call for massive federal intervention. The commission explained its rationale for higher federal expenditures succinctly: "No American—white or black—can escape the consequences of the continuing social and economic decay of our cities." It urged that programs be established or expanded to create jobs, improve education, and provide decent and affordable housing.

The commission did not present a cost estimate for carrying out its recommendations. It asserted that the American economy was strong enough to pay for the programs it urged, even with a war going on. But it also recognized that a tax increase might be necessary to address urban problems. The commission argued that the country must marshal the will to pay the toll for meeting "the vital needs of the nation." Its appeal echoed Lindsay's remarks in an interview with the *Washington Post* in January 1968. At that time, he had argued that American citizens had the means to mitigate the urban crisis. What they lacked, he said, "is the will."[37]

President Johnson was not pleased with the Kerner Commission report. Although he agreed with its arguments on improving conditions in urban slums, he was angry that the commission had not given him enough credit for the civil rights legislation he had promoted and the programs he had launched to combat poverty. Further, the report's appeal for increasing spending by what Califano called "several orders of magnitude" went far beyond what was politically possible. The president was locked in a struggle with Congress over an income-tax surcharge that he needed to pay for the Vietnam War. Congress was demanding that he cut domestic spending as a price for approving the surcharge, and now the Kerner Commission was asking for large increases. Johnson complained that he had not realized when he appointed the commission that the "son-of-a-bitch" Lindsay would wield so much clout.

As a result of his frustration and annoyance, the president refused to officially accept the specially bound presidential copy of the report or to sign thank-you letters to members of the commission. Eventually, Johnson provided a perfunctory statement of support for the commission's efforts but made clear that he did not agree fully with its recommendations. Roger W. Wilkins, director of the Community Relations Service in the Justice Department, told Harry McPherson that there was "widespread disappointment in the Negro community that the President has not embraced this report more enthusiastically."[38]

As Lindsay had hoped, the Kerner report received a great deal of attention. A paperback edition that was immediately published commercially sold more than 740,000 copies within a short time. As Roger Wilkins's comment indicated, the report also generated much controversy. The mayors of six cities that had suffered riots during the previous few years hailed its findings but suggested that little would happen without adequate state and federal funding. *BusinessWeek* praised the report for banishing any thoughts that it would be "another bland document for the files" and concluded that "any discussion of racial issues must take account of this grim report." The commission's charges that white racism was primarily to blame for the conditions that led to riots drew sharp criticism. Wilbur J. Cohen, whom Johnson had recently nominated as secretary of the Department of Health, Education, and Welfare, suggested that "the problem is more complicated than white racism." Richard Nixon returned to the points he had made in his *Reader's Digest* article the previous fall about the priority he assigned to ensuring law and order. "One of the major weaknesses of the President's commission is that it, in effect, blames everybody for the riots except the perpetrators," he said. "And I think that deficiency has to be dealt with first. Until we have order we can have no progress."[39]

The *Washington Afro-American* took a quite different view in an editorial. Although it agreed with the Kerner report on the need for sufficient federal funding to combat "ghetto ills," it cautioned that government spending was not enough in itself to solve the problems the commission identified. "A still greater need," it declared, "is for that portion of the majority white community which remains racist in its views to turn the spotlight on itself and its prejudices." The paper suggested that urban riots would end only if "massive steps" were taken "to uproot the racist disease in the white community."[40]

Although conditions in urban ghettos that the Kerner Commission had cited as causes of riots were clearly present in Washington, local officials were cautiously optimistic about avoiding severe disorders in the summer of 1968. The city's advantages of a large black middle class, geographical separation of ghetto areas, and a new city government headed by an African American mayor provided reason for hope. Mayor Washington walked through neighborhoods to talk with residents and gained a reputation for caring about their concerns. He also maintained contacts with local citizens, including militants, who kept him informed about "the mood of the streets." Director of Public Safety Murphy worked to improve police-community relations and to hire more black police officers. City officials met with federal authorities to make plans for responding to disturbances if they occurred. Since the District of Columbia National Guard had only a small force of about two thousand that could be mobilized in a riot, it would be reinforced with regular army troops to produce a "quick show of strength." Murphy was pleased enough with the preparations that he announced in March 1968, "I am completely confident we will be able to prevent any disorder, or shall we say serious disorder, in this city."[41]

Murphy's assurances might have eased, but they did not eliminate continuing concern about the possibility of serious riots in Washington. This remained a clear cause of worry for government officials and business leaders. They were especially troubled about Martin Luther King's plans to lead a march on Washington to lobby for huge anti-poverty programs funded by the federal government. The "Poor People's Campaign" would be waged by camping in temporary shelters on the National Mall to dramatize the hardships that needy citizens of all races in America experienced. King's campaign, which was scheduled to begin in late April, raised fears that it would mutate from peaceful demonstrations to violent disturbances. Andrew Parker, president of Woodward and Lothrop, one of the city's principal department stores, commented that although King's protests had been peaceful in the past, "the longer he's here, the longer the militant groups will have an opportunity to come into play."[42]

The early months of 1968 were a terrible time for the Johnson administration and for America. The Vietnam War was going badly, with no end in sight. News that the Pentagon wanted to increase draft calls incited howls of indignation. The economy was no longer thriving as it had a few years earlier and suffered from destabilizing inflation. College campuses were in turmoil as many students protested the war and other injustices in American society. The fears inspired by growing crime rates and the potential for, if not the likelihood of, urban violence produced anger with leaders and support for those who promised to make "law and order" a top priority. Johnson was under attack from Nixon and other Republicans on the right and from his Democratic challengers, Eugene McCarthy and Robert Kennedy, on the left. In late March, polls showed that only 36 percent of those surveyed approved of the president's job performance, down from 48 percent in January. Politically, economically, and culturally, the American public, or at least a considerable segment of it, was deeply unsettled over recent events and worried about prospects for the future. Johnson later commented, "I felt that I was being chased on all sides by a giant stampede coming at me from all directions." On March 31, 1968, the president shocked the nation by announcing that he would not seek or accept the Democratic nomination for another term in the White House.[43]

The "giant stampede" soon took a turn for the worse. Four days after Johnson's withdrawal, Martin Luther King was assassinated, and cities across the nation erupted in violence. In many urban areas, including Washington, the summer of 1968 came in April.

3

A City in Flames, April 4–5, 1968

AT 7:05 P.M., EASTERN STANDARD TIME, on Thursday, April 4, 1968, Martin Luther King Jr. was shot in the neck as he stood on the balcony of the Lorraine Motel in Memphis, Tennessee. United Press International (UPI) sent out the first public report at 7:12 p.m., and President Johnson learned the news by reading it on a ticker tape in his office that provided up-to-the-minute information. At 7:25 p.m., he received official word but few details from Attorney General Ramsey Clark. King died at 8:05 p.m. One hour later, Johnson appeared on national television and gave a three-minute address in which he mourned the death "of this outstanding leader" and appealed for calm. "I ask every citizen to reject the blind violence that has struck Dr. King, who lived by non-violence," he said. But his plea went unheeded as violent protests soon broke out in cities across the country.[1]

A crowd began to gather at the corner of 14th and U Streets in Northwest Washington when the news that King had been shot became public. The areas around the east–west corridor of U Street and the north–south corridor of 14th Street had deteriorated since their halcyon days of the 1920s and 1930s. But they were still the premier commercial center of black Washington. For about twenty blocks north of U Street, the 14th Street corridor and its offshoots hosted some three hundred businesses, including clothing, hardware, and grocery stores; appliance retailers; pharmacies; restaurants, cafes, carry-outs, and snack shops; and dry-cleaning establishments. It also featured bars, theaters, and nightclubs. In *Washington Post* editor Ben Gilbert's description, it was "a place notorious for tension and trouble" that "police considered . . . the most volatile in the city's crowded Negro sections." One example was a press conference that H. Rap Brown, chairman of the Student Nonviolent Coordinating Committee (SNCC), held at the organization's local office, two blocks north of 14th and U Streets, in July 1967. Brown declared that "violence is as American as apple pie" and warned that "if Washington doesn't come around, black folks are going to burn it down." He then went outside to continue his confrontation with "reporters who looked nervously at one another" before an appreciative crowd of about two hundred and "dozens of others" hanging out of windows."[2]

The 14th and U neighborhood was also the center of black activism in the city; the local offices of black leadership groups were clustered there. In addition to the local SNCC headquarters, the Washington offices of the Southern Christian Leadership Conference (SCLC) and the National Association for the Advancement of Colored People (NAACP) were located in the immediate area. It was natural that people gravitated toward the intersection when they learned that King had been shot. At the same time, police and civil defense intelligence units moved in to observe the scene. They found that, at first, the "mood of the group was . . . one of shock and dismay rather than of anger."[3]

The mood of the crowd became increasingly bitter after the announcement that King had died. Some individuals gathered around a transistor radio to listen to President Johnson's speech. His appeal for calm was not greeted favorably; one person shouted that King's death would "mean one thousand Detroits." By that time, Stokely Carmichael had joined the crowd, and he quickly assumed leadership. A graduate of Howard University, he happened to be in Washington during a series of speaking engagements around the country. He was no longer the SNCC national chairman, but when he heard about King's shooting, he went to the group's local office to consult with his colleagues. Although Carmichael and King took contrasting positions on the best approach to fighting racial injustice and obtaining equal rights, they agreed on their opposition to the Vietnam War. The twenty-six-year-old Carmichael admired King and looked up to him as something of an older brother. After talking with his SNCC associates, he decided that local businesses should close as a way of honoring King. He announced, "We're going to close them down now," and headed for the streets. His movements were carefully monitored by plainclothes police and intelligence sources.

Carmichael was not alone in deciding that stores in the 14th Street and U Street corridors should shut down. Other members of the crowd seemed to reach the same conclusion independently. A group of about twenty-five to thirty people fell in behind Carmichael, and they marched to a Peoples Drug Store at 14th and U Streets. Carmichael politely asked the manager of the store to close, and he immediately complied with the request. The group, made up mostly of young men, soon grew to about a hundred as it moved on to other businesses. The owners, doubtless in part because they felt intimidated, promptly agreed with demands to shutter their stores. By that time, large numbers of citizens, dazed by the news of King's assassination, lined 14th Street. They were primarily concentrated at the junction with U Street.[4]

From the second floor of the SCLC offices, Walter Fauntroy watched the growing turmoil on the streets below with foreboding. In addition to his duties as pastor of the New Bethel Baptist Church at 9th and S Streets and as vice-chairman of the District of Columbia city council, he headed the local chapter of the SCLC. King's death was a staggering blow to the thirty-five-year-old Fauntroy; the two men had been close friends since they had met as divinity students. Fauntroy was at his church when he learned of King's death; he had rushed to SCLC headquarters as soon as he heard that an angry crowd was assembling at the 14th and U intersection. Fauntroy feared that Carmichael, who had a well-earned reputation for making provocative statements, would further inflame a gathering that was already tense and restless. He went out on the street and elbowed his way through the crowd to confront Carmichael.

"This is not the way to do it, Stokely," Fauntroy cried above the noise of the crowd. "Let's not get anyone hurt. Let's cool it." Carmichael responded: "We're tired of them killing black people. We want them to close out of respect for Dr. King. . . . All we're asking them to do is close the stores." This explanation satisfied Fauntroy, who agreed that calling for stores to close was "a useful channeling of the frustration." He then dashed, with a police escort, to several local television and radio stations, where he appealed to city residents for "restraint, calm and nonviolence."[5]

The calls for calm and reason from leaders as disparate as Johnson, Carmichael, and Fauntroy soon proved to be futile. At 9:25 p.m., the first acts of vandalism and looting occurred. A window at the Peoples Drug Store that had closed at Carmichael's request was smashed. At about the same time, a fifteen-year-old boy broke the glass of the front door of the

Republic Theatre, just down the street from Peoples. He slipped between the glass fragments on the door and helped himself to a bag of popcorn. "Way to go, kid," somebody yelled.

The temper of the crowd turned more belligerent and the destruction more severe within a short time. A window of a Safeway market at 14th and Chapin Streets, five blocks north of U, was shattered and people immediately entered and began looting. One block south of the Safeway, a woman used her body to pummel the window of a television and appliance store until it broke. Carmichael and other SNCC workers tried to stop would-be looters, but their efforts could save the store's inventory for only a limited time. While this was happening, individuals and groups of up to twenty-five people began moving up and down 14th Street, smashing windows and looting stores. One resident later commented on the "force of those people" as they proceeded north from U Street. "They were masses of people, but without rhythm to the group or without coordination," he said. "It was like a live mass, like killer bees in a horror movie, and they were moving, charging, and chanting." The primary targets for looters were clothing stores, liquor stores, and pawnshops. In some cases, store owners scrawled "soul brother" on their windows, which was often but not always an effective defense.[6]

The outbursts on the night of April 4 were spontaneous. The intelligence division of the Metropolitan Police Department reported that "there were no indications that any of the mobs were organized or were being directed in any way." A twenty-one-year-old black man, recalling his experiences about two weeks after the riots ended, made clear that his own participation was not incited by others. He was unemployed and lived "in the center of the riot area." He was on the streets when the looting began, and he thought immediately that he had "a couple of watches," presumably hocked, in Kay Jewelry Store on 14th Street. The young man reasoned that if someone broke into the store, he could retrieve his watches. When he arrived at the store, however, he found that "it had already been cleaned out, which took only a matter of seconds." A little later, he watched as looters left a Pep Boys automotive and home supply store with tires, lawn mowers, and air conditioners. But he described himself as a "rational looter" who took only things he needed. He entered Pep Boys and walked out with a single sponge worth fifteen cents that he could use for washing dishes.[7]

The response of the Metropolitan Police Department to the growing violence on the streets of Washington was, at best, tentative. Despite the planning that followed the 1967 riots, the department failed to act promptly

PARK RD

IRVING ST

❺ KENYON ST

COLUMBIA RD

GEORGIA AVE

MICHIGAN AVE

FAIRMONT ST
❹

29

*McMillan
Reservoir*

CLIFTON ST

CHAPIN ST

*Howard
University*

FLORIDA AVE

*LeDroit
Park*

❷
❶   ❸

U ST

T ST

16TH ST

14TH ST

13TH ST

S ST

RHODE ISLAND AVE

NORTH CAPITOL ST

R ST   ❻

FLORIDA AVE

NEW YORK AVE

50

29

*Mount
Vernon
Square*

EYE ST

❽

MASSACHUSETTS AVE

H ST

*The
White
House*

15TH ST

14TH ST

13TH ST

11TH ST

9TH ST

7TH ST

6TH ST

G ST
F ST
E ST

4TH ST

1ST ST

*Union
Station*

❼

D ST

❾   INDIANA AVE

The Ellipse

PENNSYLVANIA AVE

C ST

0   1000   2000 ft

5280 feet = 1 mile

CONSTITUTION AVE

1. SCLC headquarters	4. Empire Market	7. D. J. Kaufman main store
2. Peoples Drug Store	5. G. C. Murphy store	8. D. J. Kaufman branch store
3. Republic Theatre	6. Manhattan Auto	9. DC Municipal Building

Riot areas in Northwest Washington. *Map by Emery Pajer*

or decisively when the rioting began. Shortly after King was shot, John S. Hughes, the deputy chief of police, requested a description of what was occurring on the streets from his intelligence sources. The department continued to monitor conditions but did not fully mobilize its forces in case of an outbreak of violence. At 9:30 p.m., Director of Public Safety Patrick Murphy told a reporter, "We're giving it the light touch. There are no great numbers of men visible." At about the same time, Fauntroy advised a police official at 14th and U to avoid summoning a large and perhaps provocative force.

The rioting began in earnest a short time later, and the "light touch" was not effective in controlling it. At 10:18, Assistant Chief of Police Jerry V. Wilson drove an unmarked car toward 14th Street in a drizzle and expressed hope that "it would rain like hell." But law enforcement officials were not that lucky. The police, with only a regular complement of men at hand, were badly outnumbered by the still-growing crowd. They attempted to seal off the riot area, but their numbers were too small to contain the disorders, and they were soon ordered to withdraw from the 14th and U intersection. Police cars that were visible were pelted with stones, bricks, and bottles, and patrolmen had little guidance on how to respond. At 10:26, one officer called into headquarters with a plea for instructions. "We're sur-rounded by a mob of about 50 people," he said. "What do we do? They're looting. Do we arrest them or do we leave? Or what the hell do we do?" The answer he and others who called in for orders received was not helpful: "Do whatever you think needs to be done."

By about 11:00 p.m., enough police officers had arrived to combat the riot aggressively. The midnight to 8:00 a.m. shift was ordered to report an hour early, and the combined force began to make arrests. The police did not fire their guns against rioters, but they formed a human wedge on 14th Street to limit access and discourage criminal activity. They brandished nightsticks against looters. Most effectively, they began the extensive use of tear gas.[8]

When supplies of tear gas ran low, the police department received assis-tance from a decidedly unconventional source. A twenty-seven-year-old man with a military bearing arrived at a police stationhouse at 16th and V Streets, about two blocks from the heart of the riot zone. He wore a cap-tain's uniform, combat ribbons, and a green beret, and he asked if he could do anything to help. Told of the need for tear gas, he offered his services. The police did not know at the time that the man was an imposter, and his act was very convincing. The "captain," later identified as a discharged army enlisted man, was driven in a police vehicle to the army's Fort Myer, just across the Potomac River in Virginia. No one questioned his authority, and he requisitioned 250 tear-gas grenades along with gas masks and steel helmets. The "captain" continued his charade for several days. It finally ended after he berated an army sergeant for failing to pay due respect to an officer. The sergeant, who had served as a paratrooper in Vietnam, had heard reports about an imposter that the army had circulated. After he reported his encounter to the police, the "captain" was arrested under federal charges of impersonating an army officer.[9]

The show of force by the police gradually curbed the looting of stores. But the problems caused by large-scale theft and damage to property were compounded by potentially even more devastating and dangerous effects of arson. The fire department responded to its first call in the riot area at 10:50 p.m., after a car on the sales lot of a Chevrolet dealer at 14th and Belmont Streets, four blocks north of U, was torched. This was the first in a series of eighteen fires that blazed over the next five and a half hours in the city. Seven of them occurred in the immediate vicinity of the riot on 14th Street, and all were definitively classified as arson. A few minutes after the fire at the car dealership started, a man attempted to burn a looted drugstore with lighted newspapers. Several women who were standing on the street shouted at him that people lived in apartments above the pharmacy. The man then tried to stamp out the flames without success, and the residents who lived above the store had to evacuate. The building was saved from destruction by a brief rainstorm.

Meanwhile, a fire was set at the Empire Super Market at 14th Street and Clifton. After looters cleaned out its inventory, a group of youths tried to burn it down. When police patrols drove by, they disappeared from sight, only to return when the squad cars moved on. They eventually succeeded in their self-appointed mission, and the fire they set "lit up [the] area like daylight," the *Washington Afro-American* reported. By the time the blaze was extinguished, the inside of the store was completely burned out. It was the most destructive fire of the night. Firefighters, like the police, received a rude welcome from people on the streets, who directed a barrage of verbal abuse at them. The rioters also hurled so many stones, bottles, and other objects that firemen wrapped wire mesh screens above the open cabs of their trucks. Finally, by 4:22 a.m. on April 5, after a night of enduring ill-treatment from citizens and weathering smoke and tear gas, the fire department reached a "period of relative calm" in which no new fires were reported.[10]

As the attacks on the police and firefighters, most of whom were white, indicated, the participants in the riot demonstrated ample measures of racial hostility. The disorders on 14th Street were not a race riot in the sense that they produced a series of direct, violent confrontations between blacks and whites. This had occurred at other times in Washington, most notably in a fierce clash between races in 1919 that resulted in thirty deaths and countless injuries. But if the outburst on the night of King's death was not a race riot, it clearly brought to the surface black resentment toward white society. "This is it, baby. The shit is going to hit the fan now," yelled one rioter shortly after the breaking of store windows and looting began. "Let's get some white motherfuckers. . . . Let's kill them all." At this juncture, Stokely Carmichael tried once again to cool passions, but the turmoil quickly gained momentum.[11]

Bonnie Perry, who was thirteen at the time of the riot and an attentive witness to what went on, later told an interviewer that some residents participated "because they just wanted to loot." She suggested, however, that those people were exceptions. "Most people did it because they were angry and were frustrated with the country. Frustrated and angry that Martin Luther King had been assassinated and frustrated that there was nothing," she recalled. "It was like there was no hope for the future." In considerably more graphic terms, an anonymous, unemployed black man expressed the rage he and others felt toward white society. He informed an interviewer about a month after the riots that the "shit of 'fuck whitey'" was "in the air." He went on to describe his anger and intense dissatisfaction. "Whiteys been jumping around here just killing us, man, like, oh man! His prices are ridiculous. His food is slop, you know," the man said. "We get the shit end of everything. And like we just supposed to take this shit and . . . I'm fed up. I think that a whole lot of the brothers, they was fed up."[12]

One of the rare face-to-face confrontations between black and white groups in the main riot area resulted in tragedy, though the details remained cloudy and the connection to the disturbances on the streets uncertain. The incident occurred after a group of four white men in their twenties pulled into a gas station on 14th Street. They were colleagues who worked for an electrical contracting company in Alexandria, Virginia. After a gathering in Alexandria where they reportedly had a few drinks, they decided for unexplained reasons to drive into Washington. They said later they knew nothing about King's death or the unsettled conditions in the city. When they stopped for gas, they got into an argument with a group of black youths, numbering, according to differing accounts, from eight to fifteen. The clash escalated to the point that the black youths attacked the white men with sticks and knives. One of the Virginians, George E. Fletcher, was stabbed in the head and neck and badly injured. In a panic, the electrical workers sped across the Potomac River to Virginia because they did not know where to find nearby medical assistance. Fletcher, a twenty-eight-year-old father of three, was pronounced dead at Fairfax Hospital. The story the men told was hard to verify, and the three survivors could not find the gas station where the assault occurred when police later drove them around the area. Whether or not the homicide was related to the violence taking place in the city, Fletcher was counted as the first fatality of the Washington riots.[13]

The disorders in Washington demonstrated that black animosity was directed not only at police and firefighters but also at white shop owners, who became the principal targets of the rioters. An unidentified twenty-four-year-old black man told an interviewer that as soon as the looting began on the evening of April 4, he thought immediately of "burning some stores." He explained that he focused on burning instead of looting "because if you hit the man in his pocketbook you really hurt him." In his view, it was too easy for shop owners to recover from a loss of their inventory. The man also argued that burning stores owned by whites was a source of "pride and dignity that one gets from destroying property that belongs to the enemy." And in his opinion, "the white man is our enemy." Mistrust between black residents and white merchants was a prominent and probably inevitable feature of life in low-income urban areas. White businessmen, like policemen, were symbols of white society for many ghetto residents, and for some, the only whites with whom they came in contact. Therefore, merchants and police officers involuntarily served as representatives of the institutions and conventions that had long denied black citizens equal political power, economic opportunity, and social status.

Many blacks had grievances with white merchants that went beyond symbolism. Black customers resented the palpably suspicious attitudes that some store owners displayed. Bonnie Perry recalled that she and her friends "hated to go in some of these stores because the white shop keepers would follow us like we were always in there stealing or something." An even greater source of ill will was the conviction among black shoppers that white merchants gouged them on prices. Business owners denied that this was a common practice and insisted that the prices they charged in ghetto areas were comparable to those in downtown or suburban stores. The extent of inequitable pricing was difficult, if not impossible, to measure, but there was no question that it occurred. Haynes Johnson, a white reporter for the

Evening Star, experienced it firsthand when he wrote his book on black life in the capital, published in 1963. He went shopping at a men's store in a downscale part of 7th Street NW and discovered that none of the suits, jackets, or slacks on the racks had a price tag. The owner gave him a price for a tweed sports coat, and assured him that it was "a good deal." Later, the same merchant quoted a higher price for the same jacket to a black customer. A US marshal told Johnson that he saw trousers priced at six dollars a pair in a downtown store that sold at three pairs for thirty-six dollars on uptown 7th Street. Black citizens suspected that this kind of dual pricing was widespread and found its existence in any degree infuriating.[14]

For their part, white merchants found that operating a business in predominantly black neighborhoods was increasingly difficult and indeed, dangerous. Many of those in the 14th and U Street corridors had run shops for many years, and they had watched with dismay as the area declined. They were often the victims of criminal activity, ranging from shoplifting to armed robbery, and they were perpetually worried about lawlessness and violence. The fear of crime that had increased dramatically in Washington over the previous few years was especially prevalent among whites whose livelihood depended on conditions in ghetto areas. An unidentified liquor store proprietor told a Senate hearing that he had been in business at the same location since 1949 and thought he had "a fine reputation" in the community. But his surroundings had recently taken a turn for the worse. "In the past three or four years there is an element of clientele . . . that is getting bad, we are getting bad language, we are getting minor threats, we have had to throw many people out," he said. As a result, he and his employees worked with "guns in our pockets, even to the point of going home with them and coming to work with them." Many of the business owners in the 14th and U area employed blacks and had always gotten along with their regular customers, and they were shocked and disheartened by the looting and destruction that took place on the night of April 4–5.

Larry Rosen grew up in Washington and owned Smith's Pharmacy, which he had purchased in 1959. He built it into a thriving business in a friendly neighborhood on 14th Street; among his most popular offerings were soda fountain treats and a breakfast menu of two eggs, toast, bacon, and coffee for fifty-nine cents. He employed several individuals from the neighborhood, including an African American pharmacist. When he learned of King's death, he called an employee who lived next to his property and was told, "they're breaking up your store." He sat up all night listening to the news on the radio. "It felt like it was something that couldn't be happening," Rosen later remarked, "but it was happening." The next morning he went to the store. "It was a mess," he recalled. "All the windows were smashed, the showcases were smashed, a lot of merchandise was gone." With his work of many years in shambles, "it was a feeling you can't describe." The next day, the store was burned down, and he never reopened. "I still don't understand why people took their frustrations out on the merchants," he said.[15]

During the evening of April 4, Mayor Walter Washington viewed the deteriorating conditions in the city with increasing concern. He had left his office after hearing of King's death and gone to his home in LeDroit Park. At about 10:00 p.m., he and his wife, Bennetta, were joined by Corporation Counsel Charles T. Duncan, the city's chief legal officer; his wife, Dorothy; and Julian R. Dugas, director of the District of Columbia's Department of Licenses and Inspections. Bennetta Washington, who was an educator with a PhD and a veteran administrator of anti-poverty programs, Charles Duncan, and Dugas ranked high among the mayor's most trusted advisers. The group watched news reports on television about the growing unrest on the streets, and at about 11:30 p.m., the mayor decided that he wanted to personally observe what was happening in the riot zones. He climbed into Charles Duncan's new Pontiac; appropriately enough, the model name of the car was Tempest. Washington and Duncan were accompanied by Dorothy Duncan, Dugas, and Paul Delaney, a reporter for the *Evening Star*.

The tour was a dispiriting exhibition for leaders who had taken office a few months earlier. As they drove on 14th Street, they witnessed a man heaving a bottle at a car, a convenience store and a hardware store being looted, and a liquor store stripped bare. One person shouted obscenities at them. In general, however, the mood of the crowds was one of "holiday gaiety." The mayor, Delaney reported, sat in "stunned silence, shaking his head." As they rode on, the city officials could see shadowy figures emerging from darkened stores with television sets, clothing, radios, and other merchandise. When Dugas remarked that most of the rioters were young people, Washington joked sardonically, "I guess this is our recreation program for the summer." None of his traveling companions laughed. By then, the group had seen enough. They made their way to the police station at 16th and V Streets, where the mayor met with Murphy and Chief John Layton.

At a 3:00 a.m. press conference, the mayor commended the police for a "remarkable job of restraint and containment." When Layton was asked about the delay in mobilizing the police force, he explained that the disorder "started without prior notice." His men, he said, had to "play a waiting game" until they had a force strong enough to disperse crowds and make arrests. At about the same time, Murphy attended a meeting at the Pentagon with high-ranking army officers and Justice Department officials. Although he felt confident that the "situation in D.C. was under control," he acknowledged that he was worried about what might happen the next night. The officials at the meeting discussed arrangements for calling up the National Guard. They agreed that after consulting with their superiors, they would meet again later in the morning.[16]

By about 4:00 a.m., in keeping with Murphy's favorable report on the situation at the Pentagon meeting, the police had established "reasonably complete control" of the area surrounding 14th Street. But disorder had spread to other parts of the city. On the 7th Street corridor stretching from Florida Avenue as far south as Pennsylvania Avenue, roving bands of rioters shattered windows at more than eighty stores, including two department stores, Hecht's and Kann's. They also broke the windows and took some items from a fashionable men's shop, D. J. Kaufman's, at 10th Street and Pennsylvania Avenue. There were sporadic reports of break-ins and looting at several stores in Northeast Washington. Nevertheless, the scale of those problems was manageable, and when Charles Duncan drove the mayor home at 4:36 a.m., they appeared to agree tacitly that the worst of the ordeal was behind them.

The participants in the night's disturbances looted at least 155 stores in the city. Police arrested 202 individuals, mostly for theft and drunkenness. George Fletcher was the only fatality. There were about 56 injuries, none serious, including 1 fireman and 5 policemen. Although fires were a constant danger, most were, in Murphy's description, "very minor in nature." The riots on the evening of King's death were alarming for government officials and many residents, and they were a great misfortune for store owners and others whose property was stolen, damaged, or destroyed. But the turmoil was eventually contained by the police and its consequences fell short of catastrophic proportions.[17]

Washington was not the only city to suffer outbreaks of violence the night of King's death. There was serious looting and destruction of property in Harlem. National Guard troops were called up in Memphis and Nashville, Tennessee, and Raleigh and Greensboro, North Carolina. Less severe disturbances took place in many other urban areas around the country. Although none of the disorders approached the level of devastation of the Detroit or Newark riots of 1967, they were troubling nevertheless, not least because of the fear that they might portend more intense convulsions.

The city of Washington during the morning of Friday, April 5, was fairly calm. District of Columbia and federal government officials were cautiously hopeful that the worst was over. They made plans for taking action if the rioting broke out again, but, mindful of the patterns in other cities during previous years, they did not expect major problems to occur during daylight hours. Their concern was that the unrest would be rekindled that night. The capital "seemed to quiet down in the early hours of the morning," Deputy Mayor Thomas Fletcher later commented. "We were getting geared up for [a] night-time breakout."[18]

President Johnson held a hastily organized meeting with civil rights leaders, including Mayor Washington, at the White House at 11:00 a.m. He warned that it would be "a catastrophe for the country" if Americans concluded that violence was the only way to address racial problems. The black leaders at the conference agreed to speak out against violence, but Walter Fauntroy and several others also emphasized that their efforts must be supported with practical measures to improve conditions in low-income urban areas. Johnson agreed that sharply increased spending to combat urban woes might be necessary to reduce the likelihood of riots, at least in the long run. With congressional leaders sitting in the room, he also urged prompt passage of the fair-housing legislation he had long advocated. When the meeting ended, most of those who attended rode in a twelve-car motorcade to the National Cathedral for a memorial service for King.[19]

At 12:05 p.m., Patrick Murphy met with Undersecretary of the Army David E. McGiffert and Deputy Attorney General Warren M. Christopher at the White House. McGiffert was the Pentagon official primarily responsible for developing plans for dealing with domestic disturbances after the Detroit and Newark riots. In that capacity, he worked closely with Christopher, a partner in one of the most prestigious law firms in Los Angeles who had joined the Justice Department in 1967. He had served as vice-chairman of the commission, chaired by John McCone, that had investigated the Watts riot of 1965. McCone described him in a letter to President Johnson as a "reliable, conscientious, loyal man . . . of good judgment." Ramsey Clark had gone to Memphis after King's assassination, which placed Christopher in charge of the Justice Department's response to the Washington riots.

Murphy, McGiffert, and Christopher quickly agreed that the District of Columbia National Guard should be called up. Its troops would assemble at the DC Armory on East Capitol Street, just west of the Anacostia River, in time to be ready for deployment by dark. The army had already placed units of active forces on alert, which meant that they would be prepared to move to their assigned destination within a specified period. One infantry company (150 men) at Fort Myer in nearby Virginia went on a one-and-a-half-hour alert and two companies went on a two-hour alert. Troops at Fort Meade, Maryland, about twenty-two miles from Washington, went on two-hour and four-hour alerts.[20]

By the time the meeting between Murphy, McGiffert, and Christopher ended, their plans were obsolete. Serious rioting resumed on 14th Street at about noon, and it quickly surged out of control. Despite the calm that seemed to prevail on the streets of Washington on the morning of April 5, trouble was brewing. One source of concern for government officials and others who wanted to ease tensions was a series of provocative statements that Stokely Carmichael made at a press conference. After trying without success to mitigate the anger of the crowds the previous evening, Carmichael had left the scene. He reappeared on Friday morning with an ominous message. "When white America killed Dr. King, she opened the eyes of every black man in this country," he said. "He was the one man in our race who was trying to reach our people to have love, compassion and mercy for what white people had done. When white America killed Dr. King . . . she declared war on us." Carmichael blasted the "honky Lyndon Johnson" and the "honky Bobby Kennedy" and suggested that the only way black people would survive was "to get some guns."

When Carmichael spoke a short time later to a rally at Howard University, however, he was somewhat less confrontational. "Stay off the streets if you don't have a gun," he shouted as he waved a pistol above his head. He predicted that "there's going to be shooting." The meaning of Carmichael's warning was debatable; it seemed to be more an appeal for caution than a call to arms. Contrary to the information that a White House staff member provided the president, he did not advise Howard students, "Don't loot—shoot." After his speech at Howard, Carmichael again vanished from public view, and the intelligence observers who tailed him lost track of his whereabouts.[21]

A more immediate and unambiguous threat to peace on the streets was the discontent among students in Washington's public schools. Mayor Washington, Murphy, and school superintendent William R. Manning had agreed that opening the schools on April 5 was essential for maintaining order. They were fearful of the consequences of closing the schools and providing an opportunity for some 150,000 students to roam the streets. But keeping schools open was not enough in itself to prevent students from contributing to a fierce renewal of violence. Although the schools presented tributes to King and urged their students to remain in class, it was apparent by mid-morning that their efforts had, in significant measure, failed. Many students simply walked out of school buildings and made their way to the sites of the previous night's looting.[22]

By noon, crowds of mostly young people, including students, unemployed residents, employed citizens who had not gone to work, would-be looters, and onlookers had gathered along the 14th Street corridor for twenty blocks north of U Street. Few police officers were in the area. The department's regular shift of 414 patrolmen city-wide was supplemented with a small force from its civil disturbance unit, but the main body of that unit was not scheduled for duty until 5:00 p.m. On 14th Street, groups of youths, including high school students, at first engaged in capers they found entertaining. They rocked cars stopped at traffic lights and made facetious threats to the occupants, who undoubtedly did not find the antics amusing.

Suddenly and spontaneously, the mood on the streets turned ugly and the activities of the crowds immensely destructive. At 12:13 p.m., a Safeway grocery store just below 14th and U was set on fire. Simultaneously, groups of three hundred or more people began to break windows and loot stores that had escaped damage the previous evening. All kinds of businesses were robbed of their inventory—grocery stores, jewelers, shoe stores, clothing retailers (including a maternity shop), office supply stores, gift shops, and especially liquor stores. At 14th and Harvard Streets, nine blocks north of U, police radio calls for assistance were described as "frantic." One officer appealed for "gas masks, gas and more troops" because, he said, "We are getting bricks here." The answer he received was, "If not enough men, withdraw from the area." By 1:40 p.m., the Military District of Washington's Intelligence Journal, which compiled information on what was happening on the streets from various sources, reported, "All of U St out of control because of rioting."[23]

Although the rioters generally did not target white individuals to vent their anger, there were appalling exceptions. On upper 14th Street, a group of young men chased a fleeing, terrified white man as a crowd of onlookers shouted, "Get him." When they caught him, they forced him to his knees. One of their number then struck the "pleading man" on the top of the head with a brick. The victim staggered away with blood running down his face, but his ordeal had not ended. The attackers tore his clothing, pummeled him with fists, and threw him to the ground. Many in the crowd taunted

Looting of a Safeway store, 14th Street and Park Road NW, April 5, 1968. *Steve Northup Photographic Archive, e_spn_0142, Dolph Briscoe Center for American History, University of Texas at Austin. Photo by Steve Northup / The Washington Post via Getty Images*

him, though some called for mercy by yelling, "Don't kill him." Finally, a police car arrived to rescue the injured man. Elsewhere on 14th Street, rioters heaved rocks at cars with white drivers, who were designated with shouts of, "There's one. Get whitey. Get him."[24]

The crisis caused by attacks on individuals and by looting was drastically heightened by the increasingly common practice of burning stores down once they were emptied of their contents. This was a crucial qualitative difference between the riots of Thursday and the much worse outbreaks of Friday. The fire department later reported that 95 percent of the fires in the city during the riots were "suspected arson." By about 1:00 p.m., eleven major fires and many lesser ones were burning along 14th Street, and some had spread from building to building to jeopardize entire blocks. The fire department was unable to deal with the magnitude of the problems it faced. Not only was it confronted with a growing number of blazes, but it also had great difficulty reaching the sites of burning buildings because of traffic tie-ups and crowds of people in the streets. Once firefighters arrived at a destination, they were often greeted by rioters who shouted racial epithets, threw objects, and tried to cut their hoses. The human costs of the arsonists' handiwork included the midday deaths of two teenagers in a blaze in a G. C. Murphy variety store. Their bodies were found in the rubble the next day.[25]

The fires of 14th Street caused serious suffering in other ways as well. One man who was worried about the safety of his wife and three children left his job as a chef to search the area for them. Eventually, he found them at his mother-in-law's residence. He received a huge shock when he returned to the site of his family's apartment. "I got home and there was no home," he recalled a few days later. The building in which he lived, along with all of his family's possessions, including recently purchased furniture, had been destroyed by fire. To make matters even worse, the restaurant in which he worked was also gutted. Although the man was grateful that his family was unharmed, he could not conceal his anger over what happened. "I've been in the war, man, and seen a lot of destruction," he told a reporter, "and this is just like the front line."[26]

Shortly after 14th Street erupted, a surge of destructive activity began a few blocks east on 7th Street NW. The 7th Street corridor had been hit with window-breaking and some looting on Thursday evening, but, as on 14th Street, the riots that broke out on Friday were more devastating by orders of magnitude. Moving north from Constitution Avenue, 7th Street passed by the National Archives, the eastern end of the F Street shopping area, and Mount Vernon Square, home of the District of Columbia's Carnegie Library. From that point, the surroundings became considerably harsher. In 1963, Haynes Johnson described the commercial area north of the library as a strip of stores, "nearly all boasting large and gaudy signs of the bargains to be found inside." It included a variety of inelegant shops, personal service businesses, and "bars and taverns, more bars and more taverns." The quality of the merchandise in upper 7th Street's stores was generally inferior to what was available on 14th Street. "This part of the street has no 'nice' specialty stores and no large department stores," Stephen Johnston, a *Washington Afro-American* reporter, commented in 1967. "Merchants here cater to the raw needs of the slums and ghetto residents."

The residents of the 7th Street corridor were "truly . . . the hopeless, the beaten, the underprivileged, the completely dispossessed," Johnston wrote. "The bitter resentment smolders" over rat-infested apartments, lack of jobs, and "a society that seems to have bypassed them." The buildings that lined upper 7th Street were typical two- and three-story late-nineteenth-century structures. They provided space for shops on the ground floor and for apartments on the higher floors.[27]

On the early afternoon of April 5, bands of looters moved freely and fearlessly on 7th Street between Mount Vernon Square and E Street to the south. Outnumbered police made no effort to stop the looting, though they tried without success to block access to commercial areas and they rescued some items from store windows that had been smashed. The first fire alarm

Looting of liquor store at 7th and O Streets NW, April 5, 1968. *Alexander Lmanian, Photographs of Washington, DC, and New Haven, Connecticut. General Collection, Beinecke Rare Book and Manuscript Library, Yale University*

on 7th Street sounded at about 1:00 p.m., and it was followed by many others. Within forty minutes, several stores were burning, and, ominously, the Military District of Washington reported that at one of them, "firemen are helpless."[28]

A revealing example of the emerging calamity was the fate of several stores and residences on the west side of 7th Street north of Mount Vernon Square between R and S Streets. There were sixteen stores on the block, and some had suffered minor damage the previous evening. But the store owners and apartment dwellers were not prepared for the violence that struck them on Friday afternoon. Irving Abraham, who owned a liquor store, Log Cabin Liquors, received a call from a former employee. "Irv, get out of that place," he warned. "It's starting up again." Abraham, along with his mother-in-law and brother-in-law, fled as quickly as possible. As they drove away, they saw the owner of a neighboring hardware store, Abraham Zevin, and shouted at him, "Go home!" Zevin's father, who had founded the store, at first refused to leave. "I've been standing here for fifty years," he said. "Why do I have to move now?" His son finally convinced him that "if we stayed we would get killed." A short distance away, Abraham Gritz was locking his shoe store when he was accosted by a crowd of looters. They stole his keys, watch, and wallet and slapped his face repeatedly. Then they moved on to stealing merchandise from his store while he managed to find a ride to his home in the suburbs.

Other shop owners on the block also closed their doors and took flight. There were thirteen residents, including three children, who lived in apartments above the stores. At first, the main problem was the tear gas that wafted up from the street after the police arrived. But as Claudia Howard was fixing dinner for her two granddaughters in her apartment above a dairy store next to Log Cabin Liquors, she heard an explosion. She and her granddaughters immediately ran out to the street, where they watched the building burn down with all their possessions in it. By that time, other buildings on the block were also ablaze. When the burning ended, ten stores, six with white owners and four with black owners, were completely destroyed. Six other stores, all owned by blacks, were undamaged. The thirteen people who lived in apartments above the gutted stores lost their homes, and in most cases, all their belongings.[29]

One other business that was burned to the ground was Manhattan Auto, which occupied four properties—a three-year-old showroom, a service department, a used-car lot, and an accessories store—at the R Street end of the block. The company had been founded at that location in 1914 as a gas station in a former feed store. It had grown into the largest dealer of foreign cars in the Washington area. But none of the buildings survived the riots of April 5. When Joe Herson, the president of Manhattan Auto, and his brother-in-law, Bernie Mills, who was the general manager, went to inspect the damage to their properties, they discovered that "it looked like we had been bombed out in an air raid." They had taken special pride in their recently built showroom and found that it, along with thirty-two cars, had been consumed by the flames. When Mills started to walk across the street to look at the used-car lot, Herson cautioned him against doing it. "These people are our neighbors," Mills protested. "The business has been here for 50 years." Herson responded, "Things are different now. Things are very different." Although Mills later remarked that it was "very traumatic to pull up roots," Manhattan Auto left 7th Street permanently and moved to the suburbs.[30]

While large sections of the 14th Street NW and 7th Street NW corridors were going up in flames, the disorders of April 5 spread disastrously to the Northeast and Southeast quadrants of the city. The center of the rioting in Northeast was the H Street corridor, which ran from North Capitol Street just above Union Station for fifteen blocks to the east, where it joined with Benning Road and Bladensburg Road. H Street, like its counterparts on 14th Street and 7th Street NW, was a major commercial center for residents of the low-income neighborhoods of Northeast. The tumult that started on Friday afternoon emulated the patterns in the other riot zones, and indeed, some of the participants had migrated from the disorders on 7th Street NW. Widespread looting of H Street stores began around 3:00 p.m. and quickly accelerated. The two dozen police officers in the area were badly outnumbered and had orders not to shoot into crowds of looters. They attempted, with limited success, to control the chaos with tear gas.

The burning of stores began promptly in the wake of looting. By about 4:00 p.m., the Military District of Washington reported that an eleven-block strip of H Street was "all in flames." The police at the scene indicated that they could "do nothing" to contain the violence, and, once again, the fire department was unable to effectively fight the blazes that spread irrepressibly. Among the H Street stores that burned to ashes was Morton's, a branch of a local department store chain that featured moderately priced merchandise. After the store was thoroughly looted, a man who had been watching from the street threw a Molotov cocktail through the broken front door. Ben Gilbert of the *Washington Post* described the results: "The gasoline exploded, lifting the roof of the store, nearly demolishing the whole building, and starting a fierce fire." Unfortunately, a teenage boy was still inside when the fire bomber ignited the store; his body, burned beyond recognition, was found a few days later.[31]

The firebombing of Morton's was not an isolated act. Some individuals had little interest in looting but took advantage of the unrest that followed King's death to burn down buildings. The number of arsonists and the number of stores they torched were imprecise. Three of them talked anonymously with a *Washington Post* reporter about four months after the riots, wearing hoods over their heads, to provide insight into their activities and motives. They revealed that they were a part of a group of twenty-five that was committed to a rebellion that would "destroy the white man."

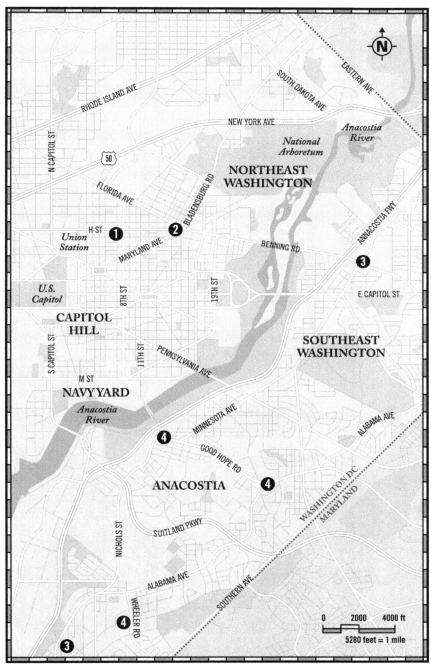

1. Morton's department store   3. Gunfire fatalities

2. Hechinger warehouse   4. Looting and burning

Riot areas in Northeast and Southeast Washington. *Map by Emery Pajer*

They made clear that they sought to "destroy the beast in any way" and that the beast was "the honkie, the whiteys." One of the men explained, "I personally want to destroy the system. The system is what suppresses our people and oppresses our people." Setting fires with dynamite stolen from construction sites and with Molotov cocktails they learned to make in the army gave them great satisfaction as a way of attacking white society. They were especially bitter toward Jewish business owners, because "they say they want to give us civil rights because they went through the same thing, and then take all the money." The men thought they had set at least twenty-five fires and insisted that "the majority of the places that were burned were burned by the mass of black people." They included among their targets shoe stores, pharmacies, fast-food restaurants, grocery markets, and especially liquor stores. It is impossible to judge the accuracy of the claims of the unidentified arsonists, but it seems clear that they and others like them were responsible for a significant, if indeterminate, share of the damage in all sections of Washington.[32]

While large portions of H Street NE were burning, serious disturbances broke out in parts of the city across the Anacostia River. It had long been the forgotten section of the capital, and its problems on April 5 did not receive nearly as much attention as the violence in other areas. But there

Burning buildings on H Street NE, April 5, 1968. *Associated Press*

were reports of extensive looting, burning buildings, and "general disor-der." Some police officers tried to gain control by carrying loaded weapons, apparently because they had not been told that they should refrain from using their guns when apprehending looters. On Friday evening, this led to questionable recourse to firearms by patrolmen who fired warning shots over the heads of rioters. Worse, it also led to the fatal shooting of two young men. In one case, at Benning Road and Minnesota Avenue NE, a fifteen-year-old bumped into a policeman's loaded and cocked pistol, which accidentally discharged and killed him. In the other case, a patrolman fired at a fleeing citizen who he thought was an armed looter. The man, who was fatally wounded, turned out to have no weapon and no loot. Although the officers who fired the shots were later cleared of wrongdoing, their actions raised tensions in the area and doubts about the soundness of police judg-ment among residents.[33]

Late in the afternoon of April 5, the F Street Mall, Washington's high-end shopping destination, was hit with looting and burning, though the consequences were less severe than in other parts of the city. The Mall was home to Washington's three leading department stores—Hecht's at F and 7th Street NW, Woodward and Lothrop at F between 10th and 11th Streets NW, and Garfinckel's at F and 14th Street NW. The F Street department stores had lost many of their customers and at least some of their aura to their suburban branches during the 1960s. But the eight-block stretch still included many upscale jewelry, clothing, and shoe stores. By about 4:00 p.m., groups of eight to twelve young people had turned their atten-tion to the street's rich looting opportunities. They were generally in a happy mood. They gamboled down F Street, "knocking out windows," the *Washington Post* reported. "They were skylarking. . . . The sound of break-ing glass mixed with [their] laughter." The looters knew what they wanted. While they did little damage to the department stores, they cleaned out several menswear and shoe shops. As tourists and local citizens waiting for buses looked on, the police took no effective steps to stop the looters. Finally, after supplies of tear gas arrived, they managed to halt the frolic on F Street, which left behind sidewalks cluttered with broken glass and aban-doned articles from plundered stores.[34]

The downtown business that suffered the worst damage was D. J. Kaufman's haberdashery, which was a short distance from F Street. The people who looted its stores at Pennsylvania Avenue and 10th Street NW and at 14th and I Streets NW were not "skylarking." Kaufman's sold expen-sive and modish men's clothing and accessories that appealed to many black customers. In mid-afternoon, rioters smashed the windows and entered the store on 14th Street. After they threatened the clerks, the owner, Oscar Dodek, told his employees by telephone to leave. Then the looting began. Crowds carried clothing out of the store, and sometimes stopped in a nearby park, Franklin Square, to try on what they had stolen. As this was going on, other looters filled a panel truck with merchandise. The store was stripped bare by about 5:00 p.m. At that point, a man stepped into the store, poured gasoline on the carpet, and lighted it. The flames reduced Kaufman's and an adjoining restaurant to burned-out shells.

Remains of D. J. Kaufman Men's Store, 14th and I Streets NW, April 5, 1968. *Alexander Lmanian, Photographs of Washington, DC, and New Haven, Connecticut. General Collection, Beinecke Rare Book and Manuscript Library, Yale University*

The main Kaufman's store on Pennsylvania Avenue fared relatively better, but this was a small consolation for the owner. As live television reports showed his property being ransacked, he watched at his home in tears. The store had suffered some minor damage the previous evening, and on Friday afternoon, it was hit much harder. Looters, including a group of black men in their twenties who drove up in two late-model Cadillacs and one Lincoln, emptied the store. But they did not burn it.[35]

Some motorists who were fleeing town on Friday afternoon had a front-row seat to watch the Kaufman's store on 14th Street looted and gutted. As the violence on the streets worsened, stores closed and many federal employees left their offices. The federal government officially shut down at 4:00 p.m., but by then many, perhaps most, workers downtown had departed for home. The result was an enormous traffic jam that made streets impassable for blocks in the city and backed up for miles on roads in the Virginia suburbs. Some commuters avoided the gridlock by walking across the bridges that led into Virginia. Those who lived in Maryland were careful to avoid driving through riot areas, which caused further congestion on other streets leading out of town. A high school student who lived in Southeast Washington but attended school in Northwest later remembered a harrowing trip home with classmates in his 1962 Plymouth Valiant. He stopped for gas, where cars driven by "white folks who were trying to get out of town" were lined up at the pumps. The owner of the gas station was in "a craze" because he "was trying to figure out if people were going to blow up his station." On the drive across the city, the student and his friends "could see people breaking into stores, busting windows out; there was a stench of tear gas all over the place." It was, he said, "one of the scariest times of my life."[36]

The long and anxious trip home for commuters was made more unpleasant by the haze of smoke that hung over large parts of the city. The fire department reported that twenty-five to thirty new fires broke out every hour on Friday, and that this rate continued for several hours. President Johnson later recalled "the sick feeling that came over me . . . as I saw the black smoke from burning buildings fill the sky over Washington." He added, "I wondered, as every American must have wondered, what we were coming to."[37]

By early Friday afternoon, it was apparent that the rampage in the city far exceeded the ability of the police and fire departments to control it. Despite the preparations for calling out National Guard and regular army troops, the decision to take this step was delayed for several hours after the rioting resumed.

When President Johnson and Mayor Washington left the memorial service for Martin Luther King at the National Cathedral shortly before 1:00 p.m., they were informed about the new outbreak of serious disorders in Northwest. Washington made several phone calls from the White House to obtain additional information, and at 1:56 p.m., he told the president that rioting in the city was "getting out of control" and that the introduction of troops was required. Johnson asked the mayor if he could use the assistance of Cyrus R. Vance, whom the president had sent as his personal representative to Detroit during the 1967 riot. Vance was a judicious, calm, and highly respected former Pentagon official who had returned to his law practice in New York. After his experiences in Detroit, he had written an influential report on handling domestic disturbances. One of his most important recommendations was that the use of tear gas was a more effective weapon to control riots than firearms. Mayor Washington responded without hesitation that he would welcome Vance's presence. The president placed a phone call to New York immediately, and within a short time, Vance was on a flight to Washington.[38]

Johnson was reluctant to order troops into the city. One reason was that some advisers, including Ramsey Clark, cautioned that placing the army in an already volatile situation could increase tensions. A more important reason was that the president feared that armed troops on the streets raised the likelihood of people getting killed. When Vance had advised him to send federal forces to Detroit the previous summer, Johnson had commented, "I guess it's just a matter of minutes before federal troops start shooting women and children." He was greatly worried about imposing the same risk on Washington. Further, he was not yet convinced that the situation in the capital merited the use of the military.[39]

At 2:00 p.m., Johnson instructed Warren Christopher to find out from the army which general would be in charge of the troops if they were called up. He also directed Christopher, Patrick Murphy, and whoever was designated as the commander of "Task Force Washington" to tour the riot zones to determine the need for troops. Christopher learned from Harold K. Johnson, the army chief of staff, that Ralph E. Haines Jr., the army vice–chief of staff, would likely serve as the head of the task force's operations. Haines was told to change from his uniform into civilian clothing and to meet Christopher and Murphy at the White House at 2:30 p.m.

Meanwhile, the city government was preparing a formal request that, after review by Christopher, would be sent to the president. The District of Columbia document, signed by Mayor Washington, Murphy, and Layton,

Deputy Attorney General Warren Christopher and Mayor Walter Washington in a tense moment, April 5, 1968. *Walter Washington Papers, Moorland-Spingarn Research Center, Howard University*

stated that "it is essential for the safety and welfare of the citizens of the District of Columbia that Federal Troops be employed as promptly as possible." Christopher delivered a presidential proclamation and an executive order to the White House at about 2:45 p.m. that would officially authorize the use of troops. Johnson waited to sign the documents until Christopher, Murphy, and Haines completed their inspection of conditions in the riot areas of Northwest and submitted their recommendations.[40]

The tour turned out to be a difficult assignment, though it was not without its humorous moments. The three men set out from the White House in an unmarked police car. Traffic was badly snarled and slowed their foray into the riot zones of 14th Street and 7th Street. They quickly concluded that the police were unable to control the disorders and that federal troops were needed. But the trio encountered severe problems communicating their judgment to the White House. They had planned to use the police radio in their car to contact the president, but they discovered to their dismay that the police network was overwhelmed and unavailable to them.

As Johnson waited with growing impatience, the three officials searched for a telephone booth. They finally found one in working order at a gas station on 7th Street, and, after waiting their turn in a line for a few minutes, Christopher got through to the president at 3:55 p.m. Johnson was "very upset" about the breakdown in communications, "but he was all business and knew a great deal about the events." Although he accepted the advice on calling out federal forces, he decided that he preferred to use regular army troops instead of the National Guard because they would be available sooner and because they were better trained for riot duty. At that point, Haines, whose shoulder had just been struck with a flying rock, joined Christopher in the phone booth and expressed his agreement. "I'm sure it must have been a very odd-looking pair—General Haines and I huddled around a telephone in a service station . . . with rioting going on all around us," Christopher later commented. "There was a whole group of people standing outside the telephone booth not knowing what we were doing, but lined up to use that telephone which was the only one working in the area."[41]

At 4:02 p.m., in accordance with legal requirements, President Johnson signed the proclamation that ordered the citizens of Washington to "cease and desist" from their unlawful activities, and one minute later, he signed the executive order authorizing the use of federal forces in the capital. He immediately called General Johnson to tell him he had signed the documents and "to get troops moving." The general informed him that thirty-eight hundred soldiers were on their way to the city and nearby areas. The president insisted that troop movements be carried out in a "low-key" manner and he hoped that their presence would have limited visibility. General Johnson cautioned that he could not "move troops without visibility." The president told the general that he wanted 3rd Infantry companies from Fort Myer to proceed without delay to the city. Later, the president instructed Joseph Califano to personally tell Mayor Washington, General Johnson, and Christopher that "police, troops, and National Guard be cautioned, to the man, to use the minimum force necessary" in their efforts to end the rioting. "If humanly possible," he said, "I don't want anybody killed."

General Johnson planned to send the first contingent of 3rd Infantry troops to the Capitol grounds, the White House, and the "disturbance area" of 14th Street. But at the request of the Secret Service, he changed this order to include only the Capitol and the White House. The Secret Service wanted to ensure that the units assigned to the White House were not diverted to other posts. At 4:50 p.m., the general spoke with Califano to clarify his instructions. They agreed that he would commit 500 men from the 3rd Infantry and move additional troops to the city in a manner that was as low-key as possible. The number of troops that first arrived was small. At 5:00 p.m., 555 men of the 6th Armored Cavalry, based at Fort

Meade, reached H Street NE, where the police had lost control earlier in the day. With the use of tear gas, they managed to curb the activities of the rioters, though not to rout them. This was the first engagement between the army and citizens in the riot areas.

While the 6th Cavalry tried to gain the upper hand on H Street, one company of 150 men from the 3rd Infantry took up positions at the Capitol. Although the Capitol grounds were quiet, the troops set up machine guns as a precautionary measure within a short time. Another 3rd Infantry company of the same size moved in from Fort Myer to guard the White House. Other army units were making their way toward the city. The District of Columbia National Guard was federalized at 5:00 p.m., but only about 40 percent of its members had reached the armory by that time because of faulty communications and traffic jams. Gradually, as the army's strength increased, its troops fanned out throughout the city. By 9:00 a.m. on Saturday, April 6, there were 8,253 troops on the ground and another 1,150 en route.[42]

Shortly after General Haines returned from his tour of the riot areas in Northwest with Christopher and Murphy, General Johnson confirmed his appointment as commander of Task Force Washington. The rules of engagement that applied to the disorders in the capital were drawn largely from the guidelines the army had developed after the 1967 riots and issued in final form just a few days before King's assassination. In his orders to Haines, Johnson directed that "minimum force, consistent with mission accomplishment, will be used by both military and civilian personnel." He specified that troops would not load or fire their weapons unless authorized by an officer "in person" or "when required to save their lives." Soldiers in the streets were instructed to use tear gas before resorting to live ammunition. Haines was given a list of options for arming the troops that would patrol the streets, and he chose one of the least provocative, which was to fix bayonets but keep them sheathed and to carry ammunition but not load it.

The troops who were stationed in Washington were authorized to "use force to prevent looting and to detain persons caught in the act of looting." They were instructed to avoid the "use of firearms except as a last resort," and, if firing shots proved necessary, they should be "aimed to wound rather than to kill." The orders that Haines received and that were relayed to the troops were purposely general and flexible. They left a great deal of discretion to officers at the scene and to individual soldiers. With the use of firearms strongly discouraged, the most effective weapons for the army were tear gas and, as more units arrived in the city, strength in numbers. An

Soldiers guarding the US Capitol. *US News & World Report Collection, U9-18951-33, Library of Congress*

individual soldier with an unloaded rifle and a sheathed bayonet was not a major deterrent to crime. But groups of trained military personnel who could protect firefighters and detain looters until police officers arrested them held out the promise of eventually restoring order.[43]

Within half an hour after President Johnson called out federal troops, Mayor Washington took another step to contain the rioting by imposing a curfew on the entire city. It would be in effect from 5:30 p.m. to 6:30 a.m. every night until further notice. The curfew directed city residents to stay off the streets and "away from public places." It prohibited the sale of liquor, beer, wine, firearms, and ammunition. It also outlawed the sale of gasoline and other flammables except when "dispensed directly into the gas tanks of motor vehicles." Curfew violators were subject to a $300 fine and ninety days in jail. Even before the mayor acted, as a further indication of the severity of the disorders in the capital, the organizers of the annual Cherry Blossom Festival, a popular tourist attraction that had begun earlier in the week, called off the event's remaining activities. The Washington Senators announced that their opening-day baseball game against the Minnesota Twins, scheduled for Monday, April 8, would be postponed.[44]

The gradual introduction of troops and the curfew had only limited immediate effect on controlling the riots on the evening of April 5, though eventually they were critical in calming the streets. The reports that came in and were listed on timelines compiled by the Military District of Washington, Task Force Washington, the District of Columbia's Office of Civil Defense, and the White House Situation Room sketched a relentless drumbeat of disasters that had already occurred and that were continuing. At 5:30 p.m., on or near 7th Street NW: "Firemen are being attacked with sticks, stones, and crow bars." At 6:35 p.m.: "Rioting continued out of control in many parts of the city." At 7:00 p.m. on Good Hope Road SE: "Heavy looting. . . . General disorder. . . . Police are voicing concern over lack of troops. They have lost control." At 8:40 p.m. in Northeast: "Three separate negro [sic] sections burning for one solid mile." At 9:07 p.m. in Northwest: "Much of 14th Street is burned out." At 10:25 p.m. in Northwest: "Extensive fire sweeping south on Georgia Avenue" (upper 7th Street NW became Georgia Avenue at Florida Avenue). At 10:28 p.m. in Northwest: General Haines reported, "Most of 14th Street is gone." At 10:50 p.m. on H Street NE: Haines disclosed, "Many stores gutted by fire and some buildings have toppled into the streets."[45]

There were still other indications of potential trouble that worried authorities. After the experiences in Newark, Detroit, and elsewhere in 1967, the
army was greatly concerned about sniper fire, and it provided instructions
to troops about how to deal with it. It warned against responding with "an
overwhelming mass of firepower" and recommended instead keeping riot
areas well-lighted and using tear gas. There were also false alarms. Reports
of a man with a rifle on the top of the National Archives building and four
men with rifles on the roof of a restaurant near the Capitol were unsettling
but proved to be incorrect. Another disturbing piece of intelligence was that
an anonymous caller had told police that "bombs have been placed in all
Washington air, train, and bus terminals." This, too, was an unfounded but
unnerving alert.[46]

While army troops, police, and firefighters struggled to gain control of
the riot zones, the police precinct in Southeast blamed Stokely Carmichael
for most of the looting and burning in its area. At about the same time,
the White House received information that Carmichael was preparing
an assault on Georgetown and intended to "burn it down." To President
Johnson, Georgetown represented the snobbish elites and Kennedy loyalists
who looked down on him. When he heard of Carmichael's alleged plans,
he smiled and exclaimed, "Goddamn! I've waited thirty-five years for this
day!" The reports of Carmichael's activities were erroneous, and intelligence
sources still did not know where he was.[47]

At about 11:00 p.m., Mayor Washington and Murphy decided to tour
the major riot zones in Northwest and in Northeast. Meanwhile, Cyrus
Vance and city council chairman John Hechinger viewed the damages
on H Street NE from Hechinger's chauffeur-driven limousine. Vance had
arrived in the city at about 5:30 p.m. after his flight from New York and his
trip from the airport in heavy traffic. His presence was a vital asset. "The
first thing he did was to calm us down, which is probably one of the greatest
contributions that he made," Deputy Mayor Fletcher recalled. "Here was a
knowledgeable man who had gone through this and who had had experience. . . . He was able to assure us that this could be handled." As Vance and
Hechinger rode down H Street, the council chairman looked ahead and
saw a building engulfed in flames. He thought at first it was his company's
central warehouse. As they drew closer, he realized it was not his building
that was burning. He also realized that his building was being looted. "My
God," he exclaimed, "they're using our forklifts!" Vance advised him to
drive up to the warehouse, and the sight of the limousine was apparently
startling or intimidating enough that the looters ran away.

At 1:20 a.m. on Saturday, April 6, Mayor Washington and Vance held a press conference to offer their evaluations of conditions in the city. The mayor expressed hope that, despite the heavy damage he saw on his tour, the streets were "settling down." He disclosed that he was most concerned about providing food and shelter to the families who lost their homes during the riots. Vance confirmed the mayor's assessment of conditions in the city. In addition to their excursion on H Street, he and Hechinger had toured the riot areas of Northwest. They found that the areas in which the worst disorders took place "appeared to be under control." Drawing on his experiences the previous summer, Vance also suggested that "the rate of destruction was considerably less here than it was in Detroit during a comparable period."[48]

The mayor and Vance ended an exhausting and sorrowful day on a cautiously optimistic note. But they did not downplay the enormity of the destruction, danger, and trauma the city had suffered since the outbreak of rioting. By mid-morning on April 6, the death toll had risen to 5. Another 734 people were treated for injuries at hospitals, including 23 policemen, 11 firefighters, and 3 soldiers. The police had made 2,123 arrests. The District of Columbia fire department, with assistance provided by fire companies from nearby suburban jurisdictions, had responded to approximately 280 calls. Although the fire department thought it had the situation under control and concluded that it no longer needed the support of neighboring communities, the destruction caused by the burning of buildings in the riot zones was distressingly apparent. "Sections of Washington, ravaged by arsonists and looters for a second night," the *Evening Star* reported, "resembled bombing scenes from World War II." At midnight, the lighted dome of the Capitol was only faintly visible because of the smoke that lingered in the sky above the city.[49]

4

"Smoldering Ruins Block after Block," April 6–12, 1968

AS WASHINGTON WAS DEALING WITH the afflictions of looting, burning, and violence on April 5, other cities across the country, large and small, were suffering similar, though less severe, ordeals. The National Guard was called out in Chicago, Detroit, and Boston as well as Little Rock, Arkansas, and Jackson, Mississippi. Units of "weekend warriors" were mobilized in other cities to be ready for deployment if necessary. Local government officials imposed curfews and prohibited liquor sales in many cities. Conditions deteriorated so badly in Chicago that President Johnson, in consultation with Mayor Richard Daley and at the request of Acting Governor Samuel Shapiro, sent in 5,000 federal troops. By late on Saturday, April 6, the toll of the disturbances in some fifty cities throughout the nation (including Washington) was 19 people dead, more than 1,000 injured, at least 4,200 arrested, and property damage of staggering proportions. The costs seemed likely to become much higher.[1]

The streets of Washington were relatively calm on Saturday morning, at least in comparison to the chaos that had reigned the previous day. At 7:35 a.m., city council chairman Hechinger suggested that "troops have quelled the disturbance and the worst is over." He added hopefully that the city "should be able to get back to normal."[2]

Nevertheless, by ordinary standards the city was still in a great deal of turmoil. Looting continued in all the troubled parts of the capital, and after the curfew was lifted at 6:30 a.m., it gained in intensity. At 11:05 a.m., the District's Office of Civil Defense noted that "the situation in D.C. is very serious at this time." Liquor stores, pharmacies, and groceries that had not been cleaned out the previous two days were especially popular targets. Although the Safeway grocery chain could not determine the full extent of the damage to its stores, it was certain that at least five had totally burned on Friday. It closed thirty-five others as a result of looting. Peoples Drug shut down seventeen of its outlets in the riot areas. During the late morning hours of April 6, there were several reports of sniper fire and other shooting incidents. Police were stoned in Northwest.

At 2:00 p.m., soul singer James Brown, who flew in from Boston at the request of Mayor Washington, went on local radio and television and, "as one soul brother to another," urged young people to "get off the streets and go home." He recalled his own experiences to encourage his fans to heed his "idea of Black Power." He told them that he had once shined shoes outside a radio station in his hometown of Augusta, Georgia, and that after working hard at his profession, he now owned the station. A few minutes after Brown's appeal, the mayor moved the beginning of the curfew up by an hour and a half to 4:00 p.m.[3]

Soldiers patrolling burned-out block of 7th Street NW, April 8, 1968. *US News & World Report Collection, U9-18949-14, Library of Congress*

Dozens of buildings were in flames, many of which were blazes from the previous day that firefighters could not douse completely and that restarted. Between Thursday night and late Saturday afternoon, the DC fire department responded to 510 calls, 312 of which were new and 198 of which were rekindles. "In my 36 years," remarked Deputy Chief Robert T. Huntington, "it's never been close to this bad." The *Los Angeles Times* ran a front-page story with a headline announcing that Washington's riot areas were "Smoldering Ruins Block after Block."[4]

By 7:00 p.m. on Saturday, twelve thousand troops had arrived for duty in Washington. The growing number of soldiers on the streets played a critical role in gradually restoring order. The troops worked in close collaboration with the police force, and both followed the orders they received from a command center that had been set up in the Municipal Building on Indiana Avenue NW. Mayor Washington, Director of Public Safety Murphy, General Haines, and Cyrus Vance spent much of their time at the command center, gathering information and making collective operational decisions. Vance got along well with the mayor and other city officials, and his experience at the Pentagon was useful in smoothing potentially rocky relations between the army and the police department. Although he was an overnight guest at the White House during his stay in Washington and

Soldiers and police frisk suspected looters on 7th Street NW, April 6, 1968. *US News and World Report Collection, U9-18943-24, Library of Congress*

was clearly the president's representative, he did not attempt to impose his views on other policymakers. "I felt he was the eyes and ears of the White House," a city official later said of Vance. "But you'd never know it, the way he acted. He didn't throw his weight around."[5]

The police and the army followed the general policies that had been defined before the riots, which were based to a substantial degree on Vance's experiences in Detroit in 1967. The city of Washington was not under martial law, and the police retained the sole authority to make arrests. The troops were enormously helpful in breaking up groups of troublemakers (often with the assistance of tear gas), enforcing the curfew by advising people on the streets to go home, detaining looters until the police hauled them off, and offering protection to firefighters. Those measures proved to be effective in significant part because, by Saturday, the scale of the rioting, though still serious, had considerably diminished.

The troops conducted their operations by navigating the riot areas in jeeps and by lining unruly streets in a show of force. If conditions were quiet, a small number of soldiers jumped from the jeeps and stood at positions where they could see and be seen. One or two soldiers generally did not attempt to stop looters by themselves. If they sighted problems they could not handle while on patrol, they called for reinforcements. If their

Police officer leads suspected looter away after arresting him, April 6, 1968. *Associated Press*

numbers were superior, they took action to keep lawbreakers from fleeing until police arrived. The police, meanwhile, loaded their vans with prisoners whom they took to rapidly filling cells to await appearances before vastly overworked judges. The police also used rented U-Haul trucks to move their forces into riot areas and to catch looters by surprise. They called their U-Haul vans "Trojan horses."[6]

The army's duties, at least after Friday's violence subsided, were not particularly dangerous. The troops stationed at the Capitol and the White House witnessed few, if any, disruptive or threatening activities. Likewise, the soldiers who patroled the streets of the riot zones were seldom under duress. But they did experience some uneasy moments. In one case, Jack Hyler, an enlisted man from Tennessee and a Vietnam veteran, rode in the first of a line of four jeeps that were responding to a fire on a residential street that joined 14th Street NW. They were followed by a large band of youths who were shouting and taunting them. The soldiers were squeezed between row houses on the narrow street and the fire at the end of the block. "I started worrying about what we should do if those kids tried to attack us," Hyler said, "use gas, load our guns, or what." The problem was solved when residents of the street came outside "and told the kids to go away and leave us alone—that we just had a job to do." To the relief of Hyler and his comrades, the youths listened to their elders and dispersed. In patroling the streets, Hyler was uncomfortable with his obligation to "take up arms against Americans in Washington." He commented that it "would have taken a lot of thought before I'd strike another American."

Other soldiers agreed with Hyler's appreciation for the support the troops received from residents of the riot areas. Thomas Oliver was an *Evening Star* reporter who was called up for duty with the DC National Guard on Friday afternoon. He spent several days patroling in Northeast, including the burned-out strip of H Street. "My company never encountered any violent action, never expended a round of ammunition," he later wrote. "But it did gas some stores, apprehended some curfew violators, and nabbed one suspect with a gun in his pocket." Oliver remembered vividly "something no one had suggested was possible during all of our civil disturbance training—the friendly attitude of people living under what almost amounted to a military occupation." Residents greeted the troops cordially and provided them with coffee and food. "Kids, hundreds of kids, pointed to us and waved, and we waved back."[7]

Despite the kindness of many residents, the occupation of the nation's capital was, in the *Washington Post*'s description, "an obviously painful . . . assignment" for soldiers. One infantry sergeant was asked how he felt about his role in occupying the nation's capital. He responded with a smile, "I can't talk to a reporter, but I think you can guess the answer." Active duty on the streets of Washington was especially awkward for African American members of the DC National Guard, which was about 25 percent black, an unusually high percentage. Warren Freeman was an eighteen-year-old student at Howard University when he enlisted as a private in 1966 to avoid getting drafted. His unit was called up for active duty the day after King's assassination. He fought heavy traffic to reach the armory, and as he put on his uniform, he realized that his assignment was to "protect life and property" from people like his own friends. "Yesterday I was running the streets with Joe and John and Paul and Richard; today I've got to keep these same people from running the streets," he recalled. "And tomorrow, when the disturbance is over, riots have been quelled and fires put out, Joe, John, Paul and Richard are the same guys I have to see and deal with."

Freeman's National Guard unit remained on duty for twelve days, and he was grateful that, although they shot off tear gas canisters, they never had to fire their weapons. They suffered some cuts and bruises, but "the most that was injured was a lot of people's pride, from the verbal assaults." Freeman later recalled that "the black soldiers were verbally assaulted worse than the white soldiers." Even so, he remained close to his friends because they understood "that I was doing what I . . . had to do," and he understood that "they were doing what they had to do at that time." Freeman decided to remain in the National Guard after the riots, and by 1988 he had risen to the rank of colonel.[8]

Freeman's comments were echoed by other National Guard soldiers. A black officer remarked, "The main problem we had was verbal abuse. The people on the street heckled our Negro troops, especially with stuff about why were they, soul brothers, guarding the white man's property." There was no evidence of ill will between black and white soldiers, who recognized that they had a common objective. Despite the hostility that some residents expressed toward black soldiers, the *Evening Star*'s Thomas Oliver welcomed the opportunity to patrol with them. "For white soldiers like me, integration never looked so good," he wrote. "Patrolling streets in the troubled areas seemed a lot less frightening along with fellow Guardsmen who were themselves Negroes." The tensions of the moment were relieved, at least on occasion, by dark humor. When the supply room at the armory refused to give a black member of the Guard a piece of equipment he requested, he responded, "Well, I guess I'm going to have to start looting."[9]

The procedures that the DC police and the army used to curb the rioting did not meet with universal approval. One critic, at least for a time, was Senator Richard B. Russell, a Democrat from Georgia who was President Johnson's mentor, confidant, and close friend. Early on Saturday afternoon, Russell called the president to complain that troops guarding the Capitol had not been issued ammunition. Russell's statements received prompt attention from General Johnson, the army chief of staff. He quickly confirmed that the troops sent to patrol the Capitol carried two magazines of ammunition. General Haines relayed this information to Joseph Califano at the White House and sent a battalion commander to brief Russell. As a result, Russell decided that he was satisfied with the army's response and declared that "General Haines' integrity remains unchallenged."[10]

Another US senator who questioned police and military policies for dealing with looters was not so easily placated. Robert C. Byrd, a Democrat from West Virginia, was chairman of the Appropriations Committee subcommittee that determined the budget for the District of Columbia. In that capacity, he was a stern critic of welfare programs in the capital, and he played an instrumental role in reducing the number of relief recipients. Byrd had grown up in a family of very limited means and believed devoutly in the virtues of hard work as the path out of poverty. "There are numerous men and women living today who lived in poverty," he said, "but they had parents who desired to work and did work."

Byrd's personal experiences informed his judgment on dealing with urban unrest. In July 1967, after the Newark riot but before the outbreak in Detroit, he voiced his views in a speech on the Senate floor. He dismissed the "usual excuses" that the riots were caused by poverty, poor living conditions, or racial discrimination. Byrd argued that many poverty-stricken Americans, both black and white, did not participate in riots and that millions of immigrants who had faced harsh discrimination upon arrival in the United States "did not react with violence in the streets." He insisted that riots would be ended only when ghetto dwellers learned that "poverty neither provides a license for laziness nor for lawlessness." Byrd called for strong measures to combat rioters. "A Government of laws cannot tolerate disrespect for, and violation of, its laws," he argued. "Those who choose to step outside the law must be punished. And those who insist upon force must be met with greater force."

Byrd's reaction to the Washington riots was in keeping with the position he had taken the previous summer. On Saturday afternoon, he called Califano to express his emphatic disapproval of the way the disorders had been handled. He asserted that "the time for restraint is ended" and recommended that adult looters be shot, though he thought they should be shot in their legs rather than fatally wounded. He also demanded to know why authorities had not declared martial law in the city. Byrd's opinions did not influence existing policies and practices, but they set the stage for the sharp criticism he offered after the riots ended.[11]

In an editorial published on Saturday, the *Evening Star* found fault with city and federal officials on a different issue—the delay in the decision to call up troops. Although it applauded the performance of the police and military in calming the streets without the shooting and bloodshed that had occurred in Newark and Detroit in 1967, it emphasized the consequences of the riots. "Large sections of the city have been smashed, burned and looted in a mindless orgy which has had nothing to do with Dr. Martin Luther King or any other grievance," it commented. The *Star* maintained that troops should have been introduced "much sooner and in larger numbers at the start" and concluded that "once violence enters the picture, it must be met, confronted, and stopped."[12]

During the day on Saturday, government officials toured the capital to survey the damage and get a firsthand look at conditions in what the *Star* called the "ravaged city." Vance, Fletcher, and Haines took a helicopter tour while the mayor walked the streets. Journalists roamed the riot zones to report on the devastation and to assess the sentiments of residents. The *Post* described the mood of the city as "resignation, bitterness." Haynes Johnson found the situation in Washington to be "unreal," especially the smoke rising above the Capitol, the army trucks with Red Cross insignias, the "Closed to Visitors" sign at the White House, and the enormous destruction in the "war area." As he entered the riot centers, he wrote, "it began to look like Newark or Detroit or Watts or any of the other datelines of trouble."

Other observers flocked to the riot areas on a lark. Large numbers of sightseers, estimated in the thousands, drove through the burned-out strips of 14th Street and 7th Street NW and past the boarded-up stores on the F Street Mall. Many of the mostly white and young visitors took snapshots as they backed up traffic on their "bizarre Saturday jaunt." They also incited resentment in the neighborhoods they explored, where they were jeered by black youths. One resident claimed that the unwanted tourists were pelted with bricks and bottles. The sightseeing activities lasted only a short time before the police barricaded the streets.[13]

The city faced problems much more urgent than gawking joyriders. As a result of the fires that burned down entire blocks and looters who cleaned out grocery stores and pharmacies, many residents of the riot areas were in desperate need of shelter, food, and medicine. At his press conference at 1:20 a.m. on Saturday, Mayor Washington suggested that the most worrisome problem in the troubled areas would be food and housing. Relief efforts to address shortages and to help those deprived of basic necessities had already begun by that time. As the rioting worsened on Friday, District and federal agencies, private companies, churches, and other organizations cooperated in a generously supported campaign to furnish assistance to local citizens.

The DC Department of Public Welfare offered food from the warehouses of its DC Village and Children's Center, a nursing home and orphanage, until supplies began to arrive from other sources. The US Department of Agriculture provided a variety of surplus food, including cheese, butter, peanut butter, chopped meat, and dry milk. Grocery stores, especially Giant Foods, a local chain, and the much-beleaguered Safeway, contributed

Citizens affected by the riots line up as volunteers bring in food and clothing to a relief center on P Street NW, April 9, 1968. *Reprinted with permission of the DC Public Library, Star Collection, ©Washington Post*

thousands of loaves of bread and half-gallon jugs of milk. Bakeries and other small businesses also chipped in. The welfare department and volunteers transported food to more than seventy emergency centers, many of them hosted by churches. On Saturday, the combined efforts of government agencies, private businesses, churches, and volunteers delivered 45,000 meals. Over the next three days, they increased the total to 344,000 meals that weighed in at 898,000 pounds. Joseph Danzansky, president of Giant Foods and chairman of a committee organized to meet the problems of food distribution, commented, "I'm just so proud of the community and the way it has rallied."[14]

Finding shelter for residents who lost their homes was potentially even more challenging than providing food. But the magnitude of the problem, at least in the short term, proved to be less imposing than originally anticipated. The city and many churches offered temporary living quarters to those who were left homeless by the riots, but to their surprise, few showed up to stay in those shelters. Officials assumed that most of the estimated two to three hundred families and individuals whose homes were destroyed sought refuge with relatives and neighbors. Nevertheless, the victims still had to locate places to live permanently. District of Columbia agencies worked closely with private groups, especially the Washington Board of Realtors, to survey the housing market. They found more than two hundred units that were available for inspection and potential occupancy. The city also arranged to cover the first month's rent for dislocated citizens, many of whom had already paid the rent on their former residences and were short of cash.

Although food and shelter were the fundamental requirements, residents of the riot areas suffered other serious deprivations. Some were in critical need of medicine. One woman, for example, needed insulin immediately and could not get a new supply because her drugstore was burned out. The people who lost their homes often lost all their possessions at the same time. The Salvation Army and churches took the lead in collecting clothing and furniture for distribution. Their efforts could ease but not eliminate the physical and emotional hardships imposed on blameless parties by rampaging rioters.[15]

The intensity of the rioting in Washington declined significantly on Saturday, but the costs of the violence continued to escalate. The *Star* reported that by about 9:00 p.m., there were 5 confirmed deaths, 781 injuries (including 2 soldiers, 17 firefighters, and 26 policemen), and hundreds of buildings looted and destroyed by fire. In addition, the police had arrested nearly 3,000 people, about 30 percent for curfew violations, another 30 percent for looting, and the rest mainly for disorderly conduct.[16]

The growing number of arrests placed severe strains on the District of Columbia's justice system. The Court of General Sessions was so flooded with cases that it stayed in continuous session over the weekend. But the extended schedule did not prevent acute difficulties. The people arrested were taken to cells in the courthouse, police headquarters, precinct stations, and other locations to await appearances before a judge. The processing of paperwork for arrestees was at best haphazard and more often incomplete. Under normal conditions, a police officer signed his name on twenty-seven forms before an alleged lawbreaker went before a judge. But this process frequently was not followed during the riots because arresting officers had to return to the streets before finishing their paperwork. With a missing or fragmentary paper trail, the courts had trouble matching prisoners in cells with the charges filed against them. Sometimes they were unable even to identify those arrested, a problem that was compounded by some detainees who used false names. The courthouse was inundated with family members looking for relatives, a frustrating and sometimes futile quest.

The judges who heard the charges against arrestees sought to proceed as promptly as possible without violating legal procedures. Those accused of minor offenses, especially curfew violations, were generally released without having to appear in court if they promised not to participate in unlawful activities and to return for trial on a later date. But the large number of detainees prevented quick action, and hundreds of people spent Saturday night in a detention facility in Virginia. Those accused of looting and other serious crimes had to post bail and pledge not to rejoin the riots. The amount required for bail was usually set at $1,000, which was beyond the means of many defendants, and few bail bondsmen were available. As a result, many of those charged with second-degree burglary, the common citation for looting, were sent back to their cells. On Sunday evening, April 7, the police department held 685 prisoners in jail. The legal machinery did not work smoothly in this unprecedented situation, but the judges did their best to administer justice and to keep serious offenders off the streets. The *Washington Post* concluded that the court system had functioned "remarkably" well under the circumstances and that "many of those involved in it performed magnificently."[17]

Government and military officials were encouraged by the reduction in looting and violence on Saturday. General Haines reported shortly before midnight that "the curfew is working well" and that he was "greatly reassured" by the signs of improved conditions. Nevertheless, the city had not returned to normal. The next day was Palm Sunday, and there were still numerous reports of looted stores, burning buildings, and break-ins. There were also occasional sniper attacks. When a sniper fired three shots at police and soldiers guarding a shopping center in Northeast on Sunday evening, it gave them, as the *Star* commented, "an instant course in battling an unseen enemy in the dark." They responded with a barrage of tear gas, and that ended the threat.[18]

The weather on Palm Sunday was clear and pleasant, and churchgoers turned out in large numbers to mourn the death of Martin Luther King. At the National Cathedral, where King had delivered a sermon the previous Sunday, the Very Reverend Francis B. Sayre Jr. wondered, "How deep will our valley of despair be before Easter comes?" Senator Robert F. Kennedy and Stokely Carmichael, who had stayed out of the public eye since his speech at Howard University two days earlier, attended services at Walter Fauntroy's Bethel Baptist Church. Fauntroy remarked that "Good Friday came early" because of King's death. He also revealed that in a telephone conversation with his old friend on March 26, King had lamented that a wave of rioting and looting in Memphis had "emanated from our . . . misguided kids" rather than from the actions of police, soldiers, or "bigoted racists." King had added, "I'm afraid, Walter, this country just isn't ready for nonviolence."

Robert F. Kennedy, Ethel Kennedy, and Walter E. Fauntroy tour 14th Street NW after Palm Sunday services, April 7, 1968. *Associated Press*

After the service, Kennedy, his wife, Ethel, and Fauntroy embarked on a walking tour of the riot areas in Northwest. When the group reached 14th and U Streets, crowds gathered to greet the senator or at least to catch a glimpse of him. This caused alarm among the soldiers on duty, who had no advance warning of the walkabout and feared that a mob was assembling. They relaxed when they learned the reason for the excitement. As Kennedy strolled north on 14th Street past scorched remains of buildings, children tugged at his sleeves and crowds cheered him. One woman seized his hand and said, "I knew you would be the first to come here, darling." Kennedy, who had recently entered the race for the Democratic presidential nomination, remarked during his tour that the conditions he observed were "extremely sad" and said that he had "some ideas about what needs to be done."[19]

President Johnson also inspected the riot zones, but he toured by helicopter. On Sunday afternoon, he flew to Andrews Air Force Base in Maryland with General William C. Westmoreland, commander of US troops in Vietnam, with whom he had conferred over the weekend. After bidding the general good-bye, he surveyed the burned-out areas on 7th Street and 14th Street NW from the air. Johnson could see little of the damage, even after the pilot lowered the helicopter's altitude, because of the smoke that was rising from the rubble. The president made no public comment on his reaction.

In the face of stifling smoke, massive destruction, sporadic looting, and other remnants of Washington's ordeal, there were signs that the rioting had run its course. The mayor suggested on Sunday evening that the city seemed to be "settling down." But, as the District's Office of Civil Defense noted, it was an "uneasy peace." City officials remained concerned about providing food and shelter for citizens in need. Despite the relief efforts that had been organized the previous day, food shortages were a serious concern because demand was so great that some emergency centers ran out of supplies. To ease the problem, Safeway reopened seven of the stores it had closed during the worst days of the rioting. But this step toward normality was compromised by half-empty shelves and the presence of armed soldiers who stood guard.[20]

The mixed signals that prevailed on Sunday gave way to increasingly normal conditions over the next few days, at least for those who were not involved in or affected by the riots. On a quiet Monday, April 8, one sign of reduced tension was that soldiers removed their bayonets, still sheathed, from their rifles. Federal government offices, downtown department stores, and city schools reopened, but they shut down early so that employees, shoppers, and students could beat the curfew home. The following day, the mayor moved the beginning of the evening curfew back to 7:00 p.m. Schools in the District and nearly all stores, banks, and other businesses were closed as a show of respect for Martin Luther King, whose funeral was held in Atlanta. On Wednesday, April 10, the mayor further eased the curfew and allowed liquor stores, if they were able, to operate on a normal schedule. Government offices, schools, and businesses resumed regular working hours. The Washington Senators were finally able to open their major-league baseball season, and, as an indicator of the trend toward normality in the capital, they lost the game.

The city soon dropped all the restrictions it had imposed to control the riots. The mayor ended the curfew on Friday, April 12, one week after it had gone into effect. The remaining controls on liquor sales by the drink were greatly eased the same day and then abolished altogether. For taking this step, the mayor joked, "I have received warm congratulations." The bans on selling firearms and gasoline in containers were lifted on April 15. Conditions were stable enough that more than half of the soldiers patrolling the streets were withdrawn on April 13, and the last contingent of troops departed the capital three days later. Mayor Washington declared on April 16 that the "city has returned to normal."[21]

As the capital gradually emerged from the crisis, Congress passed a new civil rights bill as a tribute to King. Johnson had pushed hard for a fair-housing law since 1966, but Congress had voted down his proposals. In the aftermath of King's assassination, many members of Congress changed their positions. The new law outlawed discrimination in renting or selling homes, and, the *Post* reported, was "designed to help Negroes find homes outside of riot-breeding urban ghettos." It also took a stand against urban unrest by outlawing the crossing of state lines to incite a riot and transporting firearms for use in a riot. The law was the third of Johnson's major civil rights acts, and he hailed it as "a victory for every American." But it would do little to address the ills of urban areas plagued with poverty and despair. Although it corrected a historical injustice and could benefit middle-class blacks, the *Star* lamented that it would not produce "any discernible easing of the tensions that grip our cities."[22]

The end of the rioting in Washington, however welcome, did not result in "any discernible easing of tensions." The return to calm could not obscure the highly visible fact that the "new normal" featured neighborhoods that in three days had been blighted with the ruins of homes, businesses, and entire blocks of buildings. There was palpable concern among government leaders and residents that the April riots would be repeated in even more virulent outbreaks. For that reason, arriving at sound conclusions about the causes of the disorders, the appropriate response to them, and lessons to be learned was an urgent priority.

5

"A City of Remorse"

THE END OF THE RIOTS in Washington brought a huge sense of relief to government officials, business leaders, and residents. It also left a residue of uncertainty, disorientation, and grief. "It was a city of remorse over the death of a great leader," *Washington Post* staff writer Robert C. Maynard suggested on April 10, "as well as the death of any remnant of security that 'it can't happen here.'" The disturbances increased the fear of crime that had been a prominent feature of city life long before Martin Luther King's assassination. Joseph Califano, President Johnson's chief domestic policy adviser, remarked on May 7, 1968, that the riots had caused a "loss of confidence in the community, in Congress, and in the Press, about the ability of the Government to maintain law and order in Washington." Some informed observers thought the violence in the streets might have created even greater forebodings. "Washington seems to feel that something even deeper than the law is at stake now; that the whole foundation of order, reason, and confidence which sustains a civilized community has broken down," commented *New York Times* columnist James Reston. The concerns that the riots stirred gave immediacy to a host of critical and complicated questions that demanded prompt attention. What were the costs of the riots? What caused the riots? Who were the rioters? Who were the victims? Should the riots have been handled in a more forceful way? What ended the riots? What lessons needed to be drawn to avoid, or at least reduce the chances of, a repetition of the violence that traumatized Washington?[1]

The first step in assessing the effects of the riots in Washington and in more than one hundred cities across the country was to calculate the physical toll. The property costs of the outbreaks of violence that followed King's assassination were high, though the death toll was relatively low. Forty-three lives were lost, the same number as in Detroit alone in 1967. The insurance industry estimated property damage at $45 million, which it regarded as a conservative figure. Other consequences of the riots included 5,117 fires and about twenty-four thousand arrests. The army and National Guard mobilized nearly seventy-three thousand troops for action in American cities.

The nation's capital achieved the dubious honor of incurring the greatest costs from the disorders in any American city. The death toll by April 10 was fixed at ten, but it later rose to thirteen when more bodies were discovered in the rubble of the riot zones. Two of those fatalities resulted from police gunfire (one in Northeast and one in Southeast on April 5); nobody was shot by army or National Guard troops. The number of troops deployed in Washington peaked at 15,530, of whom 13,682 belonged to the regular army and 1,848 were members of the National Guard. The rounds of ammunition fired by military personnel came to a total of only fourteen; the number of tear gas grenades launched was 5,248. Injuries totaled 1,201, including 54 police officers, 21 firefighters, and 16 soldiers. The number of people arrested was 7,640, including 4,464 for curfew violations and 1,082 for looting.[2]

Initial estimates of property damage in the capital were in the range of $10 to $15 million, but this figure was later revised to more than $27 million, which included direct and indirect property losses, the costs of marshaling troops, and expenditures by the city government. About $24 million of that total was the damage sustained by local businesses. According to a study conducted by the National Capital Planning Commission, 1,352 private businesses were damaged or destroyed during the riots. More than 40 percent of them never reopened or moved to other locations, resulting in a loss of about 4,900 jobs in the District of Columbia. Whites owned 86 percent of the business properties that were burned and looted during the riots and blacks 12 percent. A total of 645 buildings sustained damage, of which 300 were razed. One outcome was a net loss of 403 housing units in buildings that were demolished or heavily damaged, including 354 apartments, 37 rooming houses, and 12 single-family homes. The total number of displaced individuals was 2,115. Some 50 percent of the total damage occurred in the 7th Street NW corridor, 25 percent in the 14th Street NW corridor, and 15 percent in the H Street NE corridor.[3]

Although property owners, businesses, and residents in the riot areas suffered the most grievous and visible losses, the most important segment of the city's economy other than the federal government—the tourist industry—also took a serious hit. Clarence A. Arata, executive director of the Washington Convention Bureau, reported that the number of tourists and the money they spent dropped by about 30 percent after the riots. The volume of business at downtown restaurants fell 10 to 30 percent in a period of three months, and it was especially slow at the dinner hour because tourists and area residents were afraid to come downtown in the evening. Hotels reported a wave of cancellations during and after the riots. Hudson Moses, president of the Hotel Association of Washington, estimated in early May that room occupancy was down by about 20 percent overall and that some hotels had suffered a 30 to 40 percent decline.[4]

The riots clearly produced strong misgivings about the traditional spring rite of school trips to Washington. Moses reported that student tours were only 20 percent of normal levels. He attributed the sharp fall-off to "fear on the part of the citizens of this country . . . who have read and heard about all this disorder." A junior high school vice-principal in New York offered support for Moses's claim. He informed the Hotel Stratford on E Street NW on May 13 that he was canceling a three-night reservation made for his students. "No reputable bus company in New York wants to take a school group to Washington and most of the parents are concerned about their children's safety," he told the hotel. Even neighboring Fairfax County, Virginia, placed an indefinite ban on school trips to the city. "The safety of the students is our first concern," Superintendent Earl C. Funderburk said, "and we would not be fulfilling our duties if we placed them in any danger."[5]

There were two basic explanations for the outbreak of riots in Washington. The first was that they were the result of planning by agitators who incited unrest as a means of achieving their own purposes. Spiro Agnew, the governor of Maryland and soon to be Richard Nixon's running mate in the 1968 presidential campaign, asserted, for example, that the serious disorders in his state were provoked by "riot-inciting, burn-America-down" black leaders. Those who agreed with this judgment, even in less provocative terms, emphasized the need for law and order as a top priority. The other, more widely accepted, explanation for the occurrence of civil unrest was that it was the probably inevitable consequence of substandard living conditions and limited opportunities in urban ghettos. The competing views were usually more a matter of emphasis than a disagreement over the need for law and order versus improvements in struggling urban areas. They highlighted the same balancing act that had tormented Lyndon Johnson in responding to the wave of disorders since 1964—recognition of the urban crisis that produced the riots and dismay with violence as a means of redressing it.[6]

In Washington, the focus of suspicions that black militants instigated the riots was Stokely Carmichael. After his provocative speech at Howard University on Friday, April 5, intelligence sources lost track of him for a time. But once he reappeared, they reported on his activities and alleged plans to the president and other authorities. White House staff members urged his arrest. Special assistant Frederick Panzer told Johnson that pollster Louis Harris thought that having Mayor Washington arrest Carmichael would show that "black power extremists do not represent the vast majority of Negroes." The Justice Department investigated whether Carmichael could be prosecuted for inciting a riot under District of Columbia laws. Attorney General Ramsey Clark commented on *Meet the Press* on Sunday, April 7, that if Carmichael had broken the law, "he will be prosecuted with all of the diligence and all of the energies at our command." The following day, when the police department received information that Carmichael would leave town in an automobile caravan, Cyrus Vance supported arresting him if he violated the curfew.[7]

The threat that Carmichael allegedly represented was vastly exaggerated. The Washington police stated on April 5 that the riots were not incited by "racial agitators," and no evidence was found to contradict that conclusion. An anonymous looter who was interviewed shortly after the riots ended adamantly denied that he was following Carmichael's lead. "Nobody was listening to Stokely," he said. "What I did, I did because I wanted to do it, not because Stokely said to do it or because he planted the idea in my head." Walter Washington later expressed his own skepticism that Carmichael played any significant role in provoking the disorders.[8]

Most observers did not attribute the riots largely to a handful of militants and agitators. Instead, they echoed the findings of the Kerner Commission by recognizing that the roots of the disorders were deeply grounded and did not lend themselves to easy or inexpensive solutions. Syndicated columnist Carl T. Rowan, for example, argued that there were two requirements for making America "the kind of society that the world can admire and hope to emulate." The first was "a drastic revision of the American scale of values" so that the country would give "as high a priority to fighting poverty, injustice, and hopelessness at home as we have given to fighting 'communism' abroad." This obviously would be costly. The other requirement was even more difficult to accomplish: that Americans "must surrender the hatreds and hostilities that they have nurtured for a lifetime."[9]

While Rowan commented on what needed to be done to ease tensions and reduce the likelihood of future riots, another writer drew on his own experiences as an African American journalist to review the causes of the turmoil in Washington. William Raspberry went out on the streets to cover the riots for the *Washington Post*. He later reflected on what he witnessed and what he learned from talking with residents of the troubled areas. He recalled that the achievements of the civil rights movement in the early 1960s "had black America believing, for a time, that things were about to get permanently better." By 1968, however, it was clear that this was not happening for most blacks. Locally, Raspberry cited housing discrimination that turned the "Capital Beltway into a white noose around an increasingly black central city" and the "commonplace" ill-treatment of blacks by a predominantly white police force, both of which fostered growing respect for militant black leaders. In addition, there was strong resentment of "an amorphous 'Whitey,'" a term that applied to "whites who didn't want blacks in their neighborhoods or schools, who treated them unfairly on the job, who seemed to value them primarily as captive customers for overpriced merchandise." Blacks rioted, Raspberry suggested, because they were convinced they had nothing to lose and because "it was a rare opportunity for oppressed blacks to enjoy the spectacle of whites scared out of their minds."[10]

The riots in Washington were consistent with well-established patterns for domestic disorders throughout American history. Those who participated acted on rational motives. They resorted to violence because legitimate grievances were not otherwise being effectively remedied. In addition, rioters generally selected the victims of their actions discriminately in light of their own experiences or impressions. In Washington, as in other urban disorders of the 1960s, the favorite targets were often the police and white shop owners, whom many city dwellers viewed with intense animosity.

The fact that riots were rational in causation did not mean that they were rational in execution. "There is always a certain element of irrational in any given tumult," historian Paul A. Gilje has written. Civil disturbances were generally characterized by outbursts of emotion because "people got carried away with what they were doing" and the norms of society, at least for a time, did not apply. One result was that rioters in Washington burned down apartment buildings and cleaned out the inventories of grocery stores, pharmacies, and other businesses that provided essential services in their own neighborhoods. The suspension of ordinary behavior also frequently led to a "carnival-like atmosphere." As many observers remarked, this certainly was the case in Washington in 1968. *Newsweek* reported that looters "had a Mardi Gras air about them." Tom Wicker of the *New York Times* thought that most looters, "far from appearing angry or mournful at the news from Memphis, appeared to be having a good time."[11]

As Wicker suggested, there was little evidence that grief over the death of Martin Luther King had much to do with the outbreak of the riots. The "rational looter" who had taken a sponge from Pep Boys on the first night of the disturbances told an interviewer, for example, that King's assassination was "a precipitating factor" that sparked the riots. But the real cause of the burning and looting, he said, was that "people had been oppressed" and confined to poverty. It was clear that many of those who joined the disorders were not acting in the name or the principles of the slain civil rights leader. One looter who was stopped by police with several pair of stolen shoes claimed that he was honoring the memory of his "brother, Luther King." The *Washington Afro-American* commented in an editorial that there was "no question that some simply seized the opportunity to steal what they could not afford to buy and made no pretext that they were avenging Dr. King's death."

The *Afro-American* made the point that "there is no single reason covering individual motivation of participants" in the riots. It was clear, however, that the great majority of participants neither burned and looted to make a political statement nor acted with a political objective in mind. The Washington disorders were not a rebellion undertaken to accomplish a specific goal or to overthrow the power structure in the city. Instead, they were a disorganized, spontaneous eruption of frustration over the distressed conditions in which many black citizens lived and against the diminishing likelihood of prompt or meaningful improvements.[12]

Perhaps the best analogy for explaining the riots was offered by Reuben M. Jackson, who was twelve years old at the time and later became an archivist at the Smithsonian Institution. He grew up in a middle-class family in a house several blocks from the riot areas. He did not participate in the disturbances on the streets, but he and his father watched what was happening on Georgia Avenue from the roof of their home. He later suggested that the riots broke out in Washington because it was "like a crock pot" that slowly simmered until it suddenly boiled over. In what might be termed the crock pot theory, the most important causes of the riots were the conditions that had simmered in the city for a very long time before the King assassination made them boil over in violence.[13]

The assignment of primary responsibility to white society for ghetto conditions that produced the riots, which was an argument that the Kerner Commission had emphasized, elicited sharp rejoinders from conservative commentators. Syndicated columnist David Lawrence regretted the effects of racial discrimination, but he contended that "if law and order are flouted and measures are not applied to discourage violence, the American people will face more crises in the future." The *Wall Street Journal* refused to accept "collective guilt" as the reason for King's assassination or the disturbances that followed. It maintained that such a judgment not only "gives up on the human being" but also "denies individual responsibility." The paper seconded Agnew's charges by insisting that "the chaos in city after city is the work of a relatively few trouble-makers and criminals with little interest in the tragedy of Martin Luther King."[14]

The number of participants in the Washington riots was estimated in the range of 17,600 to 22,800, about one of eight residents in the affected areas. Based on rough extrapolations, this was less than 4 percent of the black population of 564,000 in the District. Drawing on the records of the District of Columbia Bail Agency, which interviewed most of those arrested on felony charges, the *Washington Post* and later a contractor for the US Department of Labor compiled a general picture of the rioters. The Bail Agency's information was slightly skewed because it did not include juveniles under age eighteen, who made up about 15 percent of the people arrested, and because it underestimated the number of women who joined the riots. Only 9 percent of those arrested were women, though it was clear to observers that females were a much higher percentage of looters on the streets. Nevertheless, the material collected by the Bail Agency was singularly useful in providing a collective portrait of the rioters.[15]

The documents showed that about 90 percent of the rioters who were arrested were black men, the great majority of whom were young. The others were women and a handful of white men (1 percent of the total). The average age of the black males was about twenty-five, which would have been somewhat lower if juveniles had been included in the tally. The participants shared a number of characteristics. Four of five had lived in Washington for more than five years, and one of three had been born in the city. Most had jobs, though the "typical rioter could not be considered well-off." They generally held low-paying, blue-collar jobs or entry-level retail store positions. Only about 30 percent of those arrested had finished high school. There were early reports that a substantial number of federal employees had been arrested, but John W. Macy Jr., chairman of the US Civil Service Commission, denounced those accounts as "grossly exaggerated." He informed President Johnson on April 25 that only twenty federal workers faced serious charges and that all of them were "low-grade employees, such as messengers and laborers."[16]

One of the individuals arrested and held by police for a time was a federal government worker who was not a "low-grade employee." Writing in the *Washington Post* under the pseudonym of P. J. Wilson, a young African American woman, identified by the paper only as a "beautiful young government girl with a master's degree," described her experiences. "Wilson" joined the riots inadvertently. After arriving home from work at about 4:00 p.m. on Friday, April 5, she received a call from a man she had been dating intermittently for about two years. He invited her to look around the riot areas "to see what is going on," and she accepted. Wilson picked him up in her sports car, and as they drove down an unnamed street, they saw looters plundering a liquor store. Suddenly, Wilson's friend jumped out of the car, headed for the store, and quickly returned with four fifths of liquor. "Great," she thought to herself. "Now I am driving the getaway car."

Wilson drove her "getaway car" for half a block before a policeman pulled her over. Despite her date's protests that she had done nothing wrong, they both were arrested for theft. At the precinct station, her date refused to give his name, and since he had been a law student, she followed his lead. A policeman at the desk told her to take a seat and warned that "he could outwait me." After an hour or so, she "began to get panicky" and provided her name. But, as the police station filled with detainees, Wilson continued to wait in limbo because the officer who had arrested her had not filled out the necessary paperwork. "I kept begging people to get me out," she recalled. "I kept repeating that I had a master's degree and a good job and I couldn't afford to have something like that on my record." Finally, after six and a half hours, a police sergeant authorized her release. He told her "to go home and not come out again because next time no one would be able to get me out of this mess." As Wilson climbed the steps to her apartment after her ordeal, she realized "how close it had been and how much I had really put on the line for some excitement."[17]

Wilson's search for excitement was a symptom of a generation gap between the rioters and at least some older African Americans. An elderly black man who, the *Washington Post* reported, "watched teen-agers dance down F Street knocking out windows and taunting police" called them "hooligans [who] ought to be locked up." Many older blacks were appalled at the violence that ravaged their own neighborhoods. One man exclaimed as fire destroyed the block where he lived, "Stupid! Stupid!"[18]

Some older citizens might have silently applauded the actions of rampaging youths. But others disapproved of the antics of those who ran the streets "in a state of exhilaration." They had experienced, or at least witnessed, the progress the civil rights movement had accomplished, which gave them reason to hope that political and economic opportunities for African Americans were improving. A younger generation, however, lacked the same historical perspective. They saw little direct benefit from the gains of the civil rights protests and increasingly turned away from the principle of non-violence that Martin Luther King and many others advocated. Instead, they looked to more militant leaders who urged, at least rhetorically, tearing down white society. "Because of decades of neglect," Robert J. Donovan of the *Los Angeles Times* wrote, "Negro neighborhoods throughout the country abound with youngsters who feel they have no stake in society and do not care a whit about the burning of buildings."[19]

Other than those who died or were seriously injured, the most tragic of the victims of the Washington riots were the individuals and families who lost their homes, their possessions, and in many cases, their jobs. As a rule, they were not responsible for the violence in the streets and were defenseless against the destruction that others wrought. The lines at the relief centers where those in need waited for food and other staples to make it through the day testified to the human costs of the riots among the neighbors of the looters and arsonists. A representative of the National Capital Planning Commission told a Senate committee in May 1969 that families that lost their homes encountered difficulties in finding housing at affordable prices and that many had to move in with relatives. The *Washington Afro-American* condemned the violence of the riots as a way of redressing grievances. "See who died in greater numbers. See who lost their homes and belongings. See who ended up in bread lines," it rebuked militants in an editorial. "The real victims of the riots were the . . . law-abiding people." John D. Jackson, an African American who served in the Metropolitan Police Department at the time, told an interviewer in 2003, "People got their frustrations out and all that, and felt good for a day or two, but that's one of the worst things that ever happened to the black community."[20]

The afflictions imposed on innocent victims were a typical outcome of riots. "Social violence . . . is always [a] human and understandable response to social inequity or restraint, just as it is always dangerous and ambiguous in its total results," historian David Grimsted has written. "Even in the best of causes, riots provide social 'red ink,'" often in the form of "flame and blood." In Washington in 1968, there was much flame but little blood, and this led to an animated controversy over the policies that law enforcement authorities followed to control the riots.[21]

In the immediate aftermath of the riots, the police department and the army received warm accolades for ending the crisis without greater loss of life. Attorney General Clark hailed the department's performance for proving the effectiveness of the "new civil disturbance techniques developed by the Justice Department after last summer's big city riots." The local chapter of the NAACP expressed appreciation for the "outstanding manner" that police and troops dealt with a "very explosive and tense situation." The *Washington Post* took a similar position in an editorial. It praised a hierarchy of priorities in which "human life has been valued ahead of property." But it also pointed out that a policy of restraint in employing force against rioters came at a high price: "It must be reckoned in the blind eye turned to open law-breaking, in the $10 million or more of property damage, in the small shopkeepers wiped out, in the sometimes capricious arrest for burglary of some looters while others were ignored."[22]

The *Post* highlighted the dilemma that faced law enforcement officials. They could authorize the use of firearms and other strong-arm tactics at a likely cost of more deaths among rioters and, as happened in Detroit and Newark in 1967, innocent bystanders. Or they could adopt a policy of restraint at a price of greater destruction and property damage. The Justice Department and the Pentagon had opted for restraint in considering how to deal with riots after the urban violence of 1967, and this approach was carried out in Washington with the favorable result of a low number of fatalities. Gilbert Gimble, a spokesman for Mayor Washington, commented that the police were told "not to be indiscriminately shooting people" to avoid "shooting kids who are stealing some shoes out of a store window."[23]

Many business owners who suffered heavy losses found fault with the ranking of priorities. They protested bitterly that the District and federal governments had not done more to protect their properties. One outraged businessman was C. D. Kaufmann, president of Kay Jewelry Stores, a national chain headquartered in Washington. In a letter to President Johnson, he complained that "everyone exercised restraint while millions of dollars worth of property inventories in this community and many others were burned, destroyed, and looted." The policy of restraint, he declared, was "an abandonment of law and order, due legal procedure and protection of property rights," and he was astonished that members of the news media and "various officials in the District are breaking their arms to pat each other on the back."

Other merchants, including local shop owners whose financial resources were more limited than those of Kay Jewelers, shared Kaufmann's opinions. Albert Schindler was co-owner of a dry-cleaning business on 14th Street that rioters turned into a "blackened smoking mess." They wrecked the machinery and burned or stole the clothing of customers. Schindler's wife later recalled that her husband had told her on Thursday, April 4, that they were buying a new house, which was "a big step for us." The next morning, he called to tell her, "Forget it. We don't have a business." Schindler was "extremely bitter" and contended that authorities should have adopted a more forceful approach to combating the riots, including shooting looters. Irving King operated a menswear shop on U Street that was looted on April 4 and burned the next day. "This disaster represents the annihilation of a lifetime of work and our entire lifetime assets," he told Senator Joseph Tydings of Maryland. He insisted that if the law had "been enforced at the outset subsequent widespread disaster could have been averted." Although many of the losses suffered by merchants were covered by insurance, in at least some cases business owners found that the damage to their property exceeded the limits of what their policies would pay. Even those with full protection faced the prospect of higher, perhaps prohibitive, premiums.[24]

The plight of riot zone merchants received sympathetic attention from some members of Congress. Senator Robert Byrd continued his harsh criticism of the government's response to the disorders. He insisted that "the criminal element understands only one language . . . and that is the language of force." In a swipe at the official policies that prevailed during the riots, Byrd added, "no criminal is afraid of a gun that is not loaded or of a policeman or soldier who is under orders not to shoot." He viewed the riots as graphic evidence of the breakdown of law and order in the United States, which he called the "foremost domestic issue in the Nation today."

In his capacity as chairman of the Senate Appropriations Subcommittee on the District of Columbia, in May 1968 Byrd conducted a series of interviews with business owners, police officers, firefighters, and others with firsthand knowledge of the riots. He held the hearings in his own office during evening hours to protect the identity of those who made appearances. When he finished, he had compiled 1,418 pages of testimony, which, he said, "uniformly . . . told a story of fear and frustration and anger."

Indeed, the merchants who testified vented their grievances with the city government, especially Director of Public Safety Patrick Murphy, for failing to act more forcefully and more promptly to thwart the riots. They also described their constant and deep-seated fear of again becoming prime targets of crime and violence. Byrd later inserted transcripts of the hearings, without providing names of witnesses who wished to remain anonymous, into the *Congressional Record*.[25]

Members of the House Committee on the District of Columbia played their customary role of holding hearings to voice their complaints about the city. They repeated many of Byrd's objections when they grilled Murphy during hearings held on May 15 and 16, 1968. Thomas G. Abernathy of Mississippi accused Murphy of adopting a "soft" position in dealing with rioters, and John Dowdy of Texas asserted that police were ordered to refrain from making arrests. Murphy made little effort to defend the policy of restraint that had guided his actions during the riots. Rather, he argued that the DC police and army troops had applied appropriate force when they had the requisite strength. He pointed out that the police detained nearly eight thousand people during the disorders, and he explained that law enforcement officers were not able to make a lot of arrests on the first night as long as they were outnumbered on the streets. "When suddenly large numbers of people violate the law, somewhat spontaneously, without adequate warning to the police," he declared, "it is a human impossibility for [a] police officer to arrest everybody who is violating the law at that particular time."

Murphy denied that police officers or soldiers had orders to stand by "while people looted without control," as some business owners and others had charged. He suggested that there were cases in which a patrolman was carrying out other duties that were "a more important assignment at that time." When Abernathy asked if he was "satisfied with the horror left in the city and the loss of all the merchandise that was carried off and the destruction," Murphy replied that he was "terribly dissatisfied with the destruction" but that he was "satisfied with the police response."[26]

The use of firearms against rioters was a much-discussed issue in the aftermath of the riots. Mayor Richard Daley of Chicago brought it to the forefront by announcing on April 15 that he had ordered police to "shoot to kill" arsonists and "shoot to maim" fleeing looters. Murphy and other law enforcement professionals argued that shooting at looters could have escalated the violence in Washington and made the disorders on the streets much more difficult to control. "We didn't shoot and they didn't shoot," an unnamed police official commented. "With all the guns we know the people have out there and all the guns that we have, I believe a miracle has occurred" by avoiding exchanges of gunfire.[27]

The Kerner Commission had warned that the "use of excessive force . . . may be inflammatory and lead to even worse disorder," and its assessment won support among observers of and participants in the Washington riots. Rufus (Catfish) Mayfield, a twenty-one-year-old black activist described by the city's tabloid, the *Washington Daily News*, as a "thoughtful young man," was asked whether "stronger action" by the police department, such as the use of billy clubs or guns, would have ended the riots sooner. He replied: "No, I think we'd have had more trouble. What we'd have had here was people going home and getting their guns. We could have had a real bloodbath." One of the rioters agreed that if police had shot looters, "there would have been a whole lot of killing on both sides."[28]

Amid much heated discussion about law enforcement's response to the riots and its consequences for businesses in the city, a few victims whose property was destroyed rebounded well. On H Street NE, Art Young's Men's Shop reopened in August 1968 after it had burned to a "cinderblock shell" during the riots. The owners were three brothers—Norman, Milton, and Joseph Hoffman—who had spent their professional lives in the retail clothing business and did not wish to leave the area. They moved into a vacant store near their ruined property and made arrangements to gradually turn over control to three of their employees, all African Americans. The Hoffman brothers explained that their employees "now own shares in the company and keys to the store." Art Young's was among the first burned-out clothing stores to reopen in the riot areas.[29]

Another victim of the riots who suffered extensive losses but recovered quickly was W. Henry Greene, a sixty-seven-year-old physician whose office was located one floor above Log Cabin Liquors on 7th Street NW. When looters hit the liquor store on Friday afternoon, April 5, and "began hollering and stampeding," he began to worry about his safety. He was especially concerned about his almost-new Mercedes-Benz that was parked on the street. After he left his office and drove home, he learned later in the evening that the entire building that housed Log Cabin Liquors had burned to the ground. Greene lost everything in his office, including five to ten thousand dollars' worth of medical equipment, several hundred dollars in cash, patients' records, certificates from professional and social organizations he had served as an officer, diplomas and licenses, and his checkbook.

W. Henry Greene in front of the rubble on 7th Street NW where Log Cabin Liquors and his medical office once stood, April 10, 1968. *Reprinted with permission of the DC Public Library, Star Collection,* ©Washington Post

"I think it happened, frankly, because people saw an opportunity to get some stuff they wanted and didn't have the money to buy," he later commented. "Whoever tried to stop that crowd that day would have been dead." Greene's insurance policy paid him only $1,000, a small percentage of his losses, but he was philosophical. "I do not believe in crying over spilt milk," he said. "The main thing is that I am alive and can continue to treat my patients." Within a few days, he opened a new office on Georgia Avenue and resumed his medical practice.[30]

Among the other victims of the riots were schoolchildren, who had a strong and often sorrowful response to what they witnessed. When District of Columbia schools opened on Monday, April 8, teachers encouraged their students to express their feelings about the weekend's turmoil in writings and drawings. Assistant Superintendent Norman W. Nickens told teachers, "REMEMBER, CLASSES SIMPLY CANNOT GO ON AS USUAL. Unusual events have occurred, and your children are preoccupied with these. . . . DO NOT FAIL THEM BY LECTURNG THEM WHEN THEY NEED TO TALK" (uppercase in original). The students expressed a wide variety of reactions to what they had seen and experienced that included fear, consternation, pride, and frequently, bewilderment. The pictures that younger boys and girls drew often showed frightened children "in burning buildings crying out in comic-strip balloons, 'Help me!'" Some elementary school students made comments such as "I thought the world was coming to an end," and "I want to [be] saved from the riot and live in another country." One child wrote: "I was afraid because people were stealing whiskey. They were going to drink it. When they drink it makes them angry."[31]

Older students offered differing, and sometimes conflicting, perspectives on the riots. Some were dismayed. One high school student commented, "It was disgraceful and inexcusable. . . . The damage done will only place a darker shadow upon the image of black people." Another student, however, said that she "actually felt good watching my people being so happy. I was so happy I could have cried." Most students condemned the burning of buildings that left people homeless and jobless. Some approved of looting as a means of getting back at merchants they thought cheated them, presumably including those who had joined in sacking stores. But others were not so sure. One talked about a white businessman who was "very nice." She remembered one customer who was a "woman with five or six kids, and . . . he used to give her milk for her kids." But during the riots, "I saw her right in [the store] pulling out everything she could." The mixed reactions of students to the violence on the streets were a poignant reflection of the jumble of emotions that prevailed in the city, among both black and white citizens, in the wake of the riots.[32]

Within a short time after the Washington riots ended, a consensus emerged across the political spectrum on what had restored order to the capital. City and federal government officials, military authorities, reporters, and other careful observers agreed that calling in a large contingent of troops to assist the Metropolitan Police Department was the critical step in containing the disorders. "The city's riot-fighters relied on a massive show of force, coupled with a minimum use of it, to end the rioting," wrote Frederick Taylor, a staff reporter for the *Wall Street Journal*.

As a corollary, there was also wide concurrence with many of the business owners whom Byrd interviewed that troops should have been introduced in Washington much sooner. Once the first units of the army and National Guard arrived in the early evening of April 5, the looting and burning gradually began to subside to manageable levels. But most of the worst destruction had already occurred. The curfew that the mayor imposed at about the same time also had a salutary effect in calming the city. It moved law-abiding citizens off the streets and allowed police and military forces to focus on a much smaller number of offenders. The experiences in dealing with the 1968 riots in Washington and elsewhere strongly suggested that urban violence should be promptly met with a formidable show of force and a street-clearing curfew. Despite the complaints of business operators and others about the policy of restraint, its use was generally viewed as the most effective and humane means of curbing violence. "Had the police been quicker on the trigger," the *New York Times* declared in an editorial, "the almost certain result in every city would have been a much longer and bloodier period of street warfare." In that regard, the recommendations of the Kerner Commission, the policies formulated in the Justice Department and the Defense Department, and the practices employed by Murphy and his counterparts in other cities were vindicated.[33]

The most important questions about containing riots and reducing violence appeared to be settled rather easily, but other related matters that also received a great deal of high-level attention were more difficult. On April 15, 1968, one day before the last troops were withdrawn, the leading civilian and military officials involved in responding to the Washington riots met at the White House to discuss what lessons they had learned and what actions needed to be taken to apply them. The meeting was chaired by Califano, and the attendees included Mayor Washington, Deputy Mayor Fletcher, and Director of Public Safety Murphy from the city, Attorney General Clark and Deputy Attorney General Christopher from the Justice Department, Undersecretary of the Army McGiffert, Generals Johnson and Haines, and Matthew Nimetz from Califano's staff. Everyone at the table agreed on the need for improved intelligence. The mayor complained that the information he was provided on the morning of April 5 was neither timely nor adequate. He commented that he "could have made a better assessment" of the troubles that were brewing if he had known more about Stokely Carmichael's activities, the protest rally at Howard University, and the unauthorized early departure from schools by many students. He suggested that the availability of current intelligence would have enabled him to make a clearer judgment on the need for federal troops. The group accepted Califano's proposal that Christopher conduct a study of the District's intelligence system with the assistance of Murphy, military officials, and the Secret Service.

McGiffert, mindful of the length of time required to station troops on the streets on the afternoon of April 5, reflected on ways to move them into troubled areas more quickly. Clark argued that placing a thousand soldiers on the streets within half an hour could be more effective than introducing several thousand over a longer period. The discussions also emphasized the importance of urging the news media to reduce tension during a civil disturbance by using "calming rather than inflammatory statements." Nobody commented on the delicacy of such a goal or the likely resistance from media outlets about a potential threat to freedom of the press. The meeting attendees agreed to assign responsibility for investigating the issues they pondered to various members of their group. A sign of the magnitude of their concern was their collective view on the possible forms of future disorders. They worried that "we must be prepared for guerrilla-type warfare, incidents in the suburbs, use of children, Castro-trained commandos, and various other possibilities, however remote they may seem now."[34]

Many of the same officials convened at the White House three weeks later. McGiffert disclosed that the army had prepared a revised deployment plan that would move one thousand troops into the city within four hours "from a cold start." This was little better than the numbers that had arrived in the riot areas on April 5. Christopher reported on new arrangements for intelligence activities in Washington, including a commitment from the FBI to share information with the District of Columbia police. Fletcher, who believed that the main difficulty during the riots "was not the lack of intelligence, but rather the lack of adequate communication," announced that this problem had been corrected with the establishment of a well-equipped command post in the Municipal Building on Indiana Avenue. It would provide direct connections with the White House and among leading city government officials, who often had been out of touch with one another during the April disorders.

While acknowledging the importance of the command center, others remained concerned with upgrading the city's intelligence networks. Murphy lamented that the city government lacked the funds it needed to further expand its intelligence capabilities. This deficiency was soon remedied with an allocation of $150,000 from the Department of the Army. The Metropolitan Police Department had an intelligence unit of ten men, who spent about half of their time on civil disorders. They collected information from contacts with other police departments, phone calls to leaders of protests or rallies, information on applications for parade permits, reports from police officers on the streets, and newspapers. The department also used undercover agents who infiltrated organizations regarded as potentially violent and reported on conditions in urban ghettos that could produce trouble. Professional intelligence officers contended that "good intelligence" was "impossible without the use of undercover agents." They insisted that agents receive extra compensation and benefits because of the dangers of their duties and the possibility that inadequate pay would turn some into double agents.[35]

The White House discussion of intelligence activities and military planning for violence in Washington took on particular urgency because of apprehensions about what might occur during the Poor People's Campaign that was soon to take place in the capital. The campaign was King's idea, designed to call attention to the plight of the poor of all races in America. He envisioned nine caravans of protesters from different sections of the country traveling to Washington and picking up supporters along the way. After they converged in the capital, they would set up camp on the National Mall. From their bivouac site, they would organize demonstrations and lobby Congress for increased funding for anti-poverty programs. King had announced in February 1968 that the goal of the campaign was a commitment from Congress to provide $30 billion for an agenda that included a guaranteed minimum income and the construction of five hundred thousand units of affordable housing per year.

After King's death, his successor as head of the Southern Christian Leadership Conference, Ralph D. Abernathy, announced that the march on Washington would go on, though it was shifted from late April to mid-May. Walter Fauntroy and other SCLC leaders negotiated a detailed agreement with several federal agencies, including the Justice Department and the National Park Service, over the use of federal land to build a temporary settlement called Resurrection City. The protest would be limited to thirty-six days (later extended), with a cap for the population of Resurrection City of three thousand. The SCLC was granted use of a fifteen-acre plot of land in West Potomac Park, just off the Mall to the south of the Lincoln Memorial and the Reflecting Pool.[36]

The prospect of a large contingent of protesters arriving in Washington had been disturbing for government officials and business owners from the time King had disclosed his plans. They worried that the Poor People's Campaign would turn violent, and their concerns intensified in the wake of the riots of early April. An unnamed attorney who was interviewed by Senator Byrd during his hearings on crime in Washington in May 1968 was asked what he regarded as the greatest source of concern for the merchants of the District. The lawyer, who was involved in efforts to provide food to Resurrection City, replied, "I would say the uncertainty of the presence of the Poor People's Campaign and what possible effect it might have on possible additional civil disturbances. . . . I think that the apprehension was brought about by the events of April 4." The District and federal officials who attended the White House conference on May 7 expressed similar views. They discussed the possibility of "preposition-ing" troops who would be ready on short notice to respond to disorders that might arise. The mayor thought this would be a good way to head off a disturbance before it gained momentum. Christopher, however, argued that placing troops in the city would contribute to a "crisis atmos-phere." Although the officials at the meeting did not reach a consensus on this matter, the agencies they represented kept careful tabs through their intelligence networks on the protesters who resided in Resurrection City.[37]

There were few signs that the shantytown adjacent to the Mall was a breeding ground for rioting. It was, however, a scene of terrible living con-ditions. The planning for Resurrection City had provided for canvas and plywood shelters, food, clean water, sanitation, trash collection, electricity, and telephones. But it had not provided for the rain, often heavy, that hit Washington during twenty-eight days of the encampment, including tor-rents of one inch or more on six days and two inches on another day. The result was a sea of ankle-deep mud and a season of misery for residents of the settlement. The number of camp occupants peaked at about 2,600 but dropped as low as 700 on some days. As the demonstration proceeded, the problems of fights, theft, drunkenness, and other unruly behavior in Resurrection City worsened. The District police who monitored the activi-ties of the protesters twice fired tear gas after youths threw stones at officers and at passing vehicles. The Poor People's Campaign failed to accomplish its goals. A rally on June 19 drew about 50,000 people, but the main achieve-ment, in the view of SCLC leaders, was that it took place peacefully.

The Poor People's Campaign ended with an ugly and potentially danger-ous confrontation with police. On the morning of June 24, 1968, after the permit for the encampment expired, about one thousand well-armed police-men arrived to clear out Resurrection City. By pre-arrangement between the SCLC and federal officials, those who remained in the settlement and another group that marched with Abernathy to the Capitol were arrested on minor charges. The SCLC regarded the arrests as a way to call attention to their cause, and the police cited about three hundred people. This part of the conclusion of the Poor People's Campaign went according to plan.

Some of the refugees from Resurrection City, however, apparently were not informed about the plan. They marched to local SCLC headquarters at 14th and U Streets NW to express their anger about the arrests and to inquire about transportation out of the city or about finding food and shelter after the encampment closed. They were joined by groups of youths from the neighborhood, and tensions began to grow. Late in the afternoon, some of those who had gathered on the streets broke windows at stores, including the Peoples Drug at 14th and U that had been an early target on April 4. The police, who had been observing events with increasing alarm, rushed to the scene and soon began to fire tear gas to disperse the crowds. But clusters of people continued to line the sidewalks of 14th Street and some threw stones at police cars and other vehicles. At 7:00 p.m., Mayor Washington sent a contingent of National Guard troops, who had been activated earlier, into the troubled area. A short time later, he imposed a curfew that would run from 9:00 p.m. to 5:30 a.m. Order was restored by midnight, and the National Guard was withdrawn the next day. About 175 people were arrested, 10 for looting and the remainder mostly for curfew violations and disorderly conduct. The police and National Guard used about one thousand tear gas grenades.[38]

A potentially major crisis had been averted as the city government diligently followed the policies and procedures installed after the April riots. The command center at the Municipal Building collected up-to-date reports on what was happening on the streets and provided means of communication among high-level District and federal officials. The police department responded quickly to the unrest on the streets with adequate supplies of tear gas. The mayor, drawing on the information gathered by the command post, acted promptly to call for assistance from the DC National Guard. The city's decisive performance drew many favorable reviews. Even Senator Byrd was impressed. "Had the same firm and prompt action been manifested in the April riot," he declared, "the city and Washington's business community would have been spared the looting, the arson, and the destruction it suffered." But residents in the affected areas were less pleased. They complained about the tear gas that lingered in the air and forced them to close their windows in hot, humid weather. Some also argued that the police engaged in overkill by responding to the disturbance with excessive use of tear gas. The mayor commented that "while resort to forceful means is unfortunate and difficult to use with precision, the action taken on June 24th brought order to a city which was threatened with serious trouble."[39]

In the minds of Mayor Washington and other city officials, they had learned and successfully applied important lessons from the April riots. They also recognized that much more difficult tasks remained to recover from those disorders. Rebuilding the burned-out areas of Northwest and Northeast would prove to be costly, controversial, and time-consuming.

6

The Long Recovery

THE END OF THE APRIL riots in Washington left behind large areas of burned-out desolation and immense problems of recovery and restoration. As early as April 9, 1968, the *Evening Star* hailed Mayor Washington's "superb exercise of leadership" and the "heartening response" of the community to provide food, shelter, and clothing to the victims of the disorders. But it also pointed out that the "much harder test of the resiliency of the District and its citizens will be faced in the long-range job of reconstruction, of restoring permanent homes, of reviving businesses senselessly and ruthlessly wiped out." The "long-range job" required not only money but also a sustained commitment and administrative competence to carry it out. Unfortunately, those attributes were in short supply in the years after the riots. As a result, large parts of the areas most affected by destruction and violence remained an unproductive wasteland for decades.[1]

In the minds of city officials and many business owners, the first requirement for reconstruction in the city was to gain and maintain control over crime. Crime rates continued to rise in the capital after the riots, and concern about this trend was compounded by fears of another similar outbreak of violence. "The pursuit of violence and lawlessness can only lead to the destruction of our city, not to its regeneration," the District of Columbia city council emphasized in a report to the mayor on May 10, 1968. "Continued threats to person or property will destroy the foundations upon which a city is built."[2]

The *Washington Post* suggested in an editorial that the District was "plagued with the aftermath of the recent riots which made a bad crime situation even worse." The editors argued that although the policy of restraint in dealing with the disorders had been justified, it produced apprehension among business owners that they would not receive police protection for their property in the future. It also seemed to have sent the message to "some young toughs" that they could engage in looting, burning, and intimidation at will. One disturbing example that supported the *Post*'s case was that some African American youths distributed flyers demanding that stores close on the birthday of Malcolm X, the black nationalist leader who had been assassinated in 1965, to honor his memory. They made "implied threats" that stores that remained open would be burned. Although few, if any, stores complied with the request, it created a great deal of unease among merchants in the city.[3]

The rise in crime rates and heightened concerns about urban unrest after the April riots in Washington and around the nation emerged as a major political issue during the 1968 presidential campaign. Richard Nixon, the front-runner for the Republican nomination, denounced the Johnson administration on the campaign stump for its failure to fight crime effectively. On May 8, 1968, he released a policy paper in which he elaborated on his attacks. He described the United States as a "lawless society" that faced the ominous prospect of becoming "an armed camp of 200 million Americans living in fear." Nixon did not address the problem of urban riots specifically, but he denied that the increasing crime rates on a day-to-day basis could be attributed mainly to poverty. "The role of poverty as a cause of the crime uprise in America," he said, "has been grossly exaggerated." A few weeks later, Nixon took aim at the situation in Washington. "The disorders and the crime and violence that are now commonplace in Washington are more than a national disgrace," he declared. "They are a cause of grave national concern."[4]

The rising crime rates that spawned fears across the nation about personal safety and public order and that Nixon sought to exploit were potent political issues. Like many other public-policy questions in 1968, they caused sharp divisions of opinion. This was especially apparent on the matter of dealing with civil disturbances. In a Gallup poll conducted in May among residents of cities with a population of more than five hundred thousand, 47 percent thought that "shooting rioters on sight" was the "best way to handle the situation." An almost equal number—49 percent—disagreed, and 4 percent had no opinion. College-educated respondents "generally" opposed a shoot-on-sight policy, as did African Americans by a margin of six to one.

Another survey, sponsored by the Kerner Commission and released in July 1968, was conducted among black citizens in fifteen cities after the 1967 riots. It found that a majority of respondents, even if they did not participate in the riots, expressed support for those who did. Their opinions, the survey concluded, were rooted in their conviction that the riots were "a spontaneous protest against unfair treatment and economic deprivation" and that they were "helpful in giving members of their race a fairer and better life." Another poll, commissioned by Vermont senator Winston Prouty and made public at about the same time, showed similar results. In three low-income neighborhoods in Washington, a "substantial minority" of those questioned in February 1968 believed that the 1967 outbursts had done more good than harm, while 63 percent disapproved of the rioting. The results of the surveys were ambiguous, but collectively, the popular views they revealed about the causes and effects of urban disorders underscored the complexities of dealing with the issue.[5]

At the same time the city government was attempting with limited success to deal with the crime problem, it was making preliminary plans for rebuilding the areas that were heavily damaged by the riots. Shortly after order was restored in Washington, the city council held a series of public meetings to solicit the ideas of citizens about what needed to be done to "best build the kind of city we all want to live in." The sessions were tense and clamorous. The members of the council were plainly annoyed when some speakers accused them of being insufficiently responsive to the needs of their constituents. Other attendees indulged in airing personal grievances rather than offering constructive opinions about how to rebuild the city. Nevertheless, the council took seriously the clear theme that came out of the meetings—that black leaders and citizens should play a major role, if not an exclusive role, in reconstructing the burned-out areas. In its report to the mayor on May 10, the council insisted that "the black community of Washington should have a central and powerful role in the planning and implementation of policies for rebuilding and recovery." But it also emphatically opposed what it called the "ideology of two separate societies." It declared that "the talents and energies of all races and economic groups are needed to make this city strong."

The council's report made some general recommendations about how to proceed with the daunting job of recovery. On the most important issue of housing, it called for improving the "woefully inadequate" choices, quantitatively and qualitatively, that were available to residents of the riot areas. It advocated the building of public housing in all sections of the city, including the affluent neighborhoods west of Rock Creek Park, and the creation of a "housing development fund" for up-front money that was required to take advantage of programs offered by the federal government. After hearing many complaints from black citizens about white merchants who overcharged for inferior goods, the council cautioned that there was no way to accurately judge the extent to which such practices occurred. But it urged that methods be found to provide credit at a reasonable rate to customers and that action be taken to lower the risks for business owners who faced higher perils and overhead costs in low-income neighborhoods. The city council's report was a wish list that cited important objectives without attempting to offer detailed solutions for the myriad problems it identified. But it was a useful blueprint for highlighting the issues the city needed to address to rebuild from the destruction caused by the riots and to improve the conditions that had caused them.[6]

Over the following few months, there were some reasons to be encouraged that the city was making headway. As early as April 9, 1968, the Metropolitan Washington Board of Trade, an alliance of business leaders that had exercised enormous informal political influence since its founding in 1889, announced that it was taking immediate action to launch a program it called JOBS (Jobs Opportunities in the Business Sector). Under a contract with the US Department of Labor, the board had pledged to persuade private industry to offer job training to 1,400 unemployed workers, including "hard-core unemployed," in the capital. At the request of Mayor Washington, the board moved up its timetable to set JOBS in motion. The program got off to a promising start by training its participants in culinary, clerical, automotive, and construction skills. Another favorable development in addressing the problems that citizens faced was that Congress enacted and the president signed legislation designed to make certain that residential and commercial property owners in the riot areas could obtain insurance at a fair price. After the April disorders, premiums for those still eligible to purchase coverage had increased by as much as 1,000 percent.[7]

A further and more readily apparent indicator of Washington's economic recovery from the riots was the revival of the tourist industry. After recording an estimated loss of $57 million from the effects of the disorders and concerns about crime, the tourist trade rebounded briskly, returning to and sometimes exceeding normal levels. By the spring of 1969, attractions were crowded, hotels were full, and restaurants were thriving. The *Washington*

Post attributed the turnaround to the absence of highly visible civil disturbances, some encouraging signs of improvement in police-community
relations, and progress on the "anti-crime front." It warned, however, "that
the calm the city is enjoying is a fragile one requiring the best efforts of everyone to maintain."[8]

The most important source of hope for the city's reconstruction was the
support it received from President Nixon after he took office in January
1969. A few days after his inauguration, Nixon, accompanied by Mayor
Washington and George W. Romney, secretary of the US Department of
Housing and Urban Development (HUD), made an unannounced visit to
the ruins of buildings on 7th Street NW. As the three officials watched a
wrecking ball take a few token whacks at the remains of what had been a
Waxie Maxie's record shop, a crowd of about two hundred gathered. Nixon
crossed the street to shake hands, and one man shouted at him, "Soul
brother!" The president smiled and told his "brother" to "help the Mayor
now." Some members of the crowd cheered.[9]

Nixon's visit to the rubble of 7th Street was more than a mere good-
will gesture. On the same day, he released a message on reducing crime
and reclaiming the damaged areas in Washington. The presidential statement was far more nuanced than Nixon's rhetorical blasts during the 1968

President Richard Nixon, Mayor Walter Washington, and HUD secretary George
Romney inspect riot damage on 7th Street NW, January 31, 1969. *Associated Press*

campaign. It readily acknowledged that Washington was a federal city and that the federal government could not "evade its responsibility for the conditions of life in the District." It affirmed that those conditions had become "intolerable" for many residents because of the increase in "raw, vicious violence." Rather than simply blaming Democratic administrations, Nixon pointed out that the city's problems had been building for a long time. Washington, he said, was "reaping a whirlwind sown . . . by rural poverty in the South, by failures in education, by racial prejudice and the sometimes explosive strains of rapid social readjustments." He held out no hope that there were quick or easy solutions for the quandaries that crime, poverty, and hatred presented. "But," he declared, "we can begin."

Nixon made recovery from the riots and improvement of conditions in the capital a priority. He proposed several steps to make the police department more effective and the administration of justice more efficient. They included expanding the DC police force by hiring a thousand new officers, and adding more judges, prosecuting attorneys, and public defenders to the court system. To address the urgent problems of restoring the devastated riot zones, Nixon announced that HUD had authorized a grant of $29.7 million for the Shaw area, including the 7th Street NW corridor. At the behest of Secretary Romney, his department approved the grant application within twenty-four hours after the city submitted it. "This unprecedented process illustrates the commitment of this Administration to meeting the urgent needs of the capital city," Nixon commented. The president encouraged Mayor Washington to seek additional funds for the other riot-torn neighborhoods, and as an interim payment, he offered $1 million for modest improvements in the 14th Street NW and H Street NE areas. Finally, in a symbolic gesture that underlined the importance the administration attached to rebuilding the city, Nixon announced that net proceeds from his inauguration eleven days earlier would be donated for city parks and playground equipment. The mayor announced that the president's message provided the grounds for an "exceedingly bright day" for the District.[10]

Despite Nixon's interest and other favorable signs, bright days for efforts to rebuild from the April disorders were distressingly rare. In late December 1968, about three weeks before Nixon's inauguration, comments by residents and store owners in the riot corridors demonstrated acute disappointment with the lack of progress and frustration with unkept promises. "A lot of promises were made at the height of the 'problem' we had in April," lamented Robert Harrison, a minister whose church was located near H Street NE, "but the enthusiasm [for] rebuilding is gone." All three of the main riot areas were distinguished by vacant lots and charred shells where buildings once stood and boarded-up windows in many of the structures that survived. During the summer of 1968, the city used a $600,000 grant from the Ford Foundation to create an organization to manage rebuilding programs, the Reconstruction and Development Corporation. A few months later, its recently appointed executive director, Brent Oldham, admitted, "There isn't too much we can spread on the record as actual accomplishments. . . . We have not been able to do a great deal."[11]

Two years after the riots, the city still could not boast of many "actual accomplishments." In May 1968, Mayor Washington and the city council had insisted that citizens of the affected areas play an important role in planning redevelopment by expressing their views on housing, commercial properties, schools, health centers, and other community sites. The mayor had imposed a time limit of one hundred days to come up with proposals. He recognized that the deadline was probably impossible to meet, but he hoped that it would inspire prompt action. Community leaders, concerned residents, and architects met weekly to discuss ideas, and canvassers who were paid $25 a day solicited input from their neighbors. In a little more than a year, citizen groups from the 7th Street and 14th Street NW and the H Street NE areas each prepared detailed plans for what they wanted to accomplish in their own sections. It was a remarkable performance. "Normally urban renewal plans take two to two and a half years to develop," observed Melvin Mister, head of the city's Redevelopment Land Agency (RLA). "This time the citizens did it in half the time."[12]

Preparing and winning approval of the plans was a critical first step, but progress on carrying them out was painfully slow. The problem was not lack of funds; HUD had allocated a total of about $58 million to the city to buy property in the riot zones. Once the RLA appraised and purchased vacant lots and run-down buildings, it would offer its newly acquired properties to private developers. This was where the process ran into serious difficulties. By April 1970, only three stores had reopened in new buildings on 14th Street NW, and some citizens complained that they were chain stores that had not consulted the planning committees. On one block of 7th Street NW that had hosted thirty-two stores, theaters, restaurants, and other businesses before the riots, the number was down to six. The commercial strip on H Street NE remained largely unimproved, and the riot-scarred stores in Southeast were abandoned and forgotten.

Would-be investors were reluctant to build in still-edgy neighborhoods, and many store owners who had suffered losses during the riots were disinclined to return. Brent Oldham of the city's Reconstruction and Development Corporation was angry with charges that his agency had failed to do its job. "Hardly an acre of public land was burned during the civil disorders of 1968. It was private land," he pointed out. "In our society you can force a man to remove a safety hazard from his property but you can't tell him to build." He was not surprised that so many merchants had permanently abandoned the city. "How do you convince private merchants to come back? They were deeply hurt," he commented. "Many felt they had performed a service and this was their reward." Under those conditions, the rebuilding process on the streets that were the centers of the riots was sluggish, or worse, mired in a standstill. Before the riots, the estimated annual sales at stores on 14th Street NW were in the range of $75 million to $100 million. In 1970, after the permanent departure of many businesses, estimated sales were less than $4 million.[13]

The RLA's performance in selling its property to commercial interests was disappointing but largely beyond its control. Its handling of the residential properties it purchased, however, was shameful. The *Washington Star-News* (a new paper formed from a merger of the *Evening Star* and the *Daily News*) called the RLA's performance a "disgrace" that created "a crisis of intolerable dimensions." In November 1973, the *Star-News* ran a three-part story on the wretched conditions in RLA housing, especially The Fairmont apartment building at 14th and Fairmont Streets NW. It was reminiscent of the reports of six years earlier on the deplorable hardships imposed on residents of Clifton Terrace Apartments, located two blocks south. The main difference was that the blame for the squalor at The Fairmont could not be assigned to a greedy slumlord but rather to an agency of the District of Columbia government. The RLA, which received about 75 percent of its funding from HUD, owned buildings that housed some thirteen thousand people in the District of Columbia. Its properties had no legal obligation to conform with the city's housing standards.

The results were clear at The Fairmont, a once congenial place to live. The *Star-News* found a litany of unaddressed problems: dreary rooms, peeling paint, deteriorating plaster, elevated levels of lead, broken pipes, leaking gas stoves, a frequent lack of heat or hot water, rats, roaches, and crime. In 1972, the RLA spent only $750,000 of its $45 million budget on maintenance of its properties. The agency explained that it purchased dilapidated buildings for the express purpose of tearing them down and that repairing them would be a waste of money. But this argument assumed that it would move its tenants into new quarters quickly, and the slowness of the recovery from the riots contributed to the failure to find suitable dwellings. "It's a miserable, lousy situation," conceded an RLA official. "The program has never been funded or geared to address these people problems." Meanwhile, those with the misfortune to live in RLA buildings suffered the consequences with no avenue of escape. Walter Washington expressed his "concern and distress" about the RLA's flawed approach to its "people problems." He had no "magic wand" to solve it, but he promised to seek ways to accelerate the pace of urban renewal, in the riot zones and elsewhere, to relieve the trials of families forced to live in housing that fell far short of minimum standards.[14]

The mayor hoped that home-rule legislation for the District of Columbia that was on the brink of becoming law would enable the city to address its housing problems more effectively. The US House of Representatives had long been the major obstacle to home rule. But the path became much easier when John McMillan, chairman of the Committee on the District of Columbia and an unrelenting opponent of home rule, lost the Democratic primary in his South Carolina district in 1972. His defeat was in part a result of the work of DC leaders, including Walter Fauntroy, who rallied the black electorate to vote for his opponent. With McMillan gone, the House passed a home-rule bill in October 1973, and Nixon, a strong supporter, signed it on December 24.The new law did not, however, end the role of Congress in the affairs of the District. It gave Congress authority over the city's finances and the power to overrule its laws. After ratification by District voters in November 1974, the city held its first election to choose its own government leaders since 1871. Walter Washington, after winning the Democratic primary in a close contest, received a popular mandate to continue in office as an elected rather than an appointed mayor.[15]

In 1978, on the tenth anniversary of the riots, the city could point to some signs that it was finally making genuine progress toward recovery. One hopeful harbinger was that The Fairmont apartments had been rehabilitated. A new apartment complex for low- and moderate-income families had opened two blocks north at 14th and Harvard Streets; there were eight thousand applications for its 406 units. The city had also added 735 housing units in Shaw and 259 in the H Street NE area. Moreover, the incidence of crime in the capital had declined to a point where sixteen other comparably sized American cities had higher arrest rates. Police-community relations had improved, at least in part because the force was about one-half African American (up from one-quarter in 1968). More surprising, Washington experienced a nascent building boom as developers constructed new office buildings in commercial areas. In some neighborhoods near the riot zones, mostly young buyers purchased run-down, but large and handsome, old houses and fixed them up.

Nevertheless, the city had not overcome the debilitating legacy of the riots. The once-bustling commercial strips on the hardest-hit streets remained largely deserted and depressed. The *Washington Post* reported that "much of 14th Street is still a disaster area." The stores that were open often sat next to empty lots or abandoned buildings covered with graffiti. Despite the housing built or rehabilitated in the riot zones, the city owned hundreds of vacant residential and commercial properties. Residents, civic leaders, and merchants placed the blame squarely on the District government. George E. Storey, a resident who worked for the federal government as a chemist for the Food and Drug Administration and who was a community activist, called the 14th Street corridor a "horror story." He groused that "waiting on the [DC] government to do something about it is like waiting on the day when you take your last breath." David Eaton, pastor of the All Souls Unitarian Church, recalled that his church and other sponsors had proposed a rebuilding project for the neighborhood in 1971. "I certainly didn't see any great assistance from the District government during the initial stages," he recalled seven years later. "We had to push the government, and only in recent months have they shown any enthusiasm."[16]

A shortage of enthusiasm and energy seemed to be a common trait in Walter Washington's administration after more than ten years in office. James Gibson, a veteran civil rights leader, pointed out that the mayor just "couldn't make things happen." When Washington decided to seek a second term as elected mayor, he lost in a tight three-way race in the Democratic primary. The winner of the primary and then the general election in November 1978 was Marion Barry. The former president of the District school board and a member of the first elected city council, he had praised Walter Washington when Lyndon Johnson appointed him mayor in 1967. One of Barry's most prominent campaign pledges was to "take the boards off" abandoned public housing projects.

The redevelopment of the riot-torn areas of the city, where boarded-up buildings were a routine sight, made, at best, limited progress under Mayor Barry. His three terms of office between 1979 and 1991 were marked by ineptness, corruption, and a lack of sustained commitment to restore the riot zones. Barry was hampered by the decline in federal funding for rebuilding that began in 1973, and he blamed President Ronald Reagan's policies for his failures to improve the city's severe housing problems. But the mayor's government was so mismanaged that it surrendered millions of dollars in federal housing assistance by not spending it properly or not filing the required paperwork. Another major impediment to restoring the riot areas was an epidemic of crack cocaine in the capital during the 1980s, which produced a sharp increase in murder and assault (while the incidence of other crimes continued to decrease). The city's ability to combat the staggering effects of the cocaine invasion was crippled by Barry's extensive reductions in the police department's budget. He cut the size of the force, which had an authorized strength of 5,100 in 1972, to 3,612 in 1981. The well-publicized growth in crime was a further deterrent to the private investment that was necessary to recover from the devastation of the riots.[17]

After an interregnum under Mayor Sharon Pratt Dixon Kelly that accomplished little and then a fourth Barry term, the District of Columbia finally gained the benefits of an able mayor. Anthony Williams had served as the city's chief financial officer in Barry's last term after Congress had removed most of the mayor's power over spending. In that capacity, he had reduced the size of the bloated bureaucracy and converted a $770 million deficit into a surplus. After he was elected mayor in 1998, he continued his efforts to make the city functional. He balanced the budget, upgraded and modernized the tax bureau, and increased spending for education and police. He trained city employees to make them more responsive to a public that was accustomed to indifference and surliness. The improvements that Williams introduced did not solve all the capital's problems, but they greatly increased confidence among investors in the city's potential for development.[18]

Another important step toward rebuilding the riot areas was the opening of a subway line that served both 7th Street and 14th Street NW. Plans for the Washington Metropolitan Area Transit Authority's rail system, universally known as Metro, had long included a "Mid-City" line that ran through Shaw and the 14th Street corridor. But it was assigned a lower priority than other Metro routes, and it was further delayed by controversies over the effects of construction on housing and over the siting of stations. Progress was also impeded by budget cuts imposed by the Reagan administration. Finally, in August 1985, Metro broke ground for what was by then called the Green Line. This immediately caused new hardships for residents. The bedrock in the area was too deep for tunneling, so Metro had to use its despised "cut and cover" methods. This meant that it dug straight down from street level and placed planks over the deep holes during construction. The result was closed streets, poor drainage, gas leaks, and other threats to convenience and safety. When the Green Line stations near

Howard University in Shaw and at 14th and U Streets opened in May 1991, it was an occasion for celebration and relief.

Virginia Ali, the owner of Ben's Chili Bowl on U Street near 14th, hailed the moment with a sign on the restaurant: "We Survived Metro." Her business had survived, and indeed, thrived in the face of many trials through the years, including the riots, the depressed state of the neighborhood that followed, the drug scourge, and Metro construction. Ali and her husband, Ben, had founded the diner in 1958. Featuring Ben Ali's own recipe for spicy chili, it quickly became a popular attraction for its food as well as a late-night social destination. Famous entertainers, such as Count Basie, Cab Calloway, Dinah Washington, Lena Horne, Harry Belafonte, and Nat King Cole, often visited after their shows in U Street clubs. By the time of the riots, Ben's Chili Bowl had acquired the status of a local institution, and it remained open and undamaged in the midst of the destruction around it. It was, Virginia Ali later reflected, a "very, very scary time" because of the violence and because she learned "what it feels like to have tear gas in your face." As a result of the failure to promptly rebuild the area, she said, "the neighborhood just went all the way down. . . . The shock [was] to have been here for so long, to see the neighborhood deteriorate down to absolutely nothing."[19]

The improvements in the city government under Anthony Williams and the opening of Metro's Green Line were major boons to the redevelopment of the riot areas. The restoration of the 14th Street corridor had begun in 1986, when Marion Barry, in one of his sounder decisions, elected to place a large, new city office building at the corner at 14th and U Streets. The Frank D. Reeves Municipal Center drew city employees and residents to the area and led to the opening of stores and restaurants. It also, in the view of *Washington Post* columnist Courtland Milloy, acted as a "white tornado" that cleared the streets "of litter and junkies."

Shortly after Metro opened, the 14th Street corridor began a full-throttle recovery. Homes that had sold for $80,000 to $90,000 suddenly commanded prices in the $150,000 range. Stores specializing in expensive furniture popped up in the area. Just north of U Street, a new development of elegant townhouses with price tags as high as $650,000 went up in the early 2000s. As the revival of 14th Street proceeded, the 7th Street NW corridor also shed the vestiges of the 1968 disorders. It was greatly aided by the construction of the massive Walter E. Washington Convention Center on the west side of 7th Street north of Mount Vernon Square. The opening of the convention center in 2003 attracted hotels, restaurants, and other businesses to a neighborhood that had never regained its footing after the riots. At the same time, new condominiums that sold for hundreds of thousands of dollars were in high demand and gave new life to the area.[20]

The reconstruction of H Street NE took longer to begin, but by the late 2000s it was clearly under way. The development was spearheaded by young professionals, many of them white, who sought housing that was cheaper than what was available in the 14th Street and 7th Street sections of Northwest. The construction of new condominiums, town houses, and rental apartments gave H Street a welcome new look, and the opening of shops, restaurants, and clubs gave it long-missing vitality. One sign of the area's heightened appeal was that former mayor Anthony Williams purchased a condominium on H Street for a reported price of more than $1 million in 2008. The District of Columbia further spurred development by building a trolley line from H Street's junction with Benning Road to Union Station. By 2015, the same forces of change had shown early indications of reaching the Anacostia section of Southeast. It was the site of several new restaurants and stores, and like other areas damaged by the 1968 riots, the price of housing increased appreciably.

After decades of neglect, the redevelopment of the 1968 riot zones was a vast improvement. But for residents of those areas, it was an uneasy blessing. The rapid rise in housing prices also meant a substantial increase in property taxes. This was a particularly heavy burden for homeowners on fixed incomes, but it was an unhappy blow for everyone affected. Virginia Ali disclosed that the property taxes on the Chili Bowl "tripled the minute they started to dig the hole for Metro." Renters faced the prospect of higher monthly payments, being forced out of rent-controlled apartments, or having their buildings torn down to make way for new development. For some residents, it raised the specter of the same kind of "Negro removal" that occurred during the urban renewal of Southwest during the 1950s. In addition to economic issues, many longtime residents of the riot centers worried about a loss of community and cultural traditions. This was an especially acute concern because the predominantly white new arrivals were moving into neighborhoods that had long been largely black. "I feel like I'm in another city," said one longtime resident. "I get the feeling I no longer belong."[21]

The replacement of barren properties in the riot areas with productive new developments did not, of course, eliminate poverty in the District of Columbia. Approximately one of five residents lived at or below the poverty line between 2010 and 2016. The poverty rate was 18.2 percent in 2016 and substantially higher for African American citizens. After the development that took place in Northwest, and after the construction of a new major-league baseball stadium in Southeast on the west side of the Anacostia River, most of the poor in Washington lived on the east side of the river. They faced the chronic problems of high unemployment, limited opportunities, inferior education, inadequate health care, and crime-ridden neighborhoods. The infant mortality rate in the District ranked among the worst in the country and last in the world among capital cities of wealthy nations. The median income for Washington between 2008 and 2013 rose at a faster pace than the rest of the nation, but so did the unemployment rate.[22]

The question arises, then, of why the nation's capital and the United States as a whole experienced recurrences of serious rioting only on rare occasions in the decades after 1968. The disorders that followed Martin Luther King's assassination were best explained as a spontaneous eruption that grew out of the despair over living conditions in distressed urban neighborhoods. The causes of urban riots identified by the Kerner Commission still prevailed and in many ways had worsened in subsequent years. It seems puzzling that the "simmering crock pot" did not boil over in Washington and other cities around the country more often.

Careful observers offered a variety of explanations for this surprisingly low incidence of serious urban disorders. One reason was the role of police departments in curbing riot activity. In October 1968, Attorney General Ramsey Clark credited the improved police training that the Justice Department had encouraged after the 1967 riots. "We have seen that through effective police action riots can be prevented," he declared, "and that prevention failing, they can be controlled with minimum loss of life and property." Police departments gave increased attention to improving their relationships with black communities in their cities as a means of reducing the likelihood of riots. They made a point of hiring more African Americans and striving to mollify the long-standing tensions that had been prominently displayed by black residents during the 1968 riots. The DC police department sought to advance this goal by establishing extensive training programs for its personnel. It also undertook efforts to encourage citizen involvement in grievance procedures and disciplinary actions against law enforcement officers. A special committee of the city council insisted that "top police officials should not tolerate even the semblance of inhuman or illegal behavior on the part of policemen." Those programs and good intentions did not solve the problem of police-community relations or end citizen complaints about police misconduct. But they did help to bring about welcome and necessary progress after 1967, when, the *Washington Post* reported, "relations between the police and the citizenry were at rock bottom.[23]

Another important reason for the decline in urban rioting after 1968 was the African American community's recognition that the primary victims of violence resided in black neighborhoods. One unnamed African American federal government official suggested in August 1969, "Black people have learned that their own people are the ones who suffer the most from the riots—in deaths, injuries, arrests, and property damage." The *New York Times* reported "a growing feeling that blacks are gradually coming into ownership of the neighborhoods where they live and that thus, they do not want them destroyed."[24]

This outlook dovetailed with a conviction that African Americans were focusing on the need for constructive change. In 1971, Mayor John Lindsay of New York and Senator Fred Harris of Oklahoma, both of whom had served on the Kerner Commission, headed a new study of urban conditions across the country. They found that although people in poor urban areas were as angry as they had been in 1967, "their anger no longer seems to be the helpless kind that can express itself only by smashing and burning." They detected a "new tough pride, self-confidence, and determination." Whitney M. Young Jr., executive director of the National Urban League, made a similar point in the last syndicated column he wrote for the *New York Amsterdam News* before his sudden death in 1971. He observed that "black people are in a period of inward-looking strengthening of our communities and institutions" and had "assumed full responsibility for our own destiny." In the District of Columbia, Mayor Washington noticed the same kind of healthy change. "I've seen a transformation," he remarked, "to a new spirit and a new day with concrete opportunities."[25]

The increasing political power of African Americans was another reason for the rarity of severe urban disorders after 1968. Beginning in the mid-1960s, black elected officials and public employees began to play prominent roles in city governments. Between 1964 and 1978, the number of African Americans who held elective office in the United States grew from about 100 to 4,300. The political advances that blacks made did not in themselves solve the problems of low-income urban areas, but they offered greater access to and perhaps more sympathy from city officials. In the nation's capital, Walter Washington suggested in 1978 that the "great rage" that blacks had shown a decade earlier had been mitigated by a more responsive political system. He pointed out that the police force was 47 percent black and that he had appointed African Americans to the positions of police chief and fire chief. He was convinced that he could not have placed blacks in those jobs in 1968. "You'd have people feeling they weren't protected," he said. "You don't have that anymore."[26]

Along with enhanced political power, the improved economic well-being of African Americans was a key reason for the low incidence of rioting. Educational and employment opportunities improved dramatically for many black citizens, especially women, and the black middle class grew accordingly. Although black median income still trailed white median income by substantial margins, it made clear gains after the 1960s. On the tenth anniversary of the publication of the Kerner Commission's report, David Ginsberg, the staff director of the study, furnished an upbeat evaluation of how conditions had changed for the better. "The black middle class is growing and they have a stake in the maintenance of civil relations," he said. "They are lending stability to the country." A well-educated black middle class had lived and worked in Washington for a long time, and opportunities increased after 1968.[27]

The infrequency of large-scale disorders in American cities could also be attributed to the decline of boundary disputes between races. Throughout American history, ethnic, religious, and racial groups had traditionally lived in segregated enclaves within cities, and violent conflicts had often arisen when one group threatened another's informally established boundaries. This pattern had clearly occurred after large numbers of blacks moved to northern cities during the Great Migration. In more recent years, racial tensions diminished because of the greater level of racial integration in cities and suburbs and the blurring of racial boundary lines. The 1968 riots in Washington were not a result of boundary conflicts between black and white citizens. But they demonstrated the undisguised antagonism of many rioters for whites, especially police officers and store owners. In subsequent years, the District of Columbia police force hired increasing numbers of African Americans, and a large percentage of white merchants left the low-income areas of the city permanently. The more limited contacts in ghetto areas between black residents and whites whom they resented might have had the effect of easing one potential source of unrest.[28]

All those considerations, in some combination, help to explain why there were so few serious riots in major cities after 1968. Still, no one can be sure of the reasons. "If things are worse, why aren't blacks rioting today?" asked Fred Harris, who co-edited a twenty-year retrospective on the Kerner

Commission report in 1988. "Nobody knows," he answered. In later years, scholars of rioting offered a similar response. As early as September 1971, William Greider, a staff writer for the *Washington Post*, raised the same issue in an article about the absence of rioting the previous summer. "Perhaps the only completely safe conclusion . . . is that no one exactly knows the reasons why," he wrote. "Still, the experts grope for explanations, admittedly speculative. They all seem to agree on one point—that riots or no riots, the essential ingredient behind the large-scale disorders of the 1960s still exists undiminished in black communities—deprivation and resentment."[29]

Those same ingredients still prevailed in many American cities, large and small, decades later.[30] They were the fundamental reasons that furious riots occurred in Los Angeles in 1992 and Baltimore in 2015, the two worst outbreaks of urban violence between 1968 and 2016. In Los Angeles, severe and sometimes vicious turmoil followed the acquittal of police officers on trial for brutally beating Rodney King, whom they had stopped for speeding and erratic driving. King was a large, muscular man, and he resisted police efforts to subdue and arrest him. When he aggressively charged one officer, the police responded by repeatedly striking him with batons and kicking him. The confrontation was filmed by a local citizen, who captured the thrashing the police administered but showed little of King's recalcitrance. The tape created a sensation on local and national television news, and it soon became, in the view of Lou Cannon, who covered the story for the *Washington Post*, "an international symbol of police brutality." The jury's refusal to convict the arresting officers immediately caused an eruption of anger and violence in south-central Los Angeles and other parts of the city.

By the time the riots ended five days later, 54 people were dead and 2,328 were injured. The value of property destroyed and damaged totaled more the $900 million. The police department had ample warning that riots might occur, but its initial response was inexplicably deliberate and inadequate. Although Mayor Tom Bradley imposed a curfew shortly after the disorders began, city and state officials were slow to request and effectively mobilize National Guard and federal troops. They failed to gain control of the streets until troops arrived and helped restore order. After the riots ended, the fundamental problems of hostility toward and suspicion of the police department in the black community remained.[31]

In Baltimore, where violence broke out after Freddie Gray's death, Mayor Stephanie Rawlings-Blake waited a few hours before requesting that Governor Larry Hogan send in the National Guard. Hogan said that he was ready to mobilize the Guard "in about 30 seconds" once the mayor asked for troops and he criticized her for the delay. The consequences of the Baltimore riots were much less serious than those in Los Angeles in 1992: no deaths and an estimated $30 million in costs to the city and local businesses (the number of injuries was not reported, though more than one hundred police officers required hospitalization). But the relatively limited effects of the disorders were a small consolation for local officials and residents. In Los Angeles and Baltimore, authorities failed to heed one of the major lessons of the 1968 disorders—that the outbreak of fierce rioting should be met by a prompt and massive show of force by police, and if necessary, National Guard and regular army units. But another, more momentous lesson of the 1968 disturbances was also poorly learned or remembered—that mutual respect in police-community relations was essential for reducing tensions that could flare into explosive violence. In both cities, the most prominent grievance that the residents of the riot areas cited was police misconduct and brutality. This complaint was not limited to cities where riots occurred, as protests across the United States over police use of excessive force, including shooting deaths, amply demonstrated.[32]

Police behavior was far from the only source of tension and discontent. The Washington disorders of 1968 clearly revealed that until and unless the problems of urban poverty and doleful living conditions are dramatically improved—and there a few indications that this is likely to occur in the foreseeable future—the possibility of outbreaks of rioting can, with a spark of some kind, turn into enormously destructive reality.

NOTES

Introduction

1. David Von Drehle, "The Roots of a Riot," *Time*, May 11, 2015, 34–39; Gilbert Sandler, "How the City's Nickname Came to Be," *Baltimore Sun*, July 18, 1995; Kevin Rector, Scott Dance, and Luke Broadwater, "Baltimore Devolves into Chaos, Violence, Looting," *Baltimore Sun*, April 28, 2015; Timothy B. Wheeler, "City Rioting Evokes Memories of 1968," *Baltimore Sun*, April 29, 2015; Erin Cox, Justin Fenton, and Luke Broadwater, "Critics Question Delay in Calling Out Guard," *Baltimore Sun*, April 29, 2015; Editorial, "Who's in Charge?," *Baltimore Sun*, April 29, 2015; Jean Marbella and Yvonne Wenger, "A Day of Relative Calm," *Baltimore Sun*, April 30, 2015; Peter Hermann, Hamil R. Harris, and Ashley Halsey III, "Rioting Rocks Baltimore," *Washington Post*, April 27, 2015; Paul Schwartzman and Ovetta Wiggins, "Mayor, Governor Spar Warily over Response to Riots," *Washington Post*, April 29, 2015; Wesley Lowery, *"They Can't Kill Us All": Ferguson, Baltimore, and a New Era in America's Racial Justice Movement* (New York: Little, Brown, 2016), 129–67; Aaron Cowan, *A Nice Place to Visit: Tourism and Urban Revitalization in the Postwar Rustbelt* (Philadelphia: Temple University Press, 2016), 127–55.

2. *Report of the National Advisory Commission on Civil Disorders* (New York: Bantam Books, 1968), 1, 115–16.
3. Leonard Downie Jr., "April 1968: Flames of Outrage," *Washington Post Magazine*, April 9, 1978, 7–9, 34, 44.
4. Richard Starnes, "D.C. Loses Its Innocence," *Washington Daily News*, April 8, 1968.
5. Alison Isenberg, *Downtown America: A History of the Place and the People Who Made It* (Chicago: University of Chicago Press, 2004), 394n60; Clay Risen, *A Nation on Fire: America in the Wake of the King Assassination* (Hoboken, NJ: John Wiley, 2009), 5–7; Peter B. Levy, "The Dream Deferred: The Assassination of Martin Luther King, Jr., and the Holy Week Uprisings of 1968," in *Baltimore '68: Riots and Rebirth in an American City*, ed. Jessica I. Elfenbein, Thomas L. Hollowak, and Elizabeth M. Nix (Philadelphia: Temple University Press, 2011), 3–25.
6. Tavis Smiley, "It's a Dignity Thing—Democracy Is Threatened by Racism and Poverty," *Time*, May 11, 2015, 39.
7. *Oxford Dictionary of English*, 3rd ed. (Oxford: Oxford University Press, 2010), 1533. The usage example of the word "riot" that the *Oxford Dictionary* provides is, coincidentally, "riots broke out in the capital." Other dictionaries use a similar definition of "riot."
8. For discussions of the use of the term "riot," see: Paul A. Gilje, *Rioting in America* (Bloomington: Indiana University Press, 1996), 4–6; Heather Ann Thompson, "Urban Uprisings: Riots or Rebellions?," in *The Columbia Guide to America in the 1960s*, ed. David Farber and Beth Bailey (New York: Columbia University Press, 2001), 109–17; Amanda I. Seligman, " 'But Burn— No': The Rest of the Crowd in Three Civil Disorders in 1960s Chicago," *Journal of Urban History* 37 (February 2011): 230–55; Alex Elkins, "Stand Our Ground: The Street Justice of Urban American Riots, 1900 to 1968," *Journal of Urban History* 42 (March 2016): 419–37.

Chapter 1

1. Russell Baker, "Fear of Racial Violence Haunts Capital," *New York Times*, June 11, 1963.
2. Russell Baker, "Behind Washington's Postcard Façade: Change, Trouble and Danger Afflict Capital," *New York Times*, June 10, 1963;

Haynes Johnson, *Dusk at the Mountain: The Negro, the Nation, and the Capital—A Report on Problems and Progress* (Garden City, NY: Doubleday and Co., 1963), 6.

3. Constance McLaughlin Green, *Washington: Volume 1, Village and Capital, 1800–1878* (Princeton: Princeton University Press, 1962), 3–5, 38–41, 106; John W. Reps, *Monumental Washington: The Planning and Development of the Capital Center* (Princeton: Princeton University Press, 1967), 5–29; Carl Abbot, *Political Terrain: Washington, DC, from Tidewater Town to Global Metropolis* (Chapel Hill: University of North Carolina Press, 1999), 26–56; Frederick Gutheim and Antoinette J. Lee, *Worthy of the Nation: Washington, DC, from L'Enfant to the National Capital Planning Commission*, 2nd ed. (Baltimore: Johns Hopkins University Press, 2006), 9–44; J. D. Dickey, *Empire of Mud: The Secret History of Washington, DC* (Guilford, CT: Lyons Press, 2014), 1–44; Alan Lessoff, *The Nation and Its City: Politics, "Corruption," and Progress in Washington, DC, 1861–1902* (Baltimore: Johns Hopkins University Press, 1994), 4.

4. Architect of the Capitol, "History of the U.S. Capitol Building," n.d., https://www.aoc.gov/history-us-capitol-building, "Capitol Dome," n.d., https://www.aoc.gov/capitol-buildings/capitol-dome (accessed May 30, 2016); Tom Lewis, *Washington: A History of Our National City* (New York: Basic Books, 2015), 95–97, 123–26; Green, *Washington: Village and Capital*, 67–68; Gutheim and Lee, *Worthy of the Nation*, 41–42, 57.

5. Howard Gillette Jr., *Between Justice and Beauty: Race, Planning, and the Failure of Urban Policy in Washington, DC* (Baltimore: Johns Hopkins University Press, 1995), 83–87; Green, *Washington: Village and Capital*, 170–71; Gutheim and Lee, *Worthy of the Nation*, 53–55, 129; Lewis, *Washington*, 118–23.

6. Constance McLaughlin Green, *Washington: Volume 2, Capital City, 1879–1950* (Princeton: Princeton University Press, 1962), 18; Green, *Washington: Village and Capital*, 344–60; Reps, *Monumental Washington*, 58–61; Gillette, *Between Justice and Beauty*, 72; Gutheim and Lee, *Worthy of the Nation*, 86–88, 90–91, 103; Dickey, *Empire of Mud*, 221–32; Lessoff, *The Nation and Its City*, 72–94.

7. Gillette, *Between Justice and Beauty*, 88–108; Gutheim and Lee, *Worthy of the Nation*, 119–43.

8. Donald E. Press, "South of the Avenue: From Murder Bay to the Federal Triangle," *Records of the Columbia Historical Society* 51 (1984): 51–70; Reps, *Monumental Washington*, 167–73; Abbot, *Political Terrain*, 104, 116; Gutheim and Lee, *Worthy of the Nation*, 182–87; Dickey, *Empire of Mud*, 196–98. Kirk Savage, *Monument Wars: Washington, DC, the National Mall, and the Transformation of the Memorial Landscape* (Berkeley: University of California Press, 2009), argues that Murder Bay was not as disreputable as commonly portrayed and that its residents "were relatively diverse in race and status" (p. 101).

9. Barbara Jeanne Fields, *Slavery and Freedom on the Middle Ground: Maryland during the Nineteenth Century* (New Haven: Yale University Press, 1985), 113; Green, *Washington: Village and Capital*, 183.

10. Kate Masur, *An Example for All the Land: Emancipation and the Struggle over Equality in Washington, DC* (Chapel Hill: University of North Carolina Press, 2010), 22–34, 55–59, 69; Constance McLaughlin Green, *The Secret City: A History of Race Relations in the Nation's Capital* (Princeton: Princeton University Press, 1967), 55–74; Fields, *Slavery and Freedom on the Middle Ground*, 109–13; Gillette, *Between Justice and Beauty*, 39–43; Savage, *Monument Wars*, 165–72.

11. Green, *Secret City*, 82–83.

12. Green, *Washington: Village and Capital*, 276, 302–303, 339–62; Lewis, *Washington*, 183–201; Dickey, *Empire of Mud*, 207.

13. Abbott, *Political Terrain*, 71–72, 99–104; Gillette, *Between Justice and Beauty*, 77; Masur, *An Example for All the Land*, 214.

14. Kathryn Allamong Jacob, " 'Like Moths to a Candle': The Nouveaux Riches Flock to Washington, 1870–1900," in *Urban Odyssey: A Multicultural History of Washington, DC*, ed. Francine Curro Cary (Washington: Smithsonian Institution Press, 1996), 79–96; Green, *Washington: Capital City*, 399–400; Green, *Washington: Village and Capital*, 332–34; Gillette, *Between Justice and Beauty*, 72, 80.

15. Gillette, *Between Justice and Beauty*, 73–77.

16. Blair A. Ruble, *Washington's U Street: A Biography* (Baltimore: Johns Hopkins University Press, 2010), 19–54; Michael Andrew Fitzpatrick, " 'A Great Agitation for Business': Black Economic

Development in Shaw," *Washington History* 2 (Fall/Winter 1990/1991): 48–73; Kathryn S. Smith, "Remembering U Street," *Washington History*, 9 (Fall/Winter 1997/1998): 28–53.

17. Ruble, *Washington's U Street*, 133–66; Green, *Washington: Capital City*, viii.

18. Gillette, *Between Justice and Beauty*, 109–23; Dickey, *Empire of Mud*, 17–18, 232.

19. Sam Smith, *Captive Capital: Colonial Life in Modern Washington* (Bloomington: Indiana University Press, 1974), 74; Green, *Secret City*, 83; Lewis, *Washington*, 190.

20. Eric S. Yellin, *Racism in the Nation's Service: Government Workers and the Color Line in Woodrow Wilson's America* (Chapel Hill: University of North Carolina Press, 2013), 2–3, 114–15; Joan Quigley, *Just Another Southern Town: Mary Church Terrell and the Struggle for Racial Justice in the Nation's Capital* (New York: Oxford University Press, 2016), 7–9; Green, *Secret City*, 119–54, 166–73, 223; Masur, *An Example for All the Land*, 158–62.

21. Erik S. Gellman, *Death Blow to Jim Crow: The National Negro Congress and the Rise of Militant Civil Rights* (Chapel Hill: University of North Carolina Press, 2012), 109–47; Green, *Secret City*, 174–80, 228–30.

22. Green, *Secret City*, 250–73.

23. John Kelly, "DC Restaurant List Is Relic from a Painful Past," *Washington Post*, October 5, 2011; Quigley, *Just Another Southern Town*, 3–6.

24. Quigley, *Just Another Southern Town*, 143–50, 163, 172, 182–83, 186–87, 207, 227.

25. Zachary M. Schrag, *The Great Society Subway: A History of the Washington Metro* (Baltimore: Johns Hopkins University Press, 2006), 17–18; Gillette, *Between Justice and Beauty*, 154; Green, *Washington: Capital City*, 89; Johnson, *Dusk at the Mountain*, 33.

26. Nicholas Lemann, *The Promised Land: The Great Black Migration and How It Changed America* (New York: Vintage Books, 1991), 5–7; Thomas J. Sugrue, *The Origins of the Urban Crisis: Race and Inequality in Postwar Detroit* (Princeton: Princeton University Press, 1996), 7–8; James N. Gregory, *The Southern Diaspora: How*

the Migrations of Black and White Southerners Transformed America
(Chapel Hill: University of North Carolina Press, 2005), 4–23;
Isabel Wilkerson, *The Warmth of Other Suns: The Epic Story of
America's Great Migration* (New York: Vintage Books, 2010), 9–11,
161, 217–18.

27. Elizabeth Clark-Lewis, *Living In, Living Out: African American
Domestics in Washington, DC, 1910–1940* (Washington,
DC: Smithsonian Institution Press, 1994), 51–81; James
Borchert, *Alley Life in Washington: Family, Community, Religion,
and Folklife in the City, 1850–1970* (Urbana: University of
Illinois Press, 1980), 219–22; Spencer R. Crew, "Melding the Old
and the New: The Modern African American Community, 1930–
1960," in *Urban Odyssey*, ed. Cary, 208–27; Green, *Secret City*,
233–34; Wilkerson, *The Warmth of Other Suns*, 177–79, 185,
262–65.

28. Stephen Grant Meyer, *As Long as They Don't Move Next
Door: Segregation and Racial Conflict in American Neighborhoods*
(Lanham, MD: Rowman and Littlefield, 2000), 7, 92–95; Carl H.
Nightingale, *Segregation: A Global History of Divided Cities*
(Chicago: University of Chicago Press, 2012), 341–58; Green, *Secret
City*, 233–37, 277, 341–58; Ruble, *Washington's U Street*, 120–21;
Sugrue, *Origins of the Urban Crisis*, 62–64; Gillette, *Between Justice
and Beauty*, 160.

29. John Hope Franklin, *Mirror to America: The Autobiography of John
Hope Franklin* (New York: Farrar, Straus, and Giroux, 2005), 216;
Johnson, *Dusk at the Mountain*, 248–49.

30. Smith, *Captive Capital*, 74–75; Ruble, *Washington's U Street*,
173–79.

31. Daniel Thursz, *Where Are They Now? A Study of the Impact of
Relocation on Former Residents of Southwest Washington Who Were
Served in an HWC Demonstration Project* (Washington, DC: Health
and Welfare Council of the National Capital Area, 1966), 1–3, 98–
104; Harry S. Jaffe and Tom Sherwood, *Dream City: Race, Power,
and the Decline of Washington, DC* (New York: Simon and Schuster,
1994), 29; Gillette, *Between Beauty and Justice*, 161–65; Ruble,
Washington's U Street, 181–85.

32. Green, *Secret City*, 262, 290–95; Ruble, *Washington's U Street*, 120–
23; Crew, "Melding the Old and the New," 216–22; "A Summer of
Change: The Civil Rights Story of Glen Echo Park," n.d., https://

www.nps.gov/glec/learn/historyculture/summer-of-change.htm (accessed July 7, 2016).

33. Paul Schwartzman and Robert E. Pierre, "From Ruin to Rebirth in DC," *Washington Post*, April 6, 2008; Green, *Secret City*, 200.

34. Green, *Secret City*, 299–305, 328–34; Johnson, *Dusk at the Mountain*, 119–35; Ruble, *Washington's U Street*, 177–78.

35. *Report of the President's Commission on Crime in the District of Columbia* (Washington, DC: Government Printing Office, 1966), 793–96; *The Challenge of Crime in a Free Society: A Report by the President's Commission on Law Enforcement and Administration of Justice* (Washington, DC: Government Printing Office, 1967), 5–6, 27–28; J. W. Anderson, "Anxiety of a City at Night Enters Politics," *Washington Post*, July 26, 1964.

36. "Story of School Crisis and Crime—The Blight in the Nation's Capital," *US News & World Report*, February 18, 1963, printed in Joint Hearing before the District of Columbia Committees of the Senate and the House of Representatives, *Crime in the District of Columbia*, 88th Cong., 1st Sess., 1963, 165–68; *Report of the President's Commission on Crime in the District of Columbia*, 20–21, 36, 56, 104–5; "DC Area Crime Rise Is Fastest in US," *Evening Star* [Washington], July 28, 1966; Johnson, *Dusk at the Mountain*, 100.

37. Bill Davidson, "A City in Trouble: The Mess in Washington," *Saturday Evening Post*, July 13, 1963, 17–23; "Negro Violence Turned against Own Race," *Chicago Daily Defender*, June 1, 1967; Ronald J. Ostrow, "Crime Fears Hold Tight Grip on Residents of Washington," *Los Angeles Times*, February 25, 1968; *Report of the President's Commission on Crime in the District of Columbia*, 853.

38. Russell Baker, "Washington's Welfare Program Is Upset by Senate Critic," *New York Times*, June 12, 1963; Baker, "Behind Washington's Postcard Façade"; Baker, "Fear of Racial Violence Haunts Capital"; Steven J. Diner, "The Nation's City," *Journal of Urban History* 24 (July 1998): 655–66.

Chapter 2

1. Russell Baker, "Fear of Racial Violence Haunts Capital," *New York Times*, June 11, 1963; Bill Davidson, "A City in Trouble: The Mess in Washington," *Saturday Evening Post*, July 13, 1963, 17–23.

2. Michael W. Flamm, *In the Heat of the Summer: The New York Riots of 1964 and the War on Crime* (Philadelphia: University of Pennsylvania Press, 2016).

3. "The Nation," *Time*, July 31, 1964, 9–11; Louis Harris, "White Anxiety Rising in Intensity over Race Issue, Street Violence," *Washington Post*, September 29, 1964; Michael W. Flamm, "The Original Long, Hot Summer," *New York Times*, July 25, 2014.

4. *Report of the National Advisory Commission on Civil Disorders* (New York: Bantam Books, 1968), 37–38; Robert Dallek, *Flawed Giant: Lyndon Johnson and His Times* (New York: Oxford University Press, 1998), 223; Randall B. Woods, *LBJ: Architect of American Ambition* (New York: Free Press, 2006), 591–92; James T. Patterson, *The Eve of Destruction: How 1965 Transformed America* (New York: Basic Books, 2012), 179–84; Joseph A. Califano, *The Triumph and Tragedy of Lyndon Johnson: The White House Years* (New York: Simon and Schuster, 1991), 48–53. For detailed accounts of the Watts riot, see Jerry Cohen and William S. Murphy, *Burn, Baby, Burn! The Los Angeles Race Riot, August 1965* (New York: Avon Books, 1966), and Gerald Horne, *Fire This Time: The Watts Uprising and the 1960s* (Charlottesville: University Press of Virginia, 1995).

5. *Report of the National Advisory Commission on Civil Disorders*, 38–40; Woods, *LBJ*, 693–94.

6. Federal Bureau of Investigation, "Racial Violence Potential in the United States This Summer," May 23, 1967, White House Central File (WHCF), Confidential File, Human Rights (HU2), Box 56 (HU2, Equality of Races), Lyndon B. Johnson Papers, Lyndon B. Johnson Library, Austin, Texas; Katherine A. Scott, *Reining in the State: Civil Society and Congress in the Vietnam and Watergate Eras* (Lawrence: University Press of Kansas, 2013), 40–41; *Report of the National Advisory Commission on Civil Disorders*, 112–15.

7. Sidney Fine, *Violence in the Model City: The Cavanaugh Administration, Race Relations, and the Detroit Riot of 1967* (East Lansing: Michigan State University Press, 2007 [1989]), 291; Kevin Mumford, *Newark: A History of Race, Rights, and Riots in America* (New York: New York University Press, 2007), 98, 125; *Report of the National Advisory Commission on Civil Disorders*, 56–69, 84–108; Michael W. Flamm, *Law and Order: Street Crime, Civil Unrest, and the Crisis of Liberalism in the 1960s* (New York: Columbia University Press, 2005), 83–103.

8. Fred Panzer to the President, June 2, 1967, The Vice President to the President, July 27, 1967, WHCF, HU2, Box 5 (HU2, 6/1/67–6/30/67), Johnson Papers; Califano, *Triumph and Tragedy of Lyndon Johnson*, 207–17; Dallek, *Flawed Giant*, 411–14.

9. "President's Address to the Nation on Civil Disorders," July 27, 1967, Box 45, Folder 11 (National Advisory on Civil Disorders), Walter E. Washington Papers, Moorland-Spingarn Research Center, Howard University, Washington, DC; Elizabeth Hinton, *From the War on Poverty to the War on Crime: The Making of Mass Incarceration in America* (Cambridge, MA: Harvard University Press, 2016), 106–7.

10. Julian E. Zelizer, introduction to the 2016 edition, *The Kerner Report: The National Advisory Commission on Civil Disorders* (Princeton: Princeton University Press, 2016), xiii–xix; Malcolm McLaughlin, *The Long Hot Summer of 1967: Urban Rebellion in America* (New York: Palgrave Macmillan, 2014), 21–24; Califano, *Triumph and Tragedy of Lyndon Johnson*, 217–19; Dallek, *Flawed Giant*, 415–17.

11. Robert C. Baker to the President, January 25, 1967, Box 86, Folder 29 (Response to DC Crime Problem), Washington Papers; WTOP Editorial, "Everyone Is Partly to Blame for the Riots," July 26–27, 1967, Box 28 (Riots and Civil Disorders), SEN90A-F7, Records of the Senate Committee on the District of Columbia, Record Group 46 (Records of the United States Senate), National Archives, Washington, DC; Jean M. White, "An Uneasy Summer Ahead for Washington," *Washington Post*, June 4, 1967; Jeremiah V. Murphy, "Negroes Feel Best Protest Is to Riot, Study Concludes," *Washington Post*, June 27, 1967; Ulf Hannerz, *Soulside: Inquiries into Ghetto Culture and Community* (New York: Columbia University Press, 1969), 169–70.

12. "'Play It Cool,' Police Chief Asks, as Unfounded Rumors Fly," *Washington Post*, July 29, 1967.

13. Stephen J. Pollak to the President, July 25, 1967, WHCF, HU2, Box 20 (HU2/FG216, 11/23/63–5/15/68), Johnson Papers.

14. Raymond Notring to the President, August 1, 1967, Stephen J. Pollak to the President, August 2, 1967, ibid.; "Negro Youths Go on Rampage in Central City," *Evening Star*, August 1, 1967; Stephen Johnston, "Fear Stalks Seventh St.," *Washington Afro-American*, August 5, 1967.

15. Report by Chief of Police John B. Layton on Police-Community Relations, April 16, 1966, Box 19 (Police Department), SEN90A-F7, Records of the Senate Committee on the District of Columbia; John P. MacKenzie, "Johnson Picks Panel to Study Crime and Recommend a Cure," *Washington Post*, July 17, 1965; "Policemen Are Warned against 'Trigger' Words," *Washington Post*, June 27, 1966; Richard Severo, "Residual Race Hatred a Big Police Problem," *Washington Post*, July 1, 1966; White, "An Uneasy Summer Ahead"; Patrick V. Murphy and Thomas Plate, *Commissioner: A View from the Top of American Law Enforcement* (New York: Simon and Schuster, 1977), 103–5; *Report of the President's Commission on Crime in the District of Columbia*, 142–44, 223–24, 793–99, 853.

16. Harry C. McPherson to the President, August 8, 1967, WHCF, HU2, Box 6 (HU2, 7/30/67–8/9/67), Johnson Papers; "District Is Relatively Calm Despite 7 Suspicious Fires," *Evening Star*, August 2, 1967; "Negro Youths Go on Rampage in Mid-City"; Harry C. McPherson, *A Political Education: A Journal of Life with Senators, Generals, Cabinet Members, and Presidents* (Boston: Little, Brown, 1972), 377.

17. Davidson, "A City in Trouble," 20–21; "Racial Crisis Deepens in Nation's Capital," *Chicago Daily Defender*, July 9, 1963; Baker, "Fear of Racial Violence Haunts Capital.

18. Remarks of the President at the Signing of the District of Columbia Appropriations Bill, July 16, 1965, Box 68 (Crime), Office Files of Charles Horsky, Johnson Papers; Thomas W. Fletcher Oral History, March 5, 1969, Johnson Library; "Text of President's View on Crime," *Washington Post*, July 27, 1965; Califano, *Triumph and Tragedy of Lyndon Johnson*, 226–28.

19. "Floor Statement by Senator Alan Bible . . . Supporting Reorganization Plan No. 3," Draft, August 5, 1967, Box 280 (Reorg Plan, Vol. IV), Office Files of James Gaither, Johnson Papers; "Walter Washington Seen as Top Choice for DC 'Mayor,'" *Washington Post*, August 24, 1967; Peter Milius, "Washington Named DC 'Mayor,'" *Washington Post*, September 7, 1967; *Congressional Record*, 89th Cong., 2d Sess., October 22, 1966, 29035; Califano, *Triumph and Tragedy of Lyndon Johnson*, 227–31; Blair A. Ruble, *Washington's U Street: A Biography* (Baltimore: Johns Hopkins University Press, 2010), 219–20.

20. Robert L. Asher, "Walter Washington: Back Home," *Washington Post*, September 7, 1967; Thomas W. Lippman, "A Model of Bureaucratic Success," *Washington Post,* September 3, 1974; Michael Kiernan, "Road to Mayor's Office Began in Jamestown," *Washington Star*, September 4, 1977; Califano, *Triumph and Tragedy of Lyndon Johnson*, 231.

21. Stephen J. Pollak to the President, August 24, 1967, Box 127 (Nominees for Council and DC Commissioners), Office Files of Charles Horsky, Larry Levinson to the President, September 6, 1967, Box 11 (DC Government), Office Files of Joseph Califano, Johnson Papers; "Politicians, Officials Laud Mayor Choice," *Evening Star*, September 6, 1967; Editorial, "'Mayor' Washington," *Evening Star*, September 7, 1967; Editorial, "Our New Government," *Washington Post*, September 7, 1967; "Historic Day for District: Reaction," *Washington Afro-American*, September 9, 1967.

22. Charles Conconi, "T. W. Fletcher, HUD Official, Gets 2nd Spot," *Evening Star*, September 6, 1967; Robert G. Kaiser, "Fletcher, City's New No. 2 Man, a 'Top Administrator,'" *Washington Post*, September 7, 1967.

23. John W. Hechinger Oral History, March 5, 1969, Johnson Library; Robert L. Asher, "President Names Hechinger Head of City Council," *Washington Post*, October 12, 1967; Scottie Smith, "News to Me: John Is a Two-Telephone Man," *Washington Post*, October 17, 1967; Califano, *Triumph and Tragedy of Lyndon Johnson*, 236–41. Johnson originally announced that his nominee for council chairman was Max Kampelman, a prominent Washington attorney and former aide to Hubert Humphrey (and later a highly praised nuclear arms agreement negotiator). But after Republican opposition arose and confirmation appeared to be uncertain, he insisted that Kampelman withdraw and then turned to Hechinger.

24. John W. Hechinger Sr. and Gavin Taylor, "Black and Blue: The DC City Council vs. Police Brutality, 1967–69," *Washington History* 11 (Fall/Winter, 1999/2000): 4–23. This article is drawn from an unpublished memoir that Hechinger wrote in 1971 about his experiences as chairman of the DC city council.

25. District of Columbia Government News Release, December 1, 1967, Box 14 (Public Safety), SEN90A-F7, Records of the Senate Committee on the District of Columbia; "City Picks New Public

Safety Czar," *Washington Post*, December 1, 1967; Murphy and Plate, *Commissioner*, 100–5.

26. DC Police Wives Association to Walter Washington, February 6, 1968, Box 20 (Metropolitan Police Department), SEN90A-F7, Records of the Senate Committee on the District of Columbia; Leonard Downie Jr., " 'They Say I Don't Act . . . Like a Policeman,' " *Washington Post*, December 2, 1967; Murphy and Plate, *Commissioner*, 107–9.

27. Walter Washington to Charles T. Duncan, November 17, 1967, Box 23, Folder 41 (Miscellaneous Government Documents), Washington Papers; Robert G. Kaiser, "It's Walter Washington's Ball on a Hazardous Field," *Washington Post*, September 18, 1967; J. W. Anderson, "Passow Study Urges Far Better Teaching," *Washington Post*, September 7, 1967; Carl Bernstein, "Landlord Is Given Jail Term," *Washington Post*, November 8, 1967; Carl Bernstein and Robert G. Kaiser, "Buildings Frigid, Filthy, Forsaken, Tenants Say," *Washington Post*, November 13, 1967; Bernstein and Kaiser, "DC Realty Operator Deals in Big Numbers," *Washington Post*, November 14, 1967; Bernstein and Kaiser, "1200 Violations Met with Broken Promises," *Washington Post*, November 15, 1967; Bernstein, "Slum Project Upsets Mayor," *Washington Post*, November 17, 1967; William Raspberry, "Fear Invades a High-Rise," *Washington Post*, November 17, 1967; Ernest Holsendolph, "Major School Changes Urged," *Evening Star*, September 7, 1967.

28. Kaiser, "It's Walter Washington's Ball."

29. Robert E. Jordan, Memorandum for the Undersecretary of the Army, January 10, 1968, Box 4 (Directorate of Military Support Reference Chronology), Background Papers for "The Role of Federal Forces in Civil Disturbances, 1945–1971," Record Group 319 (Records of the Army Staff), National Archives, College Park, MD; Joe Califano to the President, January 18, 1968, WHCF, HU2, Box 7 (HU2, 11/16/67–1/18/68), Johnson Papers; Scott, *Reining In the State*, 33–50; Murphy and Plate, *Commissioner*, 99–103.

30. Department of the Army Task Group, "Final Report: Army Preparedness in Civil Disturbance Matters," February 1, 1968, Box 1 (204-05 DA Task Group, CSM 67-316 Final Report), Deputy Chief for Military Operations, Civil Disturbance Reporting Files,

and Counterintelligence Research Project, "Civil Disturbances, CONUS—1968," April 1, 1968, Box 4 (Directorate of Military Support Reference Chronology), both in Background Papers for "The Role of Federal Forces in Civil Disturbances," Records of the Army Staff; United States Senate, Committee on the Judiciary, Subcommittee on Constitutional Rights, *Hearings on Federal Data Banks, Computers and the Bill of Rights*, 92d Cong., 1st Sess., 1971, 184–94; Paul J. Scheips, *The Role of Federal Military Forces in Domestic Disorders, 1945–1992* (Washington, DC: Center of Military History, 2005), 227–30; Scott, *Reining In the State*, 51–61.

31. Michael T. Kaufman, "Stokely Carmichael, Rights Leader Who Coined 'Black Power,' Dies at 57," *New York Times*, November 16, 1998; Peniel E. Joseph, *Stokely: A Life* (New York: Basic Civitas Books, 2014), 113–15, 125–33; US Senate, *Hearings on Federal Data Banks*, 191; Califano, *Triumph and Tragedy of Lyndon Johnson*, 220; McPherson, *Political Education*, 362–63; Flamm, *Law and Order*, 94–95.

32. Harry J. Lemley Jr. and Richard T. Knowles to the Under Secretary of the Army, March 15, 1968, David E. McGiffert, Memorandum for the Secretary of Defense, April 1, 1968, Box 21 (Civil Disturbances, Spring 1968), Background Papers for "The Role of Federal Forces in Civil Disturbances," Records of the Army Staff.

33. Minutes of Cabinet Meeting, March 13, 1968, Cabinet Papers, Johnson Papers; Carroll Kilpatrick, "City Riots Inevitable, LBJ Says," *Washington Post*, February 14, 1968.

34. Richard L. Lyons, "House GOP Assails Johnson on Riots," *Washington Post*, July 29, 1967.

35. Richard M. Nixon, "What Has Happened to America?" *Reader's Digest*, 91 (October 1967): 49–54; Rowland Evans and Robert Novak, "LBJ Ordered Crime Drive Here to Meet a Major Political Issue," *Washington Post*, December 7, 1967; George Gallup, "Crime Tops Domestic Issue List," *Washington Post*, February 28, 1968.

36. *Report of the National Advisory Commission on Civil Disorders*, 1–2; Zelizer, introduction to *The Kerner Report*, xix–xxvii; Califano, *Triumph and Tragedy of Lyndon Johnson*, 260–61; Thomas J. Hrach, *The Riot Report and the News: How the Kerner Commission Changed Media Coverage of Black America* (Amherst: University of Massachusetts Press, 2016), 100–7.

37. *Report of the National Advisory Commission on Civil Disorders*, 5–9, 16–29, 299–305, 410–83; Leroy F. Aarons, "Lethargy toward Cities Troubles Lindsay," *Washington Post*, January 6, 1968.

38. Harry C. McPherson Jr. to Joe Califano, March 1, 1968, Roger W. Wilkins to McPherson, April 4, 1968, Box 32 (Riots), Office Files of Harry McPherson, Johnson Papers; Califano, *Triumph and Tragedy of Lyndon Johnson*, 260–63; Zelizer, introduction to *The Kerner Report*, xxx–xxxiii; Randall B. Woods, *Prisoners of Hope: Lyndon B. Johnson, The Great Society, and the Limits of Liberalism* (New York: Basic Books, 2016), 363–64, 372.

39. "6 Mayors O.K. Riot Findings, Ask Financing," *Chicago Tribune*, March 4, 1968; Robert B. Semple Jr., "Nixon Scores Panel for 'Undue' Stress on White Racism," *New York Times*, March 7, 1968; "Cohen Hits Riot Report 'White Racism' Stress," *Evening Star*, March 26, 1968; Editorial, "The Warning of the Riot Commission," *Business Week*, March 9, 1968, 143; Zelizer, introduction to *The Kerner Report*, xxxiii.

40. Editorial, "Not Encouraging," *Washington Afro-American*, March 12, 1968.

41. Robert G. Kaiser and Carl Bernstein, "City Eyes US Help in Riots," *Washington Post*, February 14, 1968; Carl Bernstein, "US Guides District's Riot-Control Plan," *Washington Post*, March 2, 1968; "No Serious Disorder Expected by Murphy," *Washington Post*, March 14, 1968; Charles Conconi, "The District . . .," *Sunday Star* [Washington], March 3, 1968.

42. Claude Koprowski, "Washington Business Community Awaits King's March with Unease," *Washington Post*, March 1, 1968; Ronald Sarro, "DC Mayor Pledges to Keep Order," *Sunday Star*, March 3, 1968; Crosby S. Noyes, "Riot Threat Requires Calling Off King's March," *Evening Star*, April 4, 1968; Harry S. Jaffe and Tom Sherwood, *Dream City: Race, Power, and the Decline of Washington, DC* (New York: Simon and Schuster, 1994), 67; Ben W. Gilbert, *Ten Blocks from the White House: Anatomy of the Washington Riots of 1968* (New York: Frederick A. Praeger, 1968), 197; Woods, *Prisoners of Hope*, 364–66.

43. George Gallup, "Johnson's War and Job Ratings Sink," *Washington Post*, March 31, 1968; Jules Witcover, *The Year the Dream Died: Revisiting 1968 in America* (New York: Warner Books, 1997),

110–11; Michael A. Cohen, *American Maelstrom: The 1968 Election and the Politics of Division* (New York: Oxford University Press, 2016), 109–12; Doris Kearns, *Lyndon Johnson and the American Dream* (New York: Harper and Row, 1976), 343.

Chapter 3

1. President's Daily Diary, April 4, 1968, Lyndon B. Johnson Papers, Lyndon B. Johnson Library, Austin, Texas; "The City's Turmoil: The Night It Began," *Washington Post*, April 14, 1968; Clay Risen, *A Nation on Fire: America in the Wake of the King Assassination* (Hoboken, NJ: John Wiley, 2009), 40–42; Ben W. Gilbert, *Ten Blocks from the White House: Anatomy of the Washington Riots of 1968* (New York: Frederick A. Praeger, 1968), xi, 13–15.

2. "SNCC Leader on U Street, Tells Views," *Washington Afro-American*, July 29, 1967; Gilbert, *Ten Blocks from the White House*, 12–13.

3. "Preliminary Action and Status Reports Relating to the Mayor, Director of Public Safety, and Police Department Relative to April 1968 Disorders in the District of Columbia," *Report on Civil Disturbances in Washington, D.C.*, April 1968, File P1613, Kiplinger Library, Historical Society of Washington, DC, Washington, DC (hereafter cited as the "Mayor's Report"); Blair A. Ruble, *Washington's U Street: A Biography* (Baltimore: Johns Hopkins University Press, 2010), 176–95; Gilbert, *Ten Blocks from the White House*, 12–14.

4. "Preliminary Action and Status Reports," Mayor's Report; Leonard Downie Jr., "April 1968: Flames of Outrage," *Washington Post Magazine*, April 9, 1978, 7–9ff; Peniel E. Joseph, *Stokely: A Life* (New York: Basic Civitas Books, 2014), 253–58; "The City's Turmoil: The Night It Began"; Gilbert, *Ten Blocks from the White House*, 15–18.

5. "Looting and Arson by Crowds Spread to Center of City," *Evening Star*, April 5, 1968; "Fauntroy, Carmichael Reactions to Slaying," *Evening Star*, April 5, 1968; "The City's Turmoil: The Night It Began"; Gilbert, *Ten Blocks from the White House*, 18–19.

6. Intelligence Summary #1, April 5, 1968, Box 1 (Intelligence Journal, 0005-0700, 5 Apr 68), Emergency Planning 1968, Record Group 338

(Records of the Army Military District of Washington), National
Archives, College Park; "Preliminary Action and Status Reports,"
Mayor's Report; Thomas Morgan, "Raging Riots on 14th St.
Shattered Years' Dreams," *Washington Post*, April 4, 1978; "An
Anatomy of the Riots," *Washington Post*, April 3, 1988; Lillian
Wiggins, "Stores Looted, Rocks Thrown at DC Police," *Washington
Afro-American*, April 9, 1968; "The City's Turmoil: The Night It
Began"; "Looting and Arson by Crowds Spread to Center of City";
Gilbert, *Ten Blocks from the White House*, 20–25.

7. "Transcript of a Recorded Interview with An Anonymous
Participant" [Mr. A], April 26, 1968, pp. 2–6, Papers of the Civil
Rights Documentation Project, Moorland-Spingarn Research
Center, Howard University, Washington, DC; Intelligence
Summary #1, Records of the Army Military District of
Washington.

8. Government of the District of Columbia, Office of Civil Defense,
"Operation Bandaid One," April 4–12, 1968, pp. 1–6, Box 94, Folder
2 (Operation Bandaid One, April 4–April 12, 1968), Walter E.
Washington Papers, Moorland-Spingarn Research Center, Howard
University; Warren Christopher to Joseph Califano, April 29,
1968, Box 37 (Riots 1968: Dr. King), Office Files of James Gaither,
Johnson Papers; "Looting and Arson by Crowds Spread to Center of
City"; "The City's Turmoil: The Night It Began"; "Anatomy of the
Riots."

9. J. Theodore Crown and Walter Gold, "Fake Captain Aids Police
in Riot Crisis," *Evening Star*, April 9, 1968; "'Army Captain' Held
as an Impersonator," *Evening Star*, April 10, 1968; "Man Denies
Impersonation Charge," *Washington Post*, April 19, 1968.

10. "The District of Columbia Fire Department's Role in the Civil
Disturbances of April 4, 5, 6, 7 and 8, 1968," "Preliminary Action
and Status Reports," Mayor's Report; "Operation Bandaid One,"
5–12, Washington Papers; "Stores Looted, Rocks Thrown at
Police"; "Looting and Arson by Crowds Spread to Center of City";
"The City's Turmoil: The Night It Began"; Gilbert, *Ten Blocks from
the White House*, 50.

11. Gilbert, *Ten Blocks from the White House,* 20–21; Ruble,
Washington's U Street, 84–86.

12. Bonnie Perry Interview, October 17, 2002, pp. 10–11, MS 0769 (1968 Riots Oral History Collection), Kiplinger Library, Historical Society of Washington, DC; "Transcript of a Tape-Recorded Interview with an Anonymous Participant" [Mr. C], May 16, 1968, p. 34, Papers of the Civil Rights Documentation Project.

13. "City's 10 Riot Fatalities: Witnesses Describe Deaths," *Washington Post*, April 10, 1968; "Looting and Arson by Crowds Spread to Center of City"; Gilbert, *Ten Blocks from the White House*, 26–27.

14. "Transcript of a Tape-Recorded Interview with Anonymous 'B,'" April 24, 1968, pp. 8–9, 18, Papers of the Civil Rights Documentation Project; Bonnie Perry interview, 8, Riots Oral History Collection; *Report of the National Advisory Commission on Civil Disorders* (New York: Bantam Books, 1968), 274–77; Ulf Hannerz, *Soulside: Inquiries into Ghetto Culture and Community* (New York: Columbia University Press, 1969), 160–66; Haynes Johnson, *Dusk at the Mountain: The Negro, the Nation, and the Capital—A Report on Problems and Progress* (Garden City, NY: Doubleday and Co., 1963), 102–4.

15. *Congressional Record*, 90th Cong., 2d Sess., October 10, 1968, 30500, 30506–7, 30544–46; Jill Nelson, "Burned into the Future," *Washington Post Magazine*, April 3, 1988, 31–32.

16. After Action Report 969–68 (TF Washington, 4–16 April 68), Box 27 (MACV-J3), Military Assistance Command, Assistant Chief of Staff for Operations, Evaluation and Analysis Division, Record Group 472 (Records of the United States Forces in Southeast Asia), National Archives, College Park; Paul Delaney, "Mayor Witnesses Looting," *Evening Star*, April 5, 1968; "The City's Turmoil: The Night It Began."

17. "Chronological Sequence of Events 4–5 April 1968 (Within the Army Operations Center), Box 1 (Confidential), Immediate Office of the Chief of Staff, Records Relating to Civil Disturbances 1968, Record Group 319 (Records of the Army Staff), National Archives, College Park; "Preliminary Action and Status Reports," Mayor's Report; "Operation Bandaid One," 8–12, Washington Papers; After Action Report 969–68, Records of the United States Forces in Southeast Asia; "Looting and Arson by Crowds Spread to Center of City"; "The City's Turmoil: The Night It Began"; Gilbert, *Ten Blocks from the White House*, 40–44.

18. Thomas W. Fletcher Oral History, March 5, 1969, Johnson Library; After Action Report 969–68, Records of the United States Forces in Southeast Asia; "Chronological Sequence of Events, 4–5 April 1968, Records of the Army Staff; "Operation Bandaid One," 4, 5,10, Washington Papers; "Slaying Sends Wave of Strife Across Nation," *Evening Star*, April 5, 1968.

19. Garnett D. Horner, "Johnson Maps Plan to Avert 'Catastrophe,'" *Evening Star*, April 6, 1968; Joseph A. Califano Jr., *The Triumph and Tragedy of Lyndon Johnson: The White House Years* (New York: Simon and Schuster, 1991), 275–77; Harry McPherson, *A Political Education: A Journal of Life with Senators, Generals, Cabinet Members and Presidents* (Boston: Little, Brown, 1972), 364–69; Risen, *A Nation on Fire*, 88–89.

20. David E. McGiffert to Walter E. Washington, May 14, 1968, Box 10 (Civil Disturbances—Washington, DC, 1968), Warren Christopher, Memorandum to Files, n.d., Box 11 (April 1968 Civil Disturbances), Papers of Warren Christopher, Johnson Library; John McCone to the President, June 16, 1967, White House Central File (WHCF), FG 135 (Department of Justice), Box 187 (FG135/A, 6/15/67–5/31/68), Marshall B. Barth, Memorandum for the Record, April 5, 1968, Box 96, President's Appointment File (Diary Backup), Johnson Papers; After Action Report 969–68, Records of the United States Forces in Southeast Asia; Wolfgang Saxon, "David McGiffert, 79, Pentagon Official in 60's," *New York Times*, October 25, 2005; Robert D. Hershey Jr., "Warren Christopher, Lawyer, Negotiator and Adviser to Presidents, Dies at 85," *New York Times*, March 20, 2011.

21. Larry Temple to the President, April 5, 1968, WHCF, HU2 (Equality of Races), Box 20 (HU2/FG216, 11/23/63–5/15/68), Johnson Papers; Phil Casey, "Carmichael Warns of 'Retaliation,'" *Washington Post*, April 6, 1968; Gilbert, *Ten Blocks from the White House*, 59–67.

22. Gilbert, *Ten Blocks from the White House*, 46–48.

23. Ibid, 49–53; Intelligence Summary #4, Intelligence Journal, 5 April 1968–6 April 1968, Records of the Army Military District of Washington; "New Riots Catch Police Short," *Washington Post*, April 6, 1968; Barry Kalb and Winston Groom, "'We Don't Have a Business': The Story of One Ravaged Block," *Sunday Star* [Washington], April 14, 1968; Downie, "April 1968," 9.

24. Mary E. Stratford, "District Rioting Unleashed Ugly Emotions," *Washington Afro-American*, April 9, 1968.

25. District of Columbia Fire Department, "Preliminary Report of Civil Disturbances of April 4–April 13, 1968," Box 1 (1968 Washington, DC Riots), Selected Topics: Civil Rights, Papers of Robert C. Byrd, Robert C. Byrd Center for Congressional History and Education, Shepherd University, Shepherdstown, WV; "The District of Columbia Fire Department's Role in the Civil Disturbances of . . . 1968," Mayor's Report; "Anatomy of the Riots"; Downie, "April 1968," 9; Gilbert, *Ten Blocks from the White House*, 51, 53.

26. Orville Green, "'I Got Home and There Was No Home,' Says Fire Victim," *Washington Afro-American*, April 13, 1968.

27. Julius Duscha, "Postscript to the Story of Seventh Street," *New York Times Magazine*, June 2, 1968, 30ff; Stephen Johnston, "Fear Stalks Seventh St.," *Washington Afro-American*, August 5, 1967; Johnson, *Dusk at the Mountain*, 101–2.

28. "Operation Bandaid One," 17–18, Washington Papers; District of Columbia Fire Department, "Preliminary Report," Byrd Papers; Intelligence Journal, April 5, 1968, Records of the Army Military District of Washington; "New Riots Catch Police Short"; "Anatomy of the Riots."

29. Duscha, "Postscript to the Story of Seventh Street," 31, 43, 45, 48, 55, 58.

30. Ibid, 45; Michael Kiernan, "Auto Dealership Found New Home in Suburbs," *Washington Star*, April 3, 1978.

31. Intelligence Journal, April 5, 1968, Records of the Army Military District of Washington; District of Columbia Fire Department, "Preliminary Report," Byrd Papers; Gilbert, *Ten Blocks from the White House*, 79–82.

32. Gilbert, *Ten Blocks from the White House*, 156–77.

33. Ibid, 83–85; Intelligence Journal, April 5, 1968, Records of the Army Military District of Washington.

34. "Operation Bandaid One," 20, Washington Papers; "Arsonists and Looters Leave Parts of Capital in Shambles," *Evening Star*, April 6, 1968; Richard Wilson, "Ninth-Floor Window Offers View of Looters," *Evening Star*, April 10, 1968; Ward Just, "The City Besieged: A Study in Ironies and Contrasts," *Washington Post*, April 6, 1968.

35. Tom Wicker, "Thousands Leave Washington as Bands of Negroes Loot Stores," *New York Times*, April 6, 1968; "New Looting Flares Despite Troops," *Evening Star*, April 6, 1968; *Congressional Record*, 90th Cong., 2d Sess., October 14, 1968, 31928–30; Gilbert, *Ten Blocks from the White House*, 78–79.

36. "Operation Bandaid One," 19, Washington Papers; Wicker, "Thousands Leave Washington as Bands of Negroes Loot Stores"; Nelson, "Burned into the Future," 37.

37. District of Columbia Fire Department, "Preliminary Report," Byrd Papers; Murray Seeger, "Capital Guarded," *Los Angeles Times*, April 6, 1968; Lyndon Baines Johnson, *The Vantage Point: Perspectives of the Presidency, 1963–1968* (New York: Holt, Rinehart and Winston, 1971), 538.

38. President's Daily Diary, April 5, 1968, Johnson Papers; Cyrus Vance Oral History, November 3, 1968, Fletcher Oral History, Johnson Library. The following day, in a phone conversation with Chicago mayor Richard Daley, Johnson complained that he had waited impatiently to order troops into Washington because "the Mayor couldn't make up his mind." He told Daley, "I just cried . . . I ate my fingernails off." It is clear, however, that the mayor had informed the president within an hour after returning from King's memorial service that troops were needed. Johnson was not prepared at that time to call in the army; he elected to wait until Christopher, Murphy, and Haines reported on their tour of the riot areas. See "President Johnson's Notes on Conversation with Mayor Richard Daley," April 6, 1968 (misdated April 4, 1968), Recordings and Transcripts of Telephone Conversations and Meetings, Johnson Library.

39. Fletcher Oral History, Johnson Library; Michael W. Flamm, *Law and Order: Street Crime, Civil Unrest, and the Crisis of Liberalism in the 1960s* (New York: Columbia University Press, 2005), 92; McPherson, *A Political Education*, 365–66; Califano, *Triumph and Tragedy of Lyndon Johnson*, 279.

40. Walter E. Washington, Patrick V. Murphy, and John B. Layton, Memorandum to the President of the United States, April 5, 1968, WHCF, HU2, Box 20 (HU2/FG216, 11/23/63–5/15/68), Johnson Papers; Warren Christopher Oral History, December 2, 1968, Johnson Library; Warren Christopher to the Files, n.d., Christopher

Papers (note 20 above); Gilbert, *Ten Blocks from the White House*, 74.

41. "Chronology per General Johnson," April 15, 1968, Box 37 (Riots 1968: Dr. King), Gaither Office Files, President's Daily Diary, April 5, 1968, Johnson Papers; Christopher Oral History, Johnson Library; Christopher to the Files, n.d., Christopher Papers (note 20 above).

42. After Action Report 969–68, Records of the United States Forces in Southeast Asia; "Operation Bandaid One," 20–22, Washington Papers; "Chronology per General Johnson," April 15, 1968, Johnson Papers (note 41 above); Paul J. Scheips, *The Role of Federal Military Forces in Domestic Disorders, 1945–1992* (Washington, DC: Center of Military History, 2005), 284–92; Califano, *Triumph and Tragedy of Lyndon Johnson*, 279.

43. Harold K. Johnson to Ralph E. Haines Jr., April 5, 1968, Box 1 (General Harold K. Johnson, Civil Disturbance Papers), Immediate Office of the Army Chief of Staff (Records Relating to Civil Disturbances 1968), Records of the Army Staff; Scheips, *Role of Federal Military Forces*, 290.

44. Willard Clopton, "4000 Troops Move into District after Day of Looting and Arson," *Washington Post*, April 6, 1968; Peter Milius, "Mayor Imposes Tight Curfew," *Washington Post*, April 6, 1968; "New Fires Set Off; Curfew On Tonight; More Soldiers Due," *Evening Star*, April 6, 1968.

45. Situation Room Information Report, April 5, 1968, 5:30 p.m., Box 96 (April 4–11, 1968: Death of Martin Luther King and Riots in Major Cities), President's Appointment File (Diary Backup), Johnson Papers; After Action Report 969–68, Records of the United States Forces in Southeast Asia; Intelligence Journal, April 5, 1968, Records of the Army Military District of Washington; "Operation Bandaid One," 20, 22, Washington Papers.

46. Situation Room Information Memorandum, April 5, 1968, 9:00 p.m., WHCF, HU2, Box 20 (HU2/FG216, 11/23/63–5/15/68), Johnson Papers; Johnson to Haines, April 5, 1968, Records of the Army Staff; Intelligence Summary #4, April 5, 1968, Records of the Army Military District of Washington; "Operation Bandaid One," 20, Washington Papers.

47. Intelligence Journal, April 5, 1968, Records of the Army Military District of Washington; Califano, *Triumph and Tragedy of Lyndon Johnson*, 280.

48. "Chronological Sequences of Events Commencing with Dr. Martin Luther King's Assassination," n.d., WHCF, Confidential File, Box 56 (HU2/FG 216), Johnson Papers; Fletcher Oral History, Johnson Library; Transcript of Press Conference, April 6, 1968, Mayor's Report; "Operation Bandaid One," 25, Washington Papers; Harry S. Jaffe and Tom Sherwood, *Dream City: Race, Power, and the Decline of Washington, DC* (New York: Simon and Schuster, 1994), 80.

49. "The District of Columbia Fire Department's Role in the Civil Disturbances of April . . . 1968," Mayor's Report; "New Fires Set Off; Curfew on Tonight; More Soldiers Due"; "Arsonists and Looters Leave Parts of Capital in Shambles."

Chapter 4

1. Situation Room Information Memorandum, April 6, 1968, 8:30 a.m., White House Central File (WHCF), Confidential File, HU2 (Equality of Races), Box 56 (HU2), Papers of Lyndon B. Johnson, Lyndon B. Johnson Library, Austin, Texas; Chalmers M. Roberts and Walter H. Pincus, "3 Slain in Chicago, Many Fires Set," *Washington Post*, April 6, 1968; Ben A. Franklin, "Army Troops in Capital As Negroes Riot; Guard Sent into Chicago, Detroit, Boston," *New York Times*, April 6, 1968; "19 Dead in Rioting Across Nation," *Sunday Star* [Washington], April 7, 1968.

2. Government of the District of Columbia, Office of Civil Defense, "Operation Bandaid One," April 4–12, 1968, p. 31, Box 94, Folder 2 (Operation Bandaid One, April 4–April 12, 1968), Walter E. Washington Papers, Moorland-Spingarn Research Center, Howard University, Washington, DC.

3. "Operation Bandaid One," 27–37, Washington Papers; Editorial, "James Brown on Riots," *Washington Afro-American*, April 13, 1968; Robert L. Asher and Martin Weil, "City's Diary of Violence Goes On without Letup," *Washington Post*, April 7, 1968.

4. "DC Fire Dept. Faces Unparalleled Challenge," *Sunday Star*, April 7, 1968; Murray Seeger, "Washington Ghetto Smoldering Ruins Block after Block," *Los Angeles Times*, April 7, 1968.

5. President's Daily Diary, April 4, April 5, April 6, 1968, Johnson Papers; Thomas W. Fletcher Oral History, March 5, 1969, Johnson Library; "The Government's Policy and Functional Response," *Report on Civil Disturbances in Washington, DC*, April 1968, File P1613, Kiplinger Library, Historical Society of Washington, DC (hereafter cited as "Mayor's Report"); "Operation Bandaid One," 40, Washington Papers; Ben W. Gilbert, *Ten Blocks from the White House: Anatomy of the Washington Riots of 1968* (New York: Frederick A. Praeger, 1968), 118–19.

6. Willard Clopton Jr. and Robert G. Kaiser, "11,500 Troops Confront Rioters; Three-Day Arrest Total at 2686," *Washington Post*, April 7, 1968; Gilbert, *Ten Blocks from the White House*, 104–5.

7. Thomas Oliver, "Guard Found Duty Rough, Residents Friendly," *Evening Star* [Washington], April 21, 1968; Paul J. Scheips, *The Role of Federal Military Forces in Domestic Disorders, 1945–1992* (Washington, DC: Center of Military History, 2005), 294; Gilbert, *Ten Blocks from the White House*, 106–7.

8. Jack Eisen, "Troops Guarding D.C. Rely on C Rations, Field Kitchens," *Washington Post*, April 7, 1968; Jill Nelson, "Burned into the Future." *Washington Post Magazine*, April 3, 1988, 29–30.

9. Oliver, "Guard Found Duty Rough, Residents Friendly"; Gilbert, *Ten Blocks from the White House*, 99, 111–12.

10. After Action Report 969–68 (TF Washington, 4–16 April 68), Box 27 (MACV-J3), Military Assistance Command, Assistant Chief of Staff for Operations, Evaluation and Analysis Division, Record Group 472 (Records of the United States Forces in Southeast Asia), Matt Nimetz to Joe Califano, April 6, 1968, Box 24 (White House Files, Situation Reports), Background Papers for "The Role of Federal Forces in Civil Disturbances, 1945–1971," Record Group 319 (Records of the Army Staff), National Archives, College Park.

11. Joe Califano to the President, April 6, 1968, 2:00 p.m., WHCF, HU2, Box 20 (HU2/FG216, 11/23/63–5/18/68), Johnson Papers; Russell Baker, "Washington's Welfare Program Is Upset by Senate

Critic," *New York Times*, June 12, 1963; "Poverty: Phony Excuse for Riots? 'Yes,' Says a Key Senator," *US News & World Report*, July 31, 1967, 14.

12. Editorial, "Coping with the Violence," *Evening Star*, April 6, 1968.

13. Joe Califano to the President, April 6, 1968, 11:05 a.m., Box 24 (White House Files, Situation Reports), Background Papers for "The Role of Federal Forces in Civil Disturbances, 1945–1971," Records of the Army Staff; Califano to the President, April 6, 1968, 2:00 p.m., Johnson Papers (cited above); "Transcript of a Tape-Recorded Interview with Anonymous 'B,'" April 24, 1968, p. 38, Papers of the Civil Rights Documentation Project, Moorland-Spingarn Research Center, Howard University; Ward Just, "City's Mood: Resignation, Bitterness," *Washington Post*, April 7, 1968; Haynes Johnson, "A Washingtonian Travels His Ravaged City," *Sunday Star*, April 7, 1968; John Mathews, "Thousands of Spectators Pour into Violence-Hit Areas, Cause Traffic Jams," *Sunday Star*, April 7, 1968.

14. Transcript of Press Conference, April 6, 1968, Winifred G. Thompson to Thomas W. Fletcher, April 9, 1968, Walter F. McArdle to Fletcher, April 10, 1968, Mayor's Report; Betty James, "Emergency Food Is Available for Victims of DC Violence," *Sunday Star*, April 7, 1968; Betty James, "Agriculture Department Pouring Surplus Food into City," *Evening Star*, April 8, 1968.

15. Thompson to Fletcher, McArdle to Fletcher, Mayor's Report; "Operation Bandaid One," 51–52, Washington Papers; David Bratten and Robert J. Lewis, "New Homes for Homeless," *Evening Star*, April 10, 1968; Betty James, "Food Centers Cut, All Operable Chain Stores Open Here," *Evening Star*, April 10, 1968; Asher and Weil, "City's Diary of Violence Goes On Without Letup"; James, "Emergency Food Is Available for Victims of DC Violence."

16. Woody West, "Looting, Arson Continue, Some Easing Is Reported," *Sunday Star*, April 7, 1968.

17. John Fialka, "Rioting Cases Inundate Court Here," *Evening Star*, April 7, 1968; Situation Room Information Memorandum, April 7, 1968, 9:25 p.m., Box 24 (White House Files, Situation Reports), Background Papers for "The Role of Federal Forces in Civil Disturbances," Records of the Army Staff; Editorial, "Justice During a Crisis," *Washington Post*, April 10, 1968; Gilbert, *Ten Blocks from the White House*, 120–39.

18. After Action Report 969–68, Records of the United States Forces in Southeast Asia; "Operation Bandaid One," 47–63, Washington Papers; Barry Kalb, "Sniper Fire in District Gets Quick Response," *Evening Star*, April 8, 1968.

19. Willard Clopton Jr. and Robert G. Kaiser, "Calm Returning to Riot-Hit City," *Washington Post*, April 8, 1968; Bernadette Carey, "Sen. Kennedy Tours Areas Torn by Riots," *Washington Post*, April 8, 1968; Woody West, "DC Begins Return to Normal," *Evening Star*, April 8, 1968.

20. President's Daily Diary, April 7, 1968, Johnson Papers; "Operation Bandaid One," 61, Washington Papers; Clopton and Kaiser, "Calm Returning to Riot-Torn City."

21. Woody West, "District Eases Curfew, Liquor Rules Further," *Evening Star*, April 11, 1968; William Delaney, "District Curfew Lifted by Mayor," *Evening Star*, April 12, 1968; William Delaney, "City Calm, Troops Leaving," *Evening Star*, April 14, 1968; "DC Begins Return to Normal"; Willard Clopton Jr. and Carl W. Sims, "DC Quiet as Looting Spreads in Baltimore," *Washington Post*, April 9, 1968; Robert L. Asher, "City Curfew Eased; Soldiers Remain but Cut Patrols," *Washington Post*, April 11, 1968; Willard Clopton Jr., "DC Relaxes Curfew, Liquor Sales Further," *Washington Post*, April 12, 1968; Robert G. Kaiser, "Last Riot Bans Revoked," *Washington Post*, April 16, 1968; "An Anatomy of the Riots," *Washington Post*, April 3, 1988; "Coalition, City Officials Tell of Efforts to Dig Out," *Washington Afro-American*, April 13, 1968; Gilbert, *Ten Blocks from the White House*, 117–18.

22. Richard L. Lyons, "House Passes Civil Rights Bill," *Washington Post*, April 11, 1968; Carroll Kilpatrick, "President Signs Rights Bill," *Washington Post*, April 12, 1968; Richard Corrigan, "Realtors Skeptical of Open Housing's Impact on Ghettos," *Washington Post*, April 18, 1968; Editorial, "Civil Rights Act, 1968," *Evening Star*, April 11, 1968; Randall B. Woods, *Prisoners of Hope: Lyndon B. Johnson, the Great Society, and the Limits of Liberalism* (New York: Basic Books, 2016), 361–62.

Chapter 5

1. Minutes, "Washington, D.C. Riots and Future Planning," May 7, 1968, Box 37 (Riots 1968: Dr. King), Office Files of James

Gaither, Papers of Lyndon B. Johnson, Lyndon B. Johnson Library, Austin, Texas; Robert C. Maynard, "People Adapt in a City of Remorse," *Washington Post*, April 10, 1968; James Reston, "Washington: Aftermath of the Crisis," *New York Times*, April 10, 1968.

2. G. R. Mather to Under Secretary of the Army, June 14, 1968, Box 9 (Civil Disturbance Intelligence Activities–1968), Background Papers for "The Role of Federal Forces in Civil Disturbances, 1945–1971," Record Group 319 (Records of the Army Staff), National Archives, College Park; Robert L. Asher, "GIs Still Patrol DC; Curfew On," *Washington Post*, April 10, 1968; "US Riot Damage about $45 Million, Insurers Estimate," *Evening Star* [Washington], April 12, 1968; "Rampage and Restraint," *Time*, April 19, 1968, 15–18.

3. Lee Flor, "Cautious Insurers Estimate Riot Loss at $10–$15 Million," *Evening Star*, April 9, 1968; "An Anatomy of the Riots," *Washington Post*, April 3, 1988; Ben Gilbert, *Ten Blocks from the White House: Anatomy of the Washington Riots of 1968* (New York: Frederick A. Praeger, 1968), 119, 178; US Senate, Committee on Government Operations, Permanent Subcommittee on Investigations, *Hearings on Riots, Civil and Criminal Disorders*, 91st Cong., 1st Sess., 1969, 3121, 3174–79, 3194, 3206.

4. *Congressional Record*, 90th Cong., 2d Sess., 1968, 31958–59; Richard M. Cohen, "Restaurant Industry Shaken," *Washington Post*, July 29, 1968.

5. Bernard Diamond to Hotel Stratford, May 13, 1968, Box 1 (1968 Washington DC Riots), Selected Topics: Civil Rights, Papers of Robert C. Byrd, Robert C. Byrd Center for Congressional History and Education, Shepherd University, Shepherdstown, WV; *Congressional Record*, 90th Cong., 2d Sess., 1968, 3160; Hobart Rowan and S. Oliver Goodman, "Stores, Hotels Reel from Riot Impact," *Washington Post*, April 7, 1968; Susan Jacoby, "Fairfax Schools' Field Trips into City Banned after Riots," *Washington Post*, April 19, 1968.

6. Peter B. Levy, "The Dream Deferred: The Assassination of Martin Luther King, Jr., and the Holy Week Uprisings of 1968," in *Baltimore '68: Riots and Rebirth in an American City*, eds. Jessica I. Elfenbein, Thomas L. Hollowak, and Elizabeth M. Nix (Philadelphia: Temple University Press, 2011), 3–25.

7. Cliff Alexander to the President, April 6, 1968, Fred Panzer to the President, April 6, 1968, Box 44 (Riots Speech), Office Files of Harry McPherson, Situation Room Information Memorandum, April 8, 1968, White House Central Files (WHCF), HU2 (Equality of Races), Box 8 (HU2, 4/8/68), Johnson Papers; Memorandum for the President, April 7, 1968, 5:30 a.m., Memorandum for the President, April 8, 1968, 5:30 a.m., Box 24 (White House Files, Situation Reports), Background Papers for "The Role of Federal Forces in Civil Disturbances, 1945–1971," Records of the Army Staff; Miriam Ottenberg, "Test of New Riot Law Seen; Carmichael's Role Assessed," *Sunday Star* [Washington], April 7, 1968; "For Stokely: A Hard Look-See," *Washington Daily News*, April 8, 1968.

8. "A Transcript of a Tape-Recorded Interview with Anonymous 'B,'" April 24, 1968, p. 31, Papers of the Civil Rights Documentation Project, Moorland-Spingarn Research Center, Howard University, Washington, DC; Walter Washington Oral History, December 10, 1971, Johnson Library.

9. Carl T. Rowan, "America's Failure to Combat Racism," *Evening Star*, April 12, 1968.

10. William Raspberry, "Lessons of the Riots," *Washington Post*, April 3, 1988. The *Post* was hardly free of racial insensitivity in its own newsroom. The paper sent its entire roster of fourteen black reporters and photographers to cover the riots, and the writers phoned in their stories to the newsroom. They were indignant when they found that their white colleagues who manned the phones received the bylines in the paper because the *Post* "normally gave credit to the rewriters." See Donald A. Ritchie, *Reporting from Washington: The History of the Washington Press Corps* (New York: Oxford University Press, 2005), 265.

11. Paul A. Gilje, *Rioting in America* (Bloomington: Indiana University Press, 1996), 6–8; Thomas J. Sugrue, *Sweet Land of Liberty: The Forgotten Struggle for Civil Rights in the North* (New York: Random House, 2008), 326; "'Take Everything You Need, Baby,'" *Newsweek*, April 15, 1968, 31–33; Tom Wicker, "Thousands Leave Washington as Bands of Negroes Loot Stores," *New York Times*, April 6, 1968.

12. "A Transcript of a Recorded Interview with Anonymous Participant," [Mr. A], April 26, 1968, pp. 16–17, Papers of the Civil

Rights Documentation Project; Editorial, "Riots and the Law," *Washington Afro-American*, April 13, 1968; "'Take Everything You Need, Baby,'" 31.

13. Reuben M. Jackson Interview, October 13, 2002, p. 20, MS 0769 (1968 Riots Oral History Collection), Kiplinger Library, Historical Society of Washington, DC.

14. David Lawrence, "Tragedy of Riots Deep-Rooted," *Evening Star*, April 9, 1968; Editorial, "Dangers to Democracy," *Wall Street Journal*, April 10, 1968; Editorial, "Collective Guilt Again," *Wall Street Journal*, April 15, 1968; James W. Button, *Black Violence: Political Impact of the 1960s* (Princeton: Princeton University Press, 1978), 5–6.

15. Gilbert, *Ten Blocks from the White House*, 149, 224; Committee on Government Operations, *Hearings on Riots, Civil and Criminal Disorders*, 3207.

16. John W. Macy Jr. to the President, April 25, 1968, WHCF, HU2, Box 20 (HU2/FG 216, 11/23/63–5/15/68), Johnson Papers; Jerry Kluttz, "Only Few US Workers Reported Seized in Riots," *Washington Post*, April 19, 1968; John Fialka, "Computer Draws a Profile of DC Rioters," *Sunday Star*, November 17, 1968; Gilbert, *Ten Blocks from the White House*, 149–53.

17. P. J. Wilson, "I Am Not Built for Revolution," *Potomac* [Sunday Supplement], *Washington Post*, May 5, 1968, 10–17.

18. Willard Clopton Jr. and Robert G. Kaiser, "11,500 Troops Confront Rioters; Three-Day Arrest Total at 2686," *Washington Post*, April 7, 1968; Ward Just, "Generation Gap in the Ghetto," *Washington Post*, April 7, 1968; Carol Honsa, "Counter-Rioters Help Cool It," *Washington Post*, April 9, 1968.

19. Robert J. Donovan, "Riots Following King Tragedy Show US Is at Crossroads," *Los Angeles Times*, April 7, 1968. On generational differences, see Isabel Wilkerson, *The Warmth of Other Suns: The Epic Story of America's Great Migration* (New York: Vintage Books, 2010), 408–20.

20. John D. Jackson Interview, March 27, 2003, pp. 21–22, MS 0769, 1968 Riots Oral History Collection; Editorial, "The Violence Must End," *Washington Afro-American*, April 16, 1968; Committee on Government Operations, *Hearings on Riots, Civil and Criminal Disorders*, 3173.

21. David Grimsted, *American Mobbing, 1828–1861: Toward Civil War* (New York: Oxford University Press, 1998), viii.

22. Leonard Downie Jr., "Praise Heaped on D.C. Police," *Washington Post*, April 8, 1968; Editorial, "So Far, Well Done," *Washington Post*, April 8, 1968; Crosby S. Noyes, "District Deserves High Marks in Riot Control," *Evening Star*, April 20, 1968.

23. Ron Youngblood, " 'Shoot Order' Fans National Controversy," *Chicago Daily Defender*, April 18, 1968.

24. C. D. Kaufmann to the President, April 12, 1968, Box 67, Folder 10 (Correspondence "K"), Walter Washington Papers, Moorland-Spingarn Research Center, Howard University; Irving King to Joseph Tydings, April 6, 1968, Box 1 (1968 Washington, DC Riots), Selected Topics: Civil Rights, Byrd Papers; Barry Kalb and Winston Groom, " 'We Don't Have a Business,' " *Sunday Star*, April 14, 1968.

25. *Congressional Record*, 90th Cong. 2d Session, 1968, 30498–30548, 31036–31076, 31921–31983; Robert G. Kaiser, "Murphy: I'd Quit, Not Shoot," *Washington Post*, April 26, 1968.

26. US House of Representatives, Committee on the District of Columbia, *Hearings on Civil Disturbances in Washington*, 90th Cong., 2d Sess., 1968, 3–15.

27. Joseph Kraft, "Disorders Here Taught Control without Bloodshed," *Washington Post*, April 9, 1968; Leonard Downie Jr., "Riot Lesson: Restraint, Planning Work," *Washington Post*, April 11, 1968; Peter Milius, "Murphy Answers Critics," *Washington Post*, May 16, 1968; Youngblood, " 'Shoot Order' Fans National Controversy."

28. Michael Bernstein, "A Candid Account of DC's Darkest Hours," *Washington Daily News*, April 24, 1968; "Transcript of . . . Interview with Anonymous 'B,' " 34, Papers of the Civil Rights Documentation Project; *Report of the National Advisory Commission on Civil Disorders* (New York: Bantam Books, 1968), 329–30.

29. Claudia Levy, "Burned-Out Store Opens after Riot," *Washington Post*, August 15, 1968.

30. Herman Schaden, "Doctor Too Busy to Worry," *Evening Star*, April 10, 1968; Julius Duscha, "Postscript to the Story of Seventh Street," *New York Times Magazine*, June 2, 1968, 43, 55.

31. John Mathews and Ernest Holsendolph, "The Children Write Their Own Postscript," *New York Times Magazine*, June 2, 1968, 63; Joy Manson, "What 'Soul' Is All About," *Washington Post*, April 10, 1968.

32. John Mathews and Ernest Holsendolph, "Telling It Like It Is— DC Students Discuss the Violence," *Sunday Star*, April 14, 1968; Mathews and Holsendolph, "The Children Write Their Own Postscript," 66, 68, 73.

33. Frederick Taylor, "Quick Show of Force, Not Exotic Weapons, Quelled Capital Violence," *Wall Street Journal*, April 11, 1968; Fred P. Graham, "Police Restraint in Riots," *New York Times*, April 13, 1968; Ben A. Franklin, "Restraint in Riot Control Result of Long Planning," *New York Times*, April 14, 1968; Editorial, "Chaos Avoided," *New York Times*, April 17, 1968; William Chapman, "Containing Riots," *Washington Post*, April 13, 1968; Philip D. Carter and Peter Osnos, "Key to Riot Control: Restraint and Speedy Use of Troops," *Washington Post*, April 9, 1970.

34. Minutes, "Washington, DC Riot and Future Planning," April 15, 1968, Box 37 (Riots 1968: Dr. King), Gaither Office Files, Joe Califano to the President, April 17, 1968, WHCF, HU2, Box 20 (HU2/FG216, 11/23/63–5/15/68), Johnson Papers; Ralph E. Haines Jr., Memorandum for Record, April 15, 1968, Box 1 (Confidential), Immediate Office of the Chief of Staff: Records Relating to Civil Disturbances 1968, Records of the Army Staff.

35. Paul G. Bower to Warren Christopher, May 4, 1968, WHCF, Confidential File, HU2/FG 216, Box 56 (HU2/FG 216, Equality of Races), Minutes, May 7, 1968, Gaither Office Files (Note 1 above), Johnson Papers; Bower to Christopher, June 10, 1968, Box 9 (Civil Disturbances 1968), Bower to Christopher, July 23, 1968, Box 10 (Civil Disturbances—Washington, DC 1968), Personal Papers of Warren Christopher, Johnson Library; David E. McGiffert to Walter Washington, June 6, 1968, Box 47 (Metro Police Reports 1968), Washington Papers. There is no evidence that the city's intelligence activities extended to include the aggressive and illegal practices carried out by the FBI against civil rights advocates and radical organizations. The misconduct of the FBI and some other agencies is well covered in Katherine A. Scott, *Reining In the State: Civil Society and*

Congress in the Vietnam and Watergate Eras (Lawrence: University Press of Kansas, 2013); Elizabeth Hinton, *From the War on Poverty to the War on Crime: The Making of Mass Incarceration in America* (Cambridge, MA.: Harvard University Press, 2016); and Arthur M. Eckstein, *Bad Moon Rising: How the Weather Underground Beat the FBI and Lost the Revolution* (New Haven: Yale University Press, 2016).

36. Minutes, May 7, 1968, Gaither Office Files (Note 1 above); Randall B. Woods, *Prisoners of Hope: Lyndon B. Johnson, the Great Society, and the Limits of Liberalism* (New York: Basic Books, 2016), 364–67; Gilbert, *Ten Blocks from the White House*, 196–97.

37. Minutes, May 7, 1968, Gaither Office Files (Note 1 above); *Congressional Record*, 90th Cong., 2d Sess., 1968, 31974–76; Woods, *Prisoners of Hope*, 366–67.

38. "City Quiet After Brief Flareup," *Evening Star*, June 25, 1968; Tom Lewis, *Washington: A History of Our National City* (New York: Basic Books, 2015), 409; Gilbert, *Ten Blocks from the White House*, 197–206. For an excellent discussion of the Poor People's Campaign, see Gordon K. Mantler, *Power to the Poor: Black-Brown Coalition and the Fight for Economic Justice, 1960–1974* (Chapel Hill: University of North Carolina Press, 2013).

39. Government of the District of Columbia, City Council, "Report of the Public Safety Committee on Police-Community Relations," August 5, 1968, Box 87, Folder 10 (Report of the Public Safety Committee on Police-Community Relations, 1968), Washington Papers; Gilbert, *Ten Blocks from the White House*, 195–96, 206–7.

Chapter 6

1. Editorial, "The City's Response," *Evening Star* [Washington], April 9, 1968.

2. *Report of City Council Public Hearings on the Rebuilding and Recovery of Washington, DC from the Civil Disturbances of April, 1968*, May 10, 1968, p. 7, File P1614, Kiplinger Library, Historical Society of Washington, DC.

3. J. Griffin Rountree to Robert C. Byrd, May 17, 1968, Box 1 (1968 Washington DC Riots), Selected Topics: Civil Rights, Robert C. Byrd Papers, Robert C. Byrd Center for Congressional History and Education, Shepherd University, Shepherdstown, WV;

Leonard Kolodny to William H. Press, May 17, 1968, Box 86, Folder 31 (The Malcolm X "Problem"), Walter E. Washington Papers, Moorland-Spingarn Research Center, Howard University, Washington, DC; Editorial, "Stop the Violence," *Washington Post*, May 5, 1968.

4. Chalmers M. Roberts, "Nixon Hits Rise in Crime," *Washington Post*, May 9, 1968; "Nixon Calls Washington a Crime Capital," *Chicago Tribune*, June 23, 1968.

5. Fred Panzer to the President, May 28, 1968, HU2 (Equality of Races), Box 8 (HU2, 5/1/68–5/31/68), Lyndon B. Johnson Papers, Lyndon B. Johnson Library, Austin, Texas; William Grigg, " 'Substantial Minority' Backs Violence," *Evening Star*, July 31, 1968; Willard Clopton Jr., "Ghettos Find Benefits in Riots, Study Shows," *Washington Post*, July 31, 1968; Editorial, "A Sobering Report," *Washington Post*, August 3, 1968.

6. *Report of City Council Public Hearings on the Rebuilding and Recovery of Washington, DC*, 1–10, 19–20, 24–30, 38–40; Paul Delaney and Shirley Elder, "Group Seeks Negro Control of Riot Rebuilding Program," *Evening Star*, April 13, 1968; Betty James, "Rebuilding Powers Asked," *Evening Star*, April 24, 1968; Paul Delaney, "Urban League Gives Council Extensive Plan on Rebuilding," *Evening Star*, April 25, 1968; Bernadette Carey, "Barry Would Bar White Control of Business in Rebuilt Ghettos," *Washington Post*, April 16, 1968; Hollis I. West, "Many Voices Give View of Rebuilding," *Washington Post*, April 29, 1968.

7. Metropolitan Washington Board of Trade Press Release, April 9, 1968, "Board of Trade Newsletter," August 1968, Box 4 (Board of Trade), SEN90A-F7, Records of the Senate Committee on the District of Columbia, Record Group 46 (Records of the US Senate), National Archives, Washington, DC; George Davis, "Jobs Center Has Birthday," *Washington Post*, April 16, 1969. The JOBS program did not fulfill the hopes it raised when it began in 1968. In 1970, the Department of Labor canceled the program because of its limited success "in placing and keeping people in jobs." David R. Boldt, "Jobs Center Closes, US Bars Funds," *Washington Post*, January 3, 1970.

8. Editorial, "Washington Bounces Back," *Washington Post*, June 9, 1969.

9. Phineas R. Fiske, "President Visits Riot Site," *Washington Post*, February 1, 1969.

10. Robert L. Asher and Leonard Downie Jr., "Nixon Details Plan to Make District Safe," "Text of Nixon's Message on Crime," *Washington Post*, February 1, 1969.

11. Robert L. Asher and Robert G. Kaiser, "Broken Promises Line Riot Area Streets," *Washington Post,* December 29, 1968.

12. Claudia Levy and Leonard Downie Jr., "The Lights Are Still Out from Riots," *Washington Post*, April 5, 1970; Ann McFeatters, "Four Days in April: Grief, and Rebirth," *Washington Daily News*, March 30, 1970; Ben W. Gilbert, *Ten Blocks from the White House: Anatomy of the Washington Riots of 1968* (New York: Frederick A. Praeger, 1968), 217–18.

13. Carl Bernstein and Ivan Brandon, "Scars in People Point Up Riot Areas' Needs," *Washington Post*, April 6, 1970; Patricia Camp, "14th St. Struggles Back from Riot," *Washington Post*, April 3, 1978; Levy and Downie, "The Lights Are Still Out from Riots"; McFeatters, "Four Days in April."

14. Walter Washington to Birch Bayh, November 17, 1973, Box 47, Folder 7 (14th Street Corridor), Washington Papers; Michael Satchell and Corrie M. Anders, "Misery in Our Midst," *Washington Star-News*, November 13, 1973; Corrie M. Anders, "The Fairmont: Squalor's Way," *Washington Star-News*, November 14, 1973; Michael Satchell, "Victims of Slums: 4 Profiles," *Washington Star-News*, November 15, 1973; Editorial, "The Housing Disgrace," *Washington Star-News*, November 15, 1973. For a study of a city whose efforts to recover from the riots paralleled those of Washington in important ways, see Alyssa Ribeiro, "'A Period of Turmoil': Pittsburgh's April 1968 Riots and Their Aftermath," *Journal of Urban History*, 39 (March 2013): 147–71.

15. Blair A. Ruble, *Washington's U Street: A Biography* (Baltimore: Johns Hopkins University Press, 2010), 220–21; Howard Gillette Jr., *Between Justice and Beauty: Race, Planning, and the Failure of Urban Policy in Washington, DC* (Baltimore: Johns Hopkins University Press, 1995), 190–91; Harry S. Jaffe and Tom Sherwood, *Dream City: Race, Power, and the Decline of Washington, DC* (New York: Simon and Schuster, 1994), 100–4.

16. Michael Kiernan and Philip Shandler, "The Washington Decade: Things Sure Have Changed," *Washington Star*, September 4, 1977; Leon Dash and Phil McCombs, "New Kind of City Emerging Out of Ruins of '68 Riot," *Washington Post*, April 2, 1978; Camp, "14th St. Struggles Back from Riot."

17. Jaffe and Sherwood, *Dream City*, 112–27, 155, 188, 210–11, 223; Ruble, *Washington's U Street*, 225–26, 232, 236–37, 253.

18. Harry S. Jaffe and Tom Sherwood, *Dream City: Race, Power, and the Decline (Revival?) of Washington, DC* (n.p., 2014), 397–406. This is an updated version of Jaffe and Sherwood's 1994 book, distributed by Argo Navis Author Services.

19. Virginia Ali Interview, February 12, 2003, pp. 14, 19, 22, MS 0769 (1968 Riots Oral History Collection), Kiplinger Library, Historical Society of Washington, DC; Jill Nelson, "Burned into the Future," *Washington Post Magazine*, April 3, 1988, 33–34; Matt Schudel, "Ben Ali, 82, Whose Chili Bowl Became a DC Landmark, Dies," *Washington Post*, October 9, 2009; Zachary M. Schrag, *The Great Society Subway: A History of the Washington Metro* (Baltimore: Johns Hopkins University Press, 2006), 213–17.

20. Ruble, *Washington's U Street*, 261–69; Schrag, *Great Society Subway*, 217–18.

21. Ali Interview, 22–24, 1968 Riots Oral History Collection; Eugene L. Meyer, "Signs of Recovery in a 'Riot Corridor,'" *New York Times*, December 2, 2007; Paul Schwartzman, "A Bittersweet Renaissance," *Washington Post*, February 23, 2006; Paul Schwartzman and Robert E. Pierre, "From Ruin to Rebirth in DC," *Washington Post*, April 6, 2008; John Mintz, "Investors Reclaiming Riot Corridors," *Washington Post*, April 7, 2008; Amanda Abrams, "Anacostia in Southeast DC Is Emerging at Last," *Washington Post*, November 26, 2015; Paul Duggan, "After a Decade of Gentrification, District Sees a Surge in Families Crushed by Rent," *Washington Post*, December 24, 2016; Ruble, *Washington's U Street*, 262–68; Schrag, *Great Society Subway*, 218. On the effects of condominium conversion, see Carolyn Gallagher, *The Politics of Staying Put: Condo Conversion and Tenant Right-to-Buy in Washington, DC* (Philadelphia: Temple University Press, 2016).

22. Tim Craig, "Report Finds Rise in DC Poverty to Nearly 1 in 5 Residents," *Washington Post*, March 25, 2010; Perry Stein, "DC's Poorer Residents Are Increasingly Concentrated East of the

Anacostia," *Washington Post*, April 14, 2015; Abigail Hauslohner, "Poor DC Babies Are More than 10 Times as Likely to Die as Rich Ones," *Washington Post*, May 4, 2015; Andrew Giambrone, "More DC Residents Live in Poverty Than Before the Great Recession, Says Study," *Washington City Paper*, September 15, 2016; Michael B. Sauter, Samuel Stebbins, and Thomas C. Frohlich, "The Most Dangerous Cities in America," *Wall Street Journal*, September 27, 2016, http://247wallst.com/special-report/2016/09/27/ 25-most-dangerous-cities-in-america/4.

23. Government of the District of Columbia, City Council, "Report of the Public Safety Committee on Police-Community Relations," August 5, 1968, Box 87, Folder 10 (Report of the Public Safety Committee on Police-Community Relations), Washington Papers; Gladwin Hill, "Clark Notes Drop in Summer Riots," *New York Times*, October 4, 1968; Jack Rosenthal, "Why the Summer Was Not as Hot as It Might Have Been," *New York Times*, September 7, 1969; Peter Braestrup, "Police-Community Relations Still a Major Problem in DC," *Washington Post*, November 12, 1969; Thomas W. Lippman, "A Model of Bureaucratic Success," *Washington Post*, September 3, 1974; Fred R. Harris and Roger W. Wilkins, eds., *Quiet Riots: Race and Poverty in the United States* (New York: Pantheon, 1988).

24. John Herbers, "US Officials Say Big Riots Are Over," *New York Times*, August 24, 1969.

25. John Herbers, "Summer's Urban Violence Stirs Fears of Terrorism," *New York Times*, September 21, 1971; Whitney M. Young Jr., "An Old Story," *New York Amsterdam News*, March 20, 1971; Dash and McCombs, "New Kind of City Emerging Out of Ruins of '68 Riot."

26. William Greider, "After Dr. King: Strong Currents of Social Change," *Washington Post*, April 2, 1978; Dash and McCombs, "New Kind of City Emerging Out of Ruins of '68 Riot."

27. Kenneth Walker, "Reassessing Kerner Panel's Riot Report of the '60s," *Washington Star*, February 28, 1978; Michael B. Katz, *Why Don't American Cities Burn?* (Philadelphia: University of Pennsylvania Press, 2012), 47–77; Greider, "After Dr. King: Strong Currents of Social Change."

28. On "boundary challenges," see Katz, *Why Don't American Cities Burn?*, 83–86.

29. William Greider, "A Long, Hot Summer: Why Was It So Cool?,"
    Washington Post, September 12, 1971; Fred R. Harris, "The 1967
    Riots and the Kerner Commission," in *Quiet Riots*, eds. Harris and
    Wilkins, 5–15. For scholarly comments on the lack of certainty or
    consensus over why the serious riots of the 1960s became much less
    common in later years, see Malcolm McLaughlin, *The Long, Hot
    Summer of 1967: Urban Rebellion in America* (New York: Palgrave
    Macmillan, 2014), and David Grimsted, *American Mobbing,
    1828–1861: Toward Civil War* (New York: Oxford University Press,
    1998). McLaughlin wrote that after 1968, "The long, hot summers
    had come to an end. No one could really be certain why" (p. 159).
    Grimsted wrote that his book, "like other riot studies, offers no clue
    to why riot ended so suddenly after the violent Martin Luther King
    wake" (p. xiii).
30. For an analysis of the cause of a riot in a midsize suburban city and
    a call for further study of urban unrest outside of large urban cen-
    ters, see Thomas J. Sugrue and Andrew P. Goodman, "Plainfield
    Burning: Black Rebellion in the Suburban North," *Journal of Urban
    History* 33 (May 2007): 568–601.
31. Lou Cannon, *Official Negligence: How Rodney King and the Riots
    Changed Los Angeles and the LAPD* (Boulder: Westview Press,
    1999), 20–37, 339–51.
32. Erin Cox, Justin Fenton, and Luke Broadwater, "Critics Question
    Delay in Calling Out Guard," *Baltimore Sun*, April 29, 2015;
    "About 130 Officers Injured during Baltimore Riots Released
    from Hospital," *Baltimore Sun*, May 6, 2015; Yvonne Wenger,
    "Unrest Will Cost City $20 Million, Officials Estimate," *Baltimore
    Sun*, May 26, 2015; Peter Hermann, Hamil R. Harris, and
    Ashley Halsey III, "Rioting Rocks Baltimore: Hogan Declares
    Emergency, Activates Guard," *Washington Post*, April 27, 2015; Paul
    Schwartzman and Ovetta Wiggins, "Mayor, Governor Spar Warily
    over Response to Riots," *Washington Post*, April 29, 2015.

ESSAY ON SOURCES

The historical literature on urban rioting can be placed in three broad interpretive categories that were originally set forth by James W. Button in his book *Black Violence: Political Impact of the 1960s Riots* (Princeton: Princeton University Press, 1978). Although he referred to contemporary analysts, his categories apply to historians as well. The "conservative" position that Button outlined was that riots were aimless, irrational, and self-defeating outbursts that were often sparked by agitators and rabble-rousers. The most prominent example of this view, at least in general terms, is Fred Siegel, *The Future Once Happened Here: New York, DC, L.A., and the Fate of America's Big Cities* (San Francisco: Encounter Books, 1997). He suggests that urban poverty was not a fundamental cause of riots. In Washington, he argues, a "federal government acutely embarrassed by pictures of troops on the Capitol steps and rioting just ten blocks from the White House decided to put more money into local antipoverty efforts, as if poverty per se had been the primary issue." A new generation of militant black leaders sought to enhance their own political power by playing on white "guilt and fear" to demand greater expenditures for urban programs.

At the other end of Button's spectrum is the "radical" interpretation, which regards urban violence as rational, calculated, and politically motivated. Scholars who advance this view "contend that public responses should consist of significant increases in power and resources for the powerless and even major alterations in the existing political system." A recent example of this approach is Malcolm McLaughlin, *The Long, Hot Summer of 1967: Urban Rebellion in America* (New York: Palgrave Macmillan, 2014). He sees the aftermath of the 1967 riots as an unfulfilled opportunity to open "debate about the scope of political change in America, far wider than anything conceived since." He faults the Kerner Commission report for its refusal to support "the notion that the riots might represent a genuine . . . rejection of the prevailing order" or the idea that "the American system was fundamentally unjust."

The interpretation of urban violence that Button calls the "liberal" perspective takes a middle ground between the conservative and radical positions. It holds that riots were a rational response to racism, poverty, joblessness, and other deplorable conditions in low-income urban areas. In this framework, the best approach is not a "*major* restructuring of the existing political or economic system" but rather the adoption of reforms that would improve both living conditions and opportunities for residents of struggling neighborhoods. Examples include the Kerner Commission, *Report of the National Advisory Commission on Civil Disorders* (New York: Bantam Books, 1968); Sidney Fine, *Violence in the Model City: The Cavanaugh Administration, Race Relations, and the Detroit Riot of 1967* (East Lansing: Michigan State University Press, 2007); and Alyssa Ribeiro, "'A Period of Turmoil': Pittsburgh's April 1968 Riots and Their Aftermath," *Journal of Urban History* 39 (March 2013): 147–71.

The findings of this book strongly favor the "liberal" interpretation. In contrast to the conservative view, there is no convincing evidence that the Washington riots were set off by outside agitators seeking to accomplish their own ends. Rather, it is clear that the lamentable conditions in the 14th Street and 7th Street corridors in Northwest, the H Street corridor in Northeast, and elsewhere in the city produced anger, frustration, and political impotence that led to spontaneous outbursts of rioting. In that sense, the outbreaks were rational responses to adversity, and Martin Luther King's assassination was the spark that set them off. In contrast to the radical view, there is little to suggest that the rioters were consciously seeking to accomplish political goals or to restructure American (or Washington) political and economic institutions. For most of the participants, the evidence indicates that the riots were an opportunity to take goods without paying, to feel a sense of power and control, to show resentment toward white society, or perhaps all of the above. But that is as far as the political objectives of the riots extended. This book concurs with the conservative and liberal positions in showing that the riots were counterproductive in producing the greatest harm, sometimes tragically so, to residents of the areas in which they took place.

There is a rich variety of primary sources relating to the 1968 Washington riots. The papers of Walter E. Washington at the Moorland-Spingarn Research Center at Howard University in Washington contain uniquely valuable information. Although there is little on the days that the mayor was dealing with the riots, the papers include correspondence, reports, and other useful materials on related issues. Of particular importance is an outline prepared by the District of Columbia's Office of Civil Defense, "Operation Bandaid One," that provides a minute-to-minute listing of events during the April crisis. The Civil Rights Documentation Project at Moorland-Spingarn includes three nearly contemporaneous oral history interviews in which rioters talked frankly about their experiences and motivations.

The Kiplinger Library at the Historical Society of Washington, DC, located at Mount Vernon Square in the District, houses important materials. An especially important document is a preliminary report to the mayor in April 1968 on the activities of various agencies of the DC government during the riots, including the police and fire departments. The library also has among its holdings several excellent oral history interviews, conducted by Dana L. Schaffer in 2002 and 2003, in which city residents shared their memories and varying perspectives.

The National Archives in College Park, Maryland, has an abundance of documentary evidence on the US Army's role in the 1968 riots. There are very good materials in Record Group 338 (Records of the Army Military District of Washington) and Record Group 319 (Records of the Army Staff). The Army Staff records include a large body of evidence collected by Paul J. Scheips of the Center of Military History for his book *The Role of Federal Military Forces in Domestic Disorders, 1945–1992* (Washington, DC: Government Printing Office, 2005). One highly useful document, an After Action Report on the Washington riots, is filed in an unlikely place, Record Group 472 (Records of the United States Forces in Southeast Asia). At the National Archives in Washington, DC, Record Group 46 (Records of the United States Senate) includes the records of the Senate Committee on the District of Columbia, which has helpful materials on events leading up to the 1968 disorders.

The Lyndon B. Johnson Library in Austin, Texas, houses a wealth of important materials. In addition to the files in Johnson's presidential papers, records of members of the White House staff and collections of personal papers are essential sources on key matters such as conditions in the city, the crime problem, relations with the DC government, the decision to call out troops during the riots, and the aftermath of the crisis. Of particular importance are the office files of James Gaither, Charles Horsky, and Harry C. McPherson and the personal papers of Warren Christopher and Ramsey Clark. Several oral histories are also of value.

The Robert C. Byrd papers contain much of interest on the 1968 riots. They help to document the views of a leading proponent of law and order and an outspoken critic of the response to the disorders in Washington. They are available at the Robert C. Byrd Center for Congressional Studies and Education at Shepherd University in Shepherdstown, West Virginia.

Newspaper accounts of the riots are a singularly enlightening source of information on events and on the perspectives of participants, victims, and government officials. The *Evening Star* of Washington and the *Washington Post* provided careful and comprehensive coverage. They should be supplemented with stories that appeared in the *Washington Afro-American* and the *Washington Daily News*, both of which produced scoops of their own.

There is very little in the scholarly or popular literature about the 1968 disorders in Washington or in the other cities where rioting broke out after Martin Luther King's assassination. The best, indeed the only, monograph on the subject is Clay Risen, *A Nation on Fire: America in the Wake of the King Assassination* (Hoboken, NJ: John Wiley, 2009). Risen provides a strong narrative on the political aspects of the riots in Washington, Chicago, and Baltimore. In the case of Washington, however, he slights other important matters, such as the background history of the District of Columbia, the growing fears of racial unrest during the 1960s, the costs and the victims of the riots, and the long-term consequences. An invaluable account is a book by Ben Gilbert, a managing editor of the *Washington Post*, and his colleagues who covered the riots. The book, *Ten Blocks from the White House: Anatomy of the Washington Riots of 1968* (New York: Frederick A. Praeger, 1968), was published about six months after the disorders occurred. It provides a detailed description of events and exceedingly useful information on the rioters. The book is as much a primary source of first-hand reporting as it is a secondary source.

Other than those two books, not much has been written on the 1968 riots in Washington. There are excellent overviews of the history of the city that cover the riots only briefly: Carl Abbott, *Political Terrain: Washington, DC, from Tidewater Town to Global Metropolis* (Chapel Hill: University of North Carolina Press, 1999); Howard Gillette Jr., *Between Justice and Beauty: Race, Planning, and the Failure of Urban Policy in Washington, DC* (Baltimore: Johns Hopkins University Press, 1995); and Blair A. Ruble, *Washington's U Street: A Biography* (Baltimore: Johns Hopkins University Press, 2010). Tom Lewis, *Washington: A History of Our National City* (New York: Basic Books, 2015), has a short discussion of the riots that is factually unreliable. Harry S. Jaffe and Tom Sherwood, *Dream City: Race, Power, and the Decline of Washington, DC* (New York: Simon and Schuster, 1994), and an updated version published in 2014 (distributed by Argo Navis Author Services), is a fascinating journalistic account with much information on political events and leaders, especially Marion Barry Jr., but it too has little on the riots. Zachary M. Schrag, *The Great Society Subway: A History of the Washington Metro* (Baltimore: Johns Hopkins University Press, 2006), discusses the riots briefly as a part of a book that provides rich insight into the building of Washington's Metro system and the issues surrounding it. Dana Lanier Schaffer, "The 1968 Washington Riots in History and Memory," *Washington History* 15 (Fall/Winter 2003/2004), 4–33, is a good article-length treatment.

INDEX

Abernathy, Ralph D., 114, 115
Abernathy, Thomas G., 108
Abraham, Irving, 66–67
Agnew, Spiro, 99, 103
Ali, Ben, 129
Ali, Muhammad, 27
Ali, Virginia, 129, 130
Arata, Clarence A., 99
Art Young's Men's Shop, 109

Baker, Russell, 5–6, 23
Barry, Marion, Jr., 35, 127–28
Basie, Count (William James), 129
Belafonte, Harry, 129
Ben's Chili Bowl, 129, 130
Bradley, Tom, 134
Brooke, Edward W., 29
Brown, H. Rap, 50
Brown, James, 83
Brown v. Board of Education of Topeka, Kansas, 21
Byrd, Robert C., 88–89, 107–8, 111, 114, 116

Califano, Joseph A., Jr.
    chairs meeting on lessons
        learned, 112
    and complaints about army's
        policies, 88
    on costs of Kerner Commission
        recommendations, 46
    failure of Johnson's policies to
        prevent urban violence, 28
    on Hechinger appointment, 36
    Johnson's home rule
        lobbying, 33–34
    Kerner's performance as
        chairman, 44
    loss of confidence caused by riots, 97
    on minimum use of force by
        troops, 76
Calloway, Cab, 129
Cannon, Lou, 134
Carmichael, Stokely
    appeals for calm on DC streets,
        51, 52, 56
    attends Palm Sunday services, 93

179

Carmichael, Stokely (*cont.*)
    background, 42, 50
    blamed for riots, 42, 80, 100
    provocative statements, 51, 62
    reaction to King death, 50
    surveillance target, 42, 50, 62,
        80, 100
Cherry Blossom Festival, 79
Christopher, Warren M.
    attends White House meeting,
        112, 115
    reports on new intelligence
        arrangements, 113
    supports use of troops, 61–62, 75
    tours riot areas, 74–76
Clark, Ramsey
    advises against use of troops, 74
    calls for faster movement of
        troops, 113
    on chances of urban riots in
        1968, 43
    holds meetings with mayors and
        police chiefs, 40
    informs Johnson of King
        shooting, 49
    and Murphy appointment, 37
    praises police performance, 105
    and preparations for urban
        rioting, 40–41
    and prosecution of Carmichael,
        42, 100
    response to 1967 riots, 40–42
    statement on riot prevention and
        control, 131
Clifton Terrace Apartments,
    39–40, 125
Cohen, Wilbur J., 46
Cole, Nat King, 129
Court of General Sessions, 92
crime
    fear of, 22–23, 29–30, 43, 97, 99,
        108, 119
    House committee blames black
        majority for, 33
    rates in DC, 22, 40, 118–19, 126, 128

rates in United States, 22,
    44, 119–20

Daley, Richard J., 82, 108, 156n38
Danzansky, Joseph, 91
DC Village and Children's Center, 90
Delaney, Paul, 59
Detroit riot, 1967
    costs of, 2, 28, 98, 106
    impact on planning and preparation
        for urban violence, 29–31, 42, 61,
        74, 80, 85, 89
District of Columbia Bail Agency, 103
District of Columbia Police Wives'
    Association, 39
D. J. Kaufman's Men's Stores,
    60, 71–73
Dodek, Oscar, 72, 73
Donovan, Robert J., 105
Douglass, Frederick, 13
Dowdy, John, 108
Downie, Leonard, Jr., 3
Dugas, Julian R., 59
Duncan, Charles T., 59, 60
Duncan, Dorothy, 59

Eaton, David, 127
Empire Super Market, 55
Evening Star
    criticizes delay in calling up
        troops, 89
    description of damage to city from
        riots, 81
    on Dupont Circle as center of high
        society, 11
    on impact of fair housing law, 95
    on poverty in DC, 12–13
    praises mayor's leadership, 118
    on unrest in DC in 1967, 31
    on use of tear gas against snipers, 93
    on Washington appointment as
        mayor, 35

fair housing legislation, 61, 95
Fairmont apartment building, 125–26

Fauntroy, Walter E.
    appointed to city council, 36
    and McMillan defeat, 126
    Palm Sunday sermon, 93
    and Poor People's Campaign, 114
    tours riot areas with Kennedy, 94
    urges calm in city, 51
    at White House meeting, 61
Federal Bureau of Investigation (FBI)
    bypassed by Clark, 41
    crime index, 22
    intelligence activities, 42, 113, 166n35
    predicts 1967 riots, 27
Federal Housing Administration, 18
fire damage, 55, 64–70, 81, 84, 91,
    98, 105
Fletcher, George E., 57, 60
Fletcher, Thomas W.
    appointed deputy mayor, 35–36
    attends White House meeting, 112
    on riot preparations, 61
    tours riot zones, 89
    urges improved communications, 113
    on Vance's role, 80
Ford Foundation, 124
Frank D. Reeves Municipal
    Center, 129
Franklin, John Hope, 18–19
Freeman, Warren, 87
Funderburk, Earl C., 99

Gallup poll, 44, 119–20
Garfinckel's department store, 71
G. C. Murphy store, 64
Giant Foods, 90–91
Gilbert, Ben, 49–50, 68
Gilje, Paul A., 101–2
Gimble, Gilbert, 106
Ginsberg, David, 133
Glen Echo Amusement Park, 20
Gray, Freddie, 1, 134
Great Migration, 17, 133
Greene, W. Henry, 109–10
Gregory, Dick, 27
Greider, William, 134

Griffith, Clark, 12
Grimsted, David, 106, 172n29
Gritz, Abraham, 67

Haines, Ralph E., Jr.
    appointed commander of Task
        Force Washington, 74, 77
    attends White House meeting, 112
    at command center, 84
    reports on conditions in city,
        74, 92–93
    responds to Russell complaint, 88
    tours riot areas, 74–76, 89
Harborplace, 1
Harlem riot, 1964, 2, 25, 26
Harris, Fred, 29, 132, 133–34
Harris, Louis, 26, 100
Harrison, Robert, 123
Hechinger, John W.
    appointed as city council
        chairman, 36
    concerns about police
        behavior, 37
    predicts return to normal, 82
    tours riot areas, 80, 81
    unpublished memoir, 147n24
Hecht's department store, 16, 60, 71
Herson, Joe, 67–68
Hoffman, Joseph, 109
Hoffman, Milton, 109
Hoffman, Norman, 109
Hogan, Larry, 1, 134–35
home rule, 10, 33–34, 126
Hoover, J. Edgar, 41
Horne, Lena, 129
Howard, Claudia, 67
Howard University, 12, 20, 34–35, 39,
    62, 100, 129
Hughes, John S., 54
Humphrey, Hubert, 28
Huntington, Robert T., 84
Hyler, Jack, 86

Ickes, Harold, 14
Interdivisional Information Unit, 41

Jackson, John D., 105
Jackson, Reuben M., 102
Jefferson, Thomas, 5
Jefferson Memorial, 8
JOBS program, 121, 168n7
Johnson, Harold K., 74, 76, 77, 88
Johnson, Lady Bird, 33
Johnson, Haynes, 6, 23, 57–58, 65, 89
Johnson, Lyndon B.
    appoints city officials, 34–36, 147n23
    appoints National Advisory
        Commission on Civil Disorders,
        26, 29–30
    attacked by Republicans on
        crime, 43
    blames mayor for delay in calling in
        troops, 156n38
    and causes of riots, 26, 42, 100
    decision to call in troops, 74–76
    establishes commission on crime
        in DC, 23
    expects urban riots in 1968, 43
    helicopter tour, 94
    home rule in DC, support for, 33–36
    as "honky," 62
    impact of 1967 riots on, 2, 28, 29, 40
    jokes about burning of
        Georgetown, 80
    Kerner Commission report,
        reaction to, 46
    King death response, 49, 50, 61
    love for city of Washington, 33
    sends troops to Chicago, 82
    signs civil rights legislation,
        25, 26, 95
    on smoke from burning
        buildings, 73
Johnston, Stephen, 65

Kaiser, Robert G., 39, 40
Kampelman, Max, 147n23
Kann's department store, 60
Kaufmann, C. D., 106–7
Kay Jewelry Stores, 52, 106
Kelly, Sharon Pratt Dixon, 128

Kennedy, Ethel, 94
Kennedy, Robert F., 20, 25, 62, 93–94
Kerner Commission. See National
    Advisory Commission on Civil
    Disorders
Kerner, Otto, 29, 44
King, Irving, 107
King, Martin Luther, Jr.
    death of, 2, 48, 49
    named as demagogue, 27
    on nonviolence, 93, 105
    and Poor People's Campaign,
        47–48, 114
King, Rodney, 134

Lawrence, David, 103
Layton, John B.
    and police-community relations,
        30–31, 37
    relations with Murphy, 39
    reports on rioting of April 4, 59–60
L'Enfant, Pierre, 6
Library of Congress, 5, 7
Lincoln, Abraham, 5, 8
Lindsay, John V.
    desire that Kerner Commission
        report attract attention, 44, 46
    disliked by Johnson, 44, 46
    hires Walter Washington, 34, 35
    report on urban conditions, 1971, 132
    as vice-chairman of Kerner
        Commission, 29, 44
Log Cabin Liquors store, 66, 67, 109
Los Angeles Times, 23, 84

Macy, John W., Jr., 104
Malcolm X, 119
Manhattan Auto, 67–68
Manning, William R., 62
Maryland Science Center, 1
Mayfield, Rufus (Catfish), 109
Maynard, Robert C., 97
McCarthy, Eugene, 48
McCone, John A., 26, 61
McGiffert, David E., 61–62, 112–13

McLaughlin, Malcolm, 172n29
McMillan, James, 7–8
McMillan, John L., 33, 34, 126
McPherson, Harry C., 32, 46
Metropolitan Police Department
    anger at among black citizens,
        32, 37, 54
    budget, 128
    and DC unrest in 1967, 30, 31–32
    improves community relations, 131–32
    intelligence activities, 50, 52, 54, 113
    outnumbered by rioters, 54, 63,
        65–66, 68
    and Poor People's Campaign, 115–16
    response to violence after King
        death, 52–53, 59–60
    tear gas usage, 54–55, 67, 68, 71, 74,
        93, 98, 115, 116
Metropolitan Washington Board of
    Trade, 121
Metro subway system, 128–29
Meyers, Frank H., 16
Milloy, Courtland, 129
Mills, Bernie, 67–68
Mister, Melvin, 124
Morton's department store, 68
Moses, Hudson, 99
Murder Bay, 8, 9
Murphy, Patrick V.
    appointed director of public
        safety, 37
    attends White House meeting, 112
    on chances of riots in 1968, 47
    at command center, 84
    criticized for riot response, 108
    expanded intelligence, need for, 113
    meets with mayors and police
        chiefs, 40–41
    and opening schools on April 5, 62
    policy of restraint, 108, 112
    relations with Layton, 39
    response to riot on April 4, 54, 60
    supports calling in troops,
        61–62, 74, 75
    tour of riot areas, 74–75, 80

National Advisory Commission on
    Civil Disorders
    categories of riot severity, 27, 31
    causes of urban riots, 2, 44–46,
        100, 103
    created, 26, 29–30
    reaction to report of, 46–47
    report of, 44–46
    study of black attitudes toward
        riots, 120
    on urban riots of 1966, 27
    warns of excessive use of force, 109
National Aquarium, 1
National Archives, 5, 65, 80
National Association for the
    Advancement of Colored People
    (NAACP), 14, 15, 29, 41, 50
National Capital Planning
    Commission, 98, 105
National Gallery of Art, 8
National Negro Congress, 15
Newark, New Jersey riot of 1967
    costs of, 28, 106
    impact on planning and preparation
        for urban violence, 2, 30–31,
        61, 80, 89
Newsweek, 102
New York Amsterdam News, 132
New York Housing Authority, 34, 35
New York Times, 112, 132
Nickens, Norman W., 110
Nimetz, Matthew, 112
Nixon, Richard M.
    on causes of urban riots, 43–44
    denounces Johnson on crime, 119
    presidential statement on
        recovery, 122–23
    response to Kerner Commission
        report, 46–47
    supports home rule, 126
    visit to riot areas, 122

Obama, Barack, 2
Oldham, Brent, 124, 125
Oliver, Thomas, 86, 87

Organic Act of 1878, 10
Orioles Park at Camden Yards, 1
Oxford Dictionary of English, 4, 138n7

Panzer, Frederick, 100
Parker, Andrew, 48
Pension Building, 7
Peoples Drug Stores, 51, 83, 116
Pep Boys, 52, 102
Perry, Bonnie, 56, 57
police-community relations
    charges of police brutality, 1, 15, 28,
        32–33, 45, 134–35
    improvements in, 122, 126, 131–32
    need for improvements, 31–33, 37,
        39, 47, 135
Pollak, Stephen J., 31
Poor People's Campaign, 47–48, 114–16
population of District of Columbia,
    8–9, 16–17, 21
President's Commission on Crime in
    the District of Columbia, 23, 31
Prouty, Winston, 120

Raspberry, William, 101
Rawlings-Blake, Stephanie, 1, 134–35
Reagan, Ronald, 127, 128
Reconstruction and Development
    Corporation, 124, 125
Redevelopment Land Agency, 19–20,
    36, 124, 125–26
Republic Theatre, 52
Reston, James, 97
restrictive covenants, 18, 21
Resurrection City, 114–15
Riis, Jacob, 13
Ritchie, Donald A., 163n10
Romney, George W., 122, 123
Roosevelt, Eleanor, 14
Rosen, Larry, 58–59
Rowan, Carl T., 100–101
rules of engagement for riot troops,
    42–43, 77
Russell, Richard B., 88

Safeway stores, 52, 63, 83, 90–91, 94
Salvation Army, 91
Sayre, Francis B., Jr., 93
Schindler, Albert, 107
Shapiro, Samuel, 82
Shepherd, Alexander, 7, 10, 12
Smiley, Tavis, 3
Smithsonian Institution, 5, 7
Southern Christian Leadership
    Conference (SCLC), 41, 50, 51,
    114, 115, 116
Southwest redevelopment, 19–20, 130
Starnes, Richard, 3
State, War, and Navy Building, 7
Stone, Chuck, 25
Storey, George E., 127
Student Nonviolent Coordinating
    Committee (SNCC), 42, 50, 52
Supreme Court building, 5, 8
Supreme Court rulings, 16, 18, 21

Taylor, Frederick, 111
Terrell, Mary Church, 15–16
Thompson's Restaurant, 15–16, 20
Tobriner, Walter N., 23, 31, 39
tourist industry, 99, 121–22
Truman, Harry S., 33
Tucker, Sterling, 33
Tydings, Joseph, 107

United Press International, 49

Vance, Cyrus R.
    on arresting Carmichael, 100
    arrival in DC, 80
    background, 74
    on conditions in riot areas, 81
    as president's representative, 84–85
    tours riot areas, 80, 81, 89
VanHook, John W., 13
Vietnam War, 28, 36, 41, 42, 46, 48, 50

Wallach, Richard, 9
Wall Street Journal, 103

Walter E. Washington Convention
    Center, 129
Washington, Bennetta, 35, 59
Washington, Dinah, 129
Washington, George, 5, 7
Washington, Walter E.
    advises use of troops. 74
    appointed mayor, 34–35
    appoints Murphy, 37
    background, 34–35
    on Carmichael role in riots, 100
    and citizen role in
        redevelopment, 124
    on city's return to normal, 94–95
    at command center, 84
    on conditions at Clifton Terrace, 40
    on conditions at The Fairmont, 126
    elected mayor, 126
    imposes curfew, 79, 83, 111
    loses reelection bid, 127
    on need for better intelligence, 112
    and Nixon statement on
        recovery, 123
    opening schools on April 5, support
        for, 62
    and Poor People's
        Campaign, 116–17
    praised for response to riots, 118
    prepositioning troops, support
        for, 115
    press conference on April 6, 81, 90
    reaches out to citizens, 47
    requests early start for JOBS, 121
    sees transformation among black
        citizens, 132–33
    tours riot areas, 59, 80, 89, 122
Washington Afro-American, 31, 47, 55,
    65, 102, 105
Washington Board of Realtors, 91
Washington Convention Bureau, 99
Washington Daily News, 109
Washington Metropolitan Area
    Transit Authority, 128
Washington Monument Society, 7

Washington Post
    account of arrest by "P.
        J. Wilson," 104
    on appointment of Fletcher as
        deputy mayor, 36
    on appointment of Washington as
        mayor, 35
    on chances of riots in 1967, 30
    collective portrait of rioters, 103
    on costs of policy of restraint, 106
    on crime in DC, 119
    denies bylines to black
        reporters, 163n10
    on failure of redevelopment, 127
    on fair housing law, 95
    on generation gap among African
        Americans, 104–5
    interview with arsonists, 68
    interview with Lindsay, 45–46
    on mood of the city, 89
    on performance of court system, 92
    on police-community relations, 132
    on recovery of tourist industry, 122
    on "skylarking" looters, 71
    on soldiers' "painful"
        assignments, 86–87
Washington Senators, 12, 79, 95
Washington Star-News, 125
Watts riot, 1965, 2, 26, 28
Waxie Maxie's record shop, 122
Westmoreland, William C., 94
white backlash, 26, 27, 28
Wicker, Tom, 102
Wilkens, Roger W., 46
Wilkins, Roy, 29
Williams, Anthony, 128, 129, 130
Wilson, P. J. (pseudonym), 104
Wilson, Woodrow, 14
Woodward and Lothrop department
    store, 71

Young, Whitney M., Jr., 132

Zevin, Abraham, 67